Basic Materials
in
Music Theory

A Programed Course

EIGHTH EDITION

Paul O. Harder

Greg A Steinke

Allyn and Bacon

Boston   London   Toronto   Sydney   Tokyo   Singapore

Vice-President and Editor-in-Chief, Humanities: Joseph Opiela
Editorial Assistant: Susannah Davidson
Production Coordinator: Catherine Hetmansky
Cover Administrator: Linda Knowles
Manufacturing Buyer: Aloka Rathnam

Copyright © 1995, 1991, 1986, 1982, 1978, 1975, 1970, 1965 by Allyn & Bacon
A Simon & Schuster Company
Needham Heights, Massachusetts 02194

ISBN 0-205-17205-9

Printed in the United States of America

10 9 8 7 6 5 4 3 2 1 99 98 97 96 95 94

Contents

1.0

2.0

3.0

4.0

5.0

6.0

7.0

Contents

8.0

The Major Scale 213

9.0

The Minor Scale 229

10.0

Key Signatures 263

11.0

Triads 309

Preface to the Eighth Edition

It is a challenging task to revise a book which has already enjoyed many years of success. It is an honor to be asked to undertake the revision of this edition, and it was with some trepidation that I approached the project. However, I have had a deep belief in these books ever since I first used them as a very young theory teacher in 1967 when they were first available. With a lot of history behind me, the highest respect and regard for all of Paul Harder's diligent efforts, I now offer various revisions and enhancements which I believe keep to the original spirit of Dr. Harder's programed concept, and which I hope all users will find helpful as they work through these pages.

In making the revisions, I have tried to respond to comments which were made available to me from Dr. Harder's estate, reviewers and current users of the books. The revisions will be most apparent in additions made to the supplementary exercises, and some additions to the appendix material. In selected places throughout the book I tried to clarify definitions or to demonstrate to the reader there are always alternatives to those ideas presented, and that the reader should explore them on his/her own or in class with one's instructor. In making these changes, I hope that the differences in theoretical and analytical approaches (which I know will always be there) can work comfortably with these books and also provide many interesting points of discussion in class. I'm quite sure that Dr. Harder never intended this volume to be the final definitive answer, but rather to provide an informed point of departure to explore the many anomalies that are always to be found in musics everywhere.

The exposition of the material is presented via a step-by-step process, which, to some, may seem mechanical, but it does ensure, in general, a good understanding of the basic tenets of the materials of the so-called common practice period in music. I would emphasize that this approach does not preclude presenting alternatives nor the exploration of other possibilities of how composers may work with various cause/effect relationships as they write, rather than following any set of "rules." A very rich learning experience can be created for all concerned, instructor as well as student, by exploring together all the many exceptions to the so-called "rules" or principles. In so doing, it becomes possible to ultimately link all that is studied to actual musical literature, or to create many varieties of assignments to solidify the understanding of the basic framework presented within these pages.

The reviser is grateful both to Mildred Harder who recommended me to undertake these revisions, and to Allyn and Bacon for accepting that recommendation and providing helpful comments and support throughout the revision process. I also wish to thank Mrs. Harder for providing me access to all notes and support materials Dr. Harder used in the original creation of these books and for her ever helpful comments and moral support to complete this project. I would also thank colleagues Dr. David Stech, Dr. Margaret Mayer, Dr. Deborah Kavasch, Dr. Tim Smith, Dr. David Sills, Prof. David Foley, and Dr. Lewis Strouse for their comments, encouragement and assistance on revision ideas. I am grateful to all concerned and am most appreciative of the help they have all provided. And finally, special thanks go to my wife, Kari (who assisted with much of the computer inputting/corrections for this current edition), and my two boys, Carl and Kyle, for being patient and quiet while I worked and always offering moral support as well as helpful comments. I hope users of this volume will find many hours of rich, musical learning to enhance their developing musicianship.

GAS

Preface to the Earlier Sixth Edition

Thorough grounding in music fundamentals is necessary for serious study of music. Unless one understands the vocabulary of music terminology, it is impossible even to converse knowingly about music. This book provides training that goes beyond vocabulary; it gives students a functional understanding of matters related to the basic materials of music: time and sound. Exercises incorporated with factual material teach not only how to write and interpret various musical symbols, but also how to construct scales, intervals, and triads.

This book employs a learning system called programed instruction, a method that results in quick, thorough learning with little or no help from the instructor. Students may work at their own pace and repeat any set of drills as many times as necessary. Comprehension of the material is subject to constant evaluation, so a missed concept or error of judgment is isolated quickly, before damage is done.

Because this book provides self-paced learning and requires little supplementation, it is ideal for use as a beginning text in a course devoted to the study of tonal harmony. It is also useful in the applied studio and for a quick review before proceeding with more advanced work.

This new edition incorporates many suggestions that have been made by both students and instructors. The acoustical knowledge contained in Chapter One has been completely revised to employ terminology that has recently come into general use. Also, the order of chapters has been adjusted to provide a more logical sequence. All mastery frames have been rewritten to assess achievement more thoroughly. The supplementary assignments are all new.

The organization and methods used in this book are the product of practical classroom experiences over a period of many years. They reflect the experimentation and free exchange of ideas between faculty and students at Michigan State University and California State University, Stanislaus.

Paul O. Harder
(1923–1986)

To the Student

A programed text is designed to induce you, the student, to take an active part in the learning process. As you use this book you will, in effect, reason your way through the program with the text serving as a tutor. The subject matter is organized into a series of segments called *frames*. Most frames require a written response that you are to supply after having read and concentrated on the information given. A programed text allows you to check each response immediately, so that false concepts do not take root and your attention is focused on "right thinking." Since each frame builds upon the knowledge conveyed by previous ones, you must work your way through the program by taking each frame in sequence. With a reasonable amount of concentration you should make few mistakes, for each successive step in the program is very small.

A glance at the first page will show that it is divided into two parts. The correct answers appear on the left side. These should be covered with the answer cover, a ruler, a slip of paper, or with the hand. Check your response to a given frame by uncovering the appropriate answer. *Your answer need not always be exactly the same as that supplied by the text.* Use your common sense to decide if your answer approximates the meaning of the one given. If you should make an excessive number of errors, repeat several of the preceding frames until your comprehension is improved. If this fails to remedy your difficulty, you should seek help from your instructor.

Following each chapter summary, you will find a short series of Mastery Frames. These frames will help you assess your comprehension of the key points of the chapter. *Do not continue unless your handling of the Mastery Frames assures your mastery of the preceding material.* Along with the correct answers on the left side of the frame are references to the specific frames in the main part of the chapter that cover that subject. These references are in parentheses. This arrangement allows you to focus remedial study on the points missed. Because the Mastery Frames are concerned with the essential matters covered in each chapter, you will find that they are useful for later review. There are also Supplementary Assignments, which are primarily intended for use in a classroom setting. The answers to these assignments are contained in the *Instructor's Manual for Harder and Steinke Basic Materials in Music Theory*, which is available upon request from the publisher.

This book concentrates on the *knowledge* of music fundamentals. Knowledge alone, however, is but one aspect of your musical development. In order to be useful, knowledge about music must be related to the actual experience of music as *sound*. To that end, Eartraining Activities appear at the end of each chapter. These exercises are designed for self-study; they are coordinated with the text but are not meant to be all-inclusive. They are intended to be used to supplement other eartraining experiences. Do not approach the study of music fundamentals as merely the acquisition of knowledge; bring to bear your musical experiences as both a performer and a listener. Try to sing or play each item as it is presented. In this way, the relation of symbols to sound will become real and functional.

Basic Materials
in
Music Theory

Basic Materials
in
Music Theory

Answer Cover

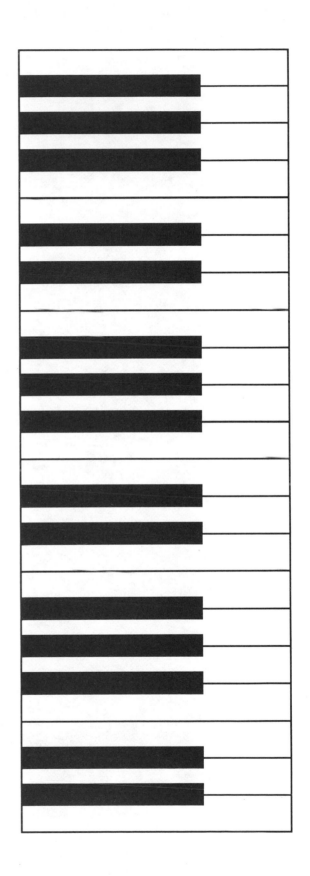

1.0
The Basic Materials of Music: Time and Sound

Time and sound are the basic materials from which music is made. In music, time is organized into patterns of duration. Sound consists of several characteristics, each of which contributes in its own way to the music. The objective of this book is to acquaint you with the terms and systems of notation that apply to the organization of time and the properties of sound. Acoustics is the scientific study of sound. The elementary acoustical facts presented in this chapter lay the groundwork for understanding the more complex materials of music.

	1.1 The source of sound is a VIBRATING OBJECT. Any object that can be made to vibrate will produce sound. *Vibrating objects* that are familiar to musicians include strings, columns of air, and metal or wooden bars or plates.
sound	A *vibrating object* is the source of _____.
	1.2 A vibrating object generates energy that is transmitted to the ear by vibrational disturbances called SOUND WAVES. These waves are transmitted as alternate compressions and rarefactions of the molecules in the atmosphere. *Sound waves* transmit energy from the vibrating
ear	object to the _____.

1.3 A simple *sound wave* may be represented as follows:

One Cycle (pitch)

Time ⟶

One complete oscillation both above and below the central axis is called a CYCLE. The example measures the *cycle* from one peak to another. How many *cycles* are represented if measured at the central axis itself?

six

_____

1.4 One complete oscillation of a sound wave is called a

cycle

_____.

1.5 Sounds are perceived subjectively as being relatively "high" or "low." This property of sound is called PITCH. The speed at which an object vibrates is affected by its physical nature, including its size, shape, and material. The faster the vibrating object vibrates, the "higher" the *pitch*. Conversely, the slower the vibrating

lower

body vibrates, the "_____" the *pitch*.

pitch

1.6 Frequency of vibration determines the_____ of the sound.

1.7 Frequency of vibration may be expressed as the number of cycles per second. Musicians are familiar with the standard of A = 440. This means that the note A (above middle C) vibrates at 440 cycles per second.

The term *cycle* lately has been supplanted by HERTZ (Abbreviation: HZ). This is to honor the nineteenth-century physicist Heinrich Hertz. As we proceed, the term *hertz* will be used instead of *cycle*.

(no response required)

higher	1.8 Will a *pitch (tone)* whose frequency is 620 *hertz* sound higher or lower than one whose frequency is 310 *hertz?* _____ Note: If you are unfamiliar with some basic principles of music notation, you may wish to cover frames 2.1 - 2.16 from chapter 2.0 before proceeding.
lower	1.9 When the frequency of a pitch is *doubled*, the resulting tone will be perceived as sounding an OCTAVE *higher*. When the frequency of a pitch is halved, the resulting tone will be an *octave* _____. *Experience this effect at the piano by playing a note such as C or A in various octaves.*
higher	1.10 Two simple sound waves are represented below: Time ⟶ Two vibrations of Wave I occur for each vibration of Wave 2. Thus Wave 1 represents a tone whose pitch (frequency) is one *octave* (higher/lower) _____ than that of Wave 2.
220	1.11 The tone whose frequency is 440 hertz is called A. The A an octave lower would have a frequency of _____ hertz.

522	1.12 The tone whose frequency is 261 hertz is called C. The C sounding an octave higher would have a frequency of _____ hertz.
lower	1.13 A tone which has a frequency one-half that of another tone will sound an octave (higher/lower) _____.
1/4	1.14 The frequency of a tone two octaves lower than a second tone is (1/2, 1/3, 1/4, 1/8) _____ the frequency of the latter.
yes	1.15 In addition to pitch, music makes use of various degrees of "loudness" or "softness" of sound. This property of sound is called INTENSITY. *Intensity* is determined by the amount of power transmitted to the ear by the sound wave. *Produce a soft sound by humming or singing; then produce the sound again, but considerably louder.* Does the louder sound require a greater expenditure of energy? _____
intensity	1.16 *Intensity* is determined by the amount of energy transmitted from the sound source to the ear and is measured by the AMPLITUDE of the sound wave. Sound waves can be compared to waves on the surface of water: the greater the agitation, the higher the waves. *Amplitude* is a measurement of _____.

	1.17 Two *simple* sound waves are represented below: 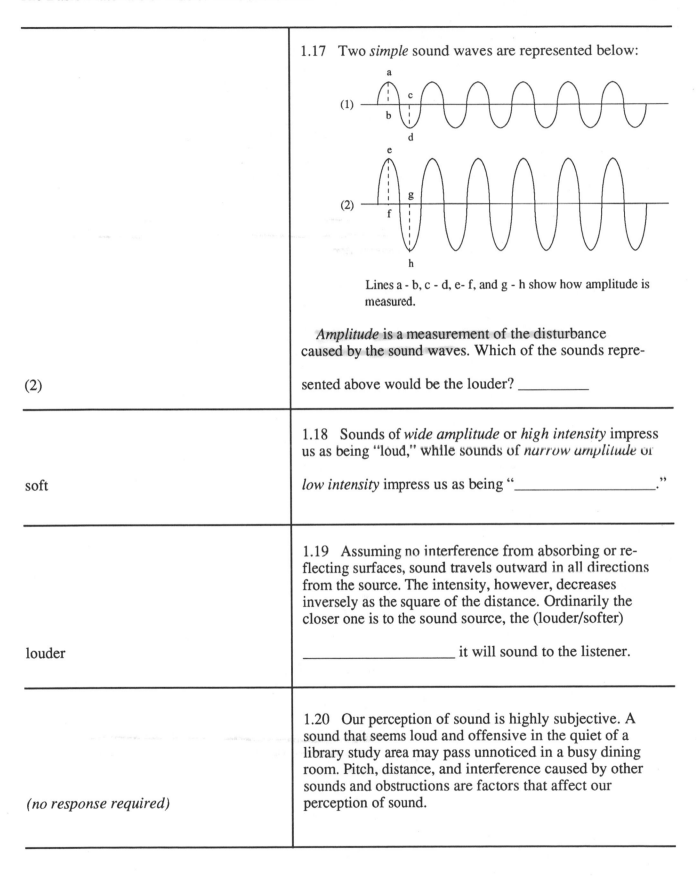 Lines a - b, c - d, e- f, and g - h show how amplitude is measured. *Amplitude* is a measurement of the disturbance caused by the sound waves. Which of the sounds represented above would be the louder? _____
(2)	
soft	1.18 Sounds of *wide amplitude* or *high intensity* impress us as being "loud," while sounds of *narrow amplitude* or *low intensity* impress us as being "_____."
louder	1.19 Assuming no interference from absorbing or reflecting surfaces, sound travels outward in all directions from the source. The intensity, however, decreases inversely as the square of the distance. Ordinarily the closer one is to the sound source, the (louder/softer) _____ it will sound to the listener.
(no response required)	1.20 Our perception of sound is highly subjective. A sound that seems loud and offensive in the quiet of a library study area may pass unnoticed in a busy dining room. Pitch, distance, and interference caused by other sounds and obstructions are factors that affect our perception of sound.

soft

1.21   Excluding other factors, sounds of high intensity impress us as being loud, while sounds of low intensity

impress us as being _____.

waves

1.22   Tones produced by various sound sources have their own distinctive *tone quality*. This property of sound is also called TIMBRE. In addition to pitch and intensity,

timbre is transmitted to the ear by sound _____.

1st Harmonic   2nd Harmonic

One Cycle

1.23   Sounds from different sound sources vary in quality because most sounds are not a single pitch, but consist of a complex of pitches called HARMONICS.* These pitches are the result of the sound source (a string or column of air, for example) vibrating not only in its entire length, but also simultaneously in 1/2, 1/3, 1/4, etc., of its length. The result is a complex sound wave that transmits all of the frequencies produced by the source.

   The number, distribution, and relative intensity of the *harmonics* contained in a sound are chiefly responsible for its *timbre*.

(no response required)

*The term "partials" is also used for these pitches.

1.24 The complex of simultaneously sounding pitches generated from a fundamental that determine the timbre of a tone is called the HARMONIC SERIES. Theoretically, the *harmonic series* extends indefinitely; but for our purposes, the naming of the first eight *harmonics* will suffice.*

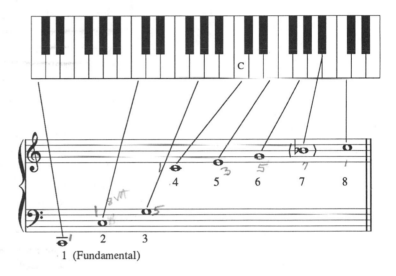

1 (Fundamental)

The example above shows that the *harmonic* with

the lowest frequency is called the _____.

fundamental

*To avoid confusion, the practice of referring to the harmonics other than the first (fundamental) as "overtones" (i.e., notes 2 through 8 above) generally has been abandoned.

1.25 Not all of the tones of the *harmonic series* are present in some musical sounds. The tuning fork, for example, produces a "pure" sound consisting of the first *harmonic* only; a closed tube, such as a stopped organ pipe, produces only the odd-numbered *harmonics*.

The number of *harmonics* present, and their relative

intensity, determines the _____ of the sound.

timbre

1.26 *Timbre* is a technical term that refers to the quality of a sound. *Tone color* is a descriptive term that refers to the same phenomenon. Reference to the visual effect of color is appropriate in the context of sound because sounds often impress us a being "bright" or "dark," or even suggesting specific colors. Some individuals are endowed with "colored hearing," a condition called *synesthesia*, in which sounds produce accompanying visualization of colors.

Factors other than harmonics affect our perception of timbre. These include the physical nature of the sound source, the acoustical characteristics of the place in which the sound is heard, and also the subjective response of the listener.

Generally, the greater the number of harmonics present in a sound, the "richer" the effect will be. In comparison, a sound with few audible harmonics will sound "pure." Such a tone may be no less beautiful, but the timbre will be different.

The terms *timbre, tone quality,* and *tone color* refer to the same characteristics of sound. *True*

true

(True/False) _____

(no response required)

1.27 The harmonic series (shown in Frame 1.24) has been introduced here to help explain what causes different timbres. It has importance in other areas of music study such as harmony and orchestration. Because you will make use of the harmonic series in future study, you should try to learn its structure and be able to play and write it on any pitch. This should be possible once you have mastered intervals, keys and key signatures later on in this study.

1.28 The structure of the harmonic series is the same regardless of the pitch of the fundamental — the series of tones is identical.

Is the fundamental considered to be one of the

yes

harmonics of a sound? _____

(1) pitch
 	
(2) intensity
 	
(3) timbre
(any order)
	1.29 List the three *properties of sound* that have been examined to this point.
	
	        (1) _____
	
	        (2) _____
	
	        (3) _____

(no response required)	1.30 Since time is one of the basic materials of music, DURATION of sound is an important factor. Even though time is required for the vibrations that produce sound to occur, *duration* is generally not regarded as a property of sound. In music, however, the *duration* of sounds is an important consideration. Patterns of *duration* create the element of music called RHYTHM. Because of its importance to music, *duration* will be included here as the fourth *property of sound*.
rhythm	1.31 The term RHYTHM applies to all aspects of time in music, including *duration*. Music utilizes sounds ranging from very short to very long, and our system of notation is designed to indicate with precision the exact duration required. All aspects of duration are part of the basic element of music called _____.
time	1.32 Is *rhythm* primarily a matter of time or sound? _____
(your opinion)	1.33 Can you conceive of *rhythm* without sound? _____
duration	1.34 The property of sound that refers to the "length" of of tones is called _____.

	1.35 The basic materials of music are TIME and SOUND. Durations of sounds are combined to produce rhythm. Duration is one of the properties of sound. Name the other three.
(1) pitch	(1) _____
(2) intensity	(2) _____
(3) timbre *(any order)*	(3) _____

Summary

Sound is produced by a *vibrating object* that transmits energy in the form of *sound waves* to the ear. The *four properties of sound* that concern musicians are summarized below:

1. *Pitch* is the perceived "highness" or "lowness" of sound and varies according to the *frequency* of vibration — higher frequencies produce higher pitches. Each time the frequency is doubled, the pitch is raised one *octave*.
2. *Intensity* is the "loudness" or "softness" of a sound, and is the result of the *amplitude* of the sound wave. This in turn is a reflection of the amount of energy emanating from the sound source.
3. *Timbre* refers to the "quality" ("brightness" and "darkness") of a sound and results, in part, from the number, relative intensity, and distribution of the *harmonics* present. Other factors such as the physical nature of the sound source, acoustics of the listening space, and the subjective response of the listener may also play a role in the perception of *timbre*.
4. *Duration* and patterns thereof are especially important for musicians because they are concerned with *rhythm* — one of the basic elements of music.

Mastery Frames

vibrating (Frames 1.1–1.2)	1–1 The source of sound is a _____ object.
sound waves (1.2)	1–2 Alternate compressions and rarefactions of the molecules in the atmosphere transmit energy in the form of _____ _____ to the ear.
true (1.3–1.4)	1–3 One complete oscillation of a sound wave is called a cycle. (True/False) _____
pitch (1.5–1.6)	1–4 The frequency at which an object vibrates determines the _____ of the sound.
620 (1.7)	1–5 A tone with the frequency of 620 hertz is vibrating at the rate of _____ cycles per second.
octave (1.9–1.14)	1–6 A tone with a frequency twice that of another is said to be an _____ higher.
intensity (1.15)	1–7 The property of sound that refers to the "loudness" or "softness" of a tone is called _____.

True (1.16–1.18)	1–8 Amplitude is a measure of the energy transmitted to the ear. (True/False) _____
timbre (1.22)	1–9 The property of sound that refers to the quality of a tone is called _____.
harmonics (1.23)	1–10 Most musical tones consist of a complex of pitches. Those pitches are called _____.
harmonic (1.24–1.28)	1–11 The entire complex of pitches that constitutes the total sound is called the _____ series.

Supplementary Assignments

Assignment 1–1   Name: _____

1. The field of science that is concerned with the phenomena of sound is called

   _____.

2. Sound is an auditory sensation caused by vibrations that reach the ear by means of

   _____ _____.

3. The source of sound is a _____ object.

4. Name several objects that are capable of producing sound.

   (1) _____

   (2) _____

   (3) _____

   (4) _____

5. Name the property of sound that relates to the "highness" or "lowness" of sound.

   _____

6. What determines the pitch of a sound? _____

7. Explain the meaning of the designation "100 hertz."

   _____

   _____

8. Complete the table by providing the missing information.

	Frequency
Two octaves higher	_____
One octave higher	_____
Original tone	440
One octave lower	_____
Two octaves lower	_____

9. Name the property of sound that relates to the volume of sound. _____

   _____

10. What effect does distance have upon the volume of sound? _____

_____

11. The individual pitches that combine to produce a complex sound are called

_____.

12. To what does the term *timbre* refer? _____

_____

13. The harmonic series through the eighth harmonic with C in the fundamental is
     shown below. Write the series on F in the space provided. *(If you are inexperienced
     in musical notation, attempt to imitate the pattern from the 1st line.)*

14. Select the item on the right that corresponds to each term on the left. *(Write the
     appropriate letter.)*

_____	1. Amplitude	A. Loudness/softness
_____	2. Timbre	B. Partials
_____	3. Vibrating object	C. 2:1 frequency ratio
_____	4. Harmonics	D. Time
_____	5. Pitch	E. Tone quality
_____	6. Fundamental	F. Energy transmitted by sound waves
_____	7. Duration	G. Cycles per second
_____	8. Intensity	H. Transmit sound
_____	9. Hertz	I. Highness/lowness
_____	10. Sound waves	J. First harmonic
_____	11. Octave	K. Source of sound

15. Rhythm is concerned with the basic material of music called _____.

16. Which frequency would produce the "higher" tone? _____
         a. 620 vibrations per second   b. 310 vibrations per second

17. A tone whose frequency is double that of another sounds an _____ higher.

Eartraining Activities

INTRODUCTION

Full musical comprehension requires both the ear and the mind: sounds and their related symbols must be *sensed* as well as *understood.* An extensive eartraining program is usually needed to develop aural discrimination. These eartraining activities, however, have a more modest objective: to reinforce your understanding of the material presented in this book. The exercises are suggestive rather than comprehensive. In most cases, they do not provide sufficient drill for developing aural mastery. They should, on the other hand, be a useful supplement to class experiences. They may also serve as models for further self-help.

Musicians must become acutely sensitive to sounds and time relations. For you to develop sensitivity, more than just passive listening is required. You must analyze both the sounds and the way those sounds affect you. By being aware of your response to musical stimuli, you will enlarge your mastery of musical expression.

This book has been designed to help you acquire musical knowledge largely on your own. These eartraining activities are provided to help achieve this goal. The exercises may be used by you alone or along with another person, each checking the other. Some exercises may seem simple, even naive, but they serve an important function: to encourage sensitive, critical, and analytical listening.

1. Tap, or strike with a pencil, any object which happens to be near you. Listen for differences in effect; analyze your responses to these simple stimuli. Are the sounds soothing/stimulating, hard/soft, high/low, short/long?

2. Notice the effect sounds that are near by or far away have on you.

3. Pluck a stretched rubber band. Listen to variations of pitch and observe how the rubber band vibrates as the tension is varied.

4. At the piano, play notes that are within your vocal range and match their pitches with your voice.

5. Play notes outside your vocal range and match them within your vocal range.

6. Sing octave intervals, both up and down. *(Check yourself at a keyboard.)*

7. Sing the tones of the natural harmonic series on various pitches. Bring the tone within your vocal range as in the following:

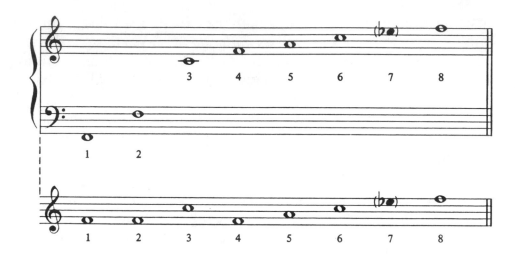

2.0
The Notation of Pitch

Various musical terms and symbols are used to refer to the organization of time and the properties of sound. In this chapter we shall study the notation of one aspect of sound, that of *pitch*. Our system of notation originated many centuries ago when tonal materials were much more limited than now. The system was not designed for the highly chromatic music that eventually evolved. The result is that the notation of pitch is unnecessarily complex. Prevalent usage, however, causes even minor changes to be resisted. Modern notation is an imperfect, but nevertheless effective, visual representation of the "high" and "low" effects produced by tones of different pitch.

	2.1 Five parallel horizontal lines with intervening spaces are used to notate the pitch of tones. This device is called a STAFF (plural: staves or staffs).
	The *staff* is used to notate the property of sound
pitch	called _____.
staff	2.2 The five horizontal parallel lines with intervening spaces used for the notation of pitch are called the _____.
seen (and written) (*The effect of a note can be imagined, but this is not an auditory sensation.*)	2.3 The written symbols which represent tones are called NOTES. *Tones* can be heard, whereas *notes* can be _____.

no. *(It is the representation of a sound.)*	2.4 A *tone* is a musical sound. Is a *note* also a sound? _____
higher	2.5 The *lines* and *spaces* of the *staff* are numbered from the bottom to the top. LINES SPACES The fourth space is (higher/lower) _____ than the fourth line.

staff	2.6 The first seven letters of the alphabet (A through G) are used to name the *notes* which are placed on the various lines and spaces of the staff.
	     Signs are placed at the left on the *staff* to identify a particular line. These signs are called CLEFS.
	     A *clef* sign is used to name a particular line of
	
	 the _____.

G	2.7 The modern *clef* signs are stylized forms of the Gothic letters G, F, and C. The TREBLE CLEF establishes the location of the note G on the second line of the staff, which passes through the lower curved half of the clef sign. The *treble clef* identifies the second line of the staff as _____.
(etc.)	2.8 Write several examples of the *treble clef*.

2.9 By reference to the note established by the clef, the location of other notes can be established.

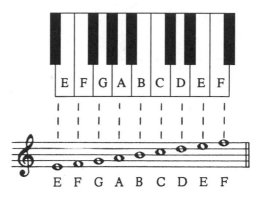

Since the lines and spaces represent an alphabetical sequence, all notes follow automatically once one pitch is located by the clef.

The *treble clef* places the note G on the _____ line of the staff.

second

2.10 Write the name of each note.

C, G, A, E, F, E, D

2.11 The BASS CLEF establishes the location of the note F on the fourth line of the staff, which passes between the two dots of the clef sign.

The *bass clef* identifies the fourth line of the

staff as _____.

F

2.12   Write several examples of the *bass clef*.

𝄢 𝄢 𝄢   (etc.)

---

fourth

2.13   The note F is located on the _____ line of the staff when the bass clef is used.

2.14   By reference to the note established by the clef, the location of the remaining notes can be established.

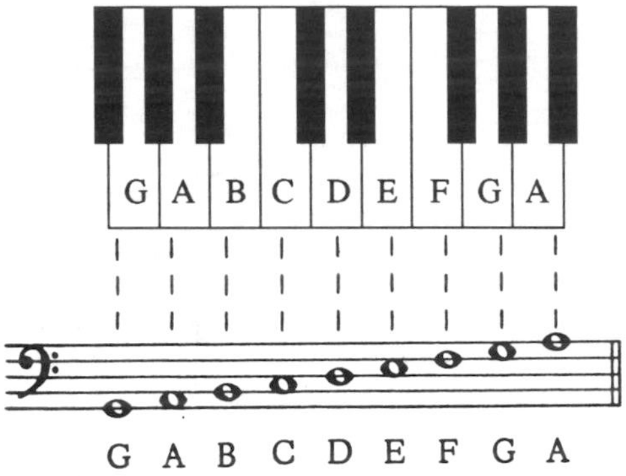

G   A   B   C   D   E   F   G   A

E

The *bass clef* identifies the third space as _____ .

2.15   Write the name of each note.

D, A, G, E, F, G, C

—   —   —   —   —   —   —

2.16   The letter names of the lines and spaces of the staff change according to the clef. Whereas the second line of the staff is G when the *treble clef*

B

is used, the second line is _____ when the *bass clef* is used.

2.17   Write the name of each note.

C, E, G, A, F, E

2.18   The C-CLEF establishes the location of the note C.*

The line which passes through the center of the

C-clef is _____.

C

* This note is actually "middle C." The precise meaning of this term is explained later in this chapter. (See Frames 2.35–.36.)

2.19   The C-clef can be placed on various lines of the staff.

TENOR CLEF (4th line)   ALTO CLEF (3rd line)

MEZZO-SOPRANO CLEF   SOPRANO CLEF
(2nd line)   (1st line)

The C-clef is not always located on the same line, but in each case the line which passes through the center

of the clef is _____.

C

Note: There are other usages of each of these clefs (treble, bass and C) if one examines the entire musical literature. What is presented in this text represents the most common usages today.

	2.20 In modern notation, the ALTO CLEF is mainly used by the viola with occasional use in trombone music. The TENOR CLEF is used by the 'cello, trombone, and bassoon. Other C-clefs are found mainly in older editions of choral music and are seldom used today.*
	Write several examples of the *alto clef*.
𝄡 𝄡 𝄡 (etc.)	
	*The C-clefs are introduced here to enable you to interpret them if necessary as they are used in much instrumental music. Only the treble and bass clefs are used in later chapters of this book as they tend to be the clefs generally used in music notation, especially in music theory study .
the third	2.21 On which line of the staff does the note C occur when the *alto clef* is used? _____
B, E, G, F, A, G, D	2.22 Write the name of each note.
𝄡 𝄡 𝄡 (etc.)	2.23 Write several examples of the *tenor clef*.
the fourth	2.24 On which line of the staff does the note C occur when the *tenor clef* is used?_____
G, E, C, A, D, E, B	2.25 Write the name of each note.

bass	2.26 The three clefs used in modern music notation are the C-clef, the treble clef, and the _____ clef.
staff	2.27 The range of a *staff* may be extended by the use of LEDGER LINES.* These lines are added above or below a staff and are spaced the same as the lines of the staff itself. The alphabetical succession of notes continues as on the staff. *Ledger lines* are used to extend the range of the _____. *The spelling *leger lines* is occasionally used.
C	2.28 Extension of the staff by means of ledger lines is shown below:  The note on the second ledger line above the staff when the treble clef is used is _____.
D	2.29 Extension of the staff by means of ledger lines is shown below: 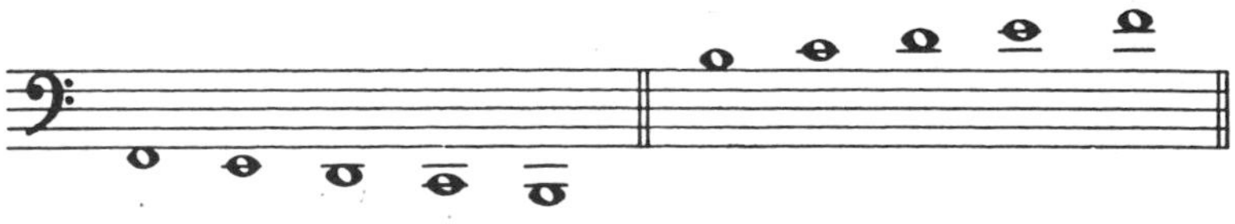 The note on the second space below the staff when the bass clef is used is _____.

2.30   Write the name of each note.

(1) A, C, B, G, D
(2) G, D, B, A, C

2.31   Write the name of each note.

(1) D, B, C, F, E
(2) C, B, E, F, D

2.32   Write the name of each note.

B, C, C, B, D, A

2.33   Write the name of each note.

A, B, C, D, B, C

2.34 The treble and bass clefs are placed upon two staves joined by a vertical line and a brace at the left to form the GRAND STAFF.

The *grand staff* is used for the notation of piano music, and is useful for other purposes, since it is capable of representing the full range of virtually all musical media. The grand staff employs the

_____ clef and the _____ clef.

treble, bass
(any order)

2.35 A note placed on the first ledger line above the bass staff represents the same pitch as a note placed on the first ledger line below the treble staff. This note is called MIDDLE C.

middle C

Middle C derives its name from the fact that

it is located in the middle of the _____ staff.

grand

This note is also approximately in the middle of the piano keyboard. Locate this note at the piano.

2.36 Other notes in addition to *middle C* can be notated
on either the treble staff or the bass staff.
    Rewrite the notes on the bass staff so they will
sound the same.

2.37   Rewrite the notes on the treble staff so they will
sound the same.

2.38   Rewrite the notes on the alto staff so they will
sound the same.

2.39 Rewrite the notes on the bass staff so they will *sound the same*.

2.40 Rewrite the notes on the tenor staff so they will *sound the same*.

2.41 Rewrite the notes on the treble staff so they will *sound the same*.

2.42 It is impractical to use more than three or four ledger lines, since notes become more difficult to read as the number of ledger lines increases. In order to avoid the excessive use of ledger lines, the treble staff may be extended upward and the bass staff extended downward by the use of the OTTAVA sign (*8 - - ¬*, *8va - - ¬*, or sometimes *8ve - - - ¬*).*
Notes over which the *ottava* sign is placed sound an octave higher than written; notes below which the *ottava* sign is placed sound an octave lower than written.

    The *ottava* sign is used to avoid the excessive

ledger lines   use of _____ _____.

_____

*Recent practice gives preference to *8 - - ¬* .

2.43 Observe the use of the ottava sign below:

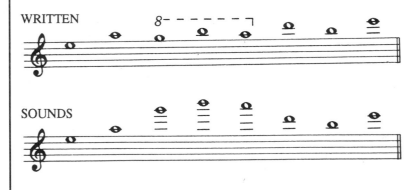

WRITTEN

SOUNDS

    The dotted line following the *8* indicates the notes affected by the sign.

    All notes over which the ottava sign appears are

higher   to be played an octave _____.

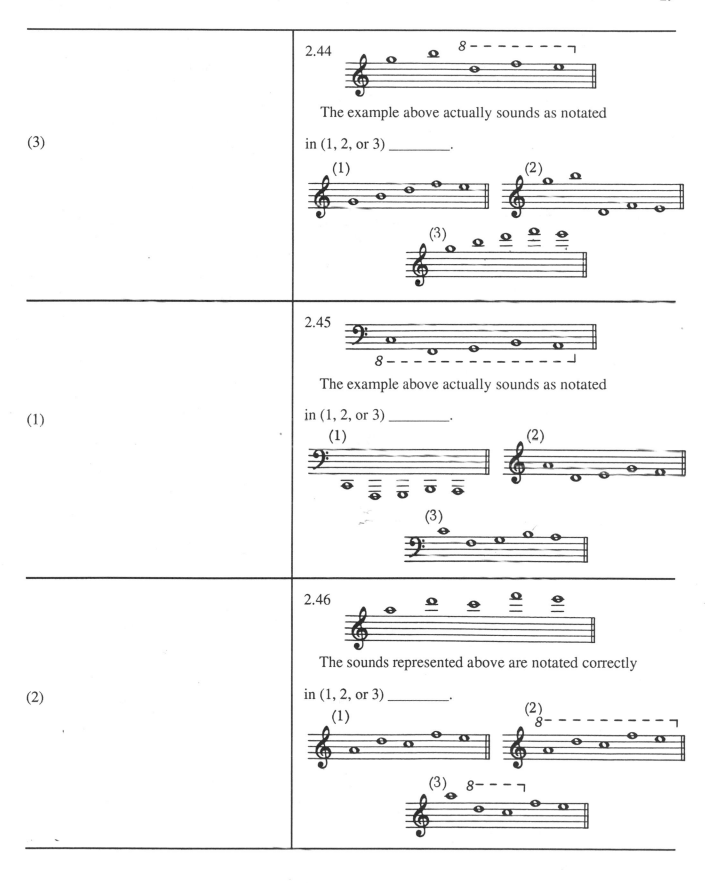

2.44

The example above actually sounds as notated

in (1, 2, or 3) _____.

(3)

(1)

(2)

(3)

2.45

The example above actually sounds as notated

in (1, 2, or 3) _____.

(1)

(1)

(2)

(3)

2.46

The sounds represented above are notated correctly

in (1, 2, or 3) _____.

(1)

(2)

(3)

2.47 Rewrite the passage below so it will *sound the same*, avoiding all use of ledger lines. *(Use the ottava sign.)*

2.48 Rewrite the passage below so it will *sound the same. (Use the ottava sign only for those notes which lie below the staff.)*

2.49 Each note as written below notates the *same pitch.* (True/False) _____

true

2.50 Each note as written below notates the *same pitch.* (True/False) _____

true

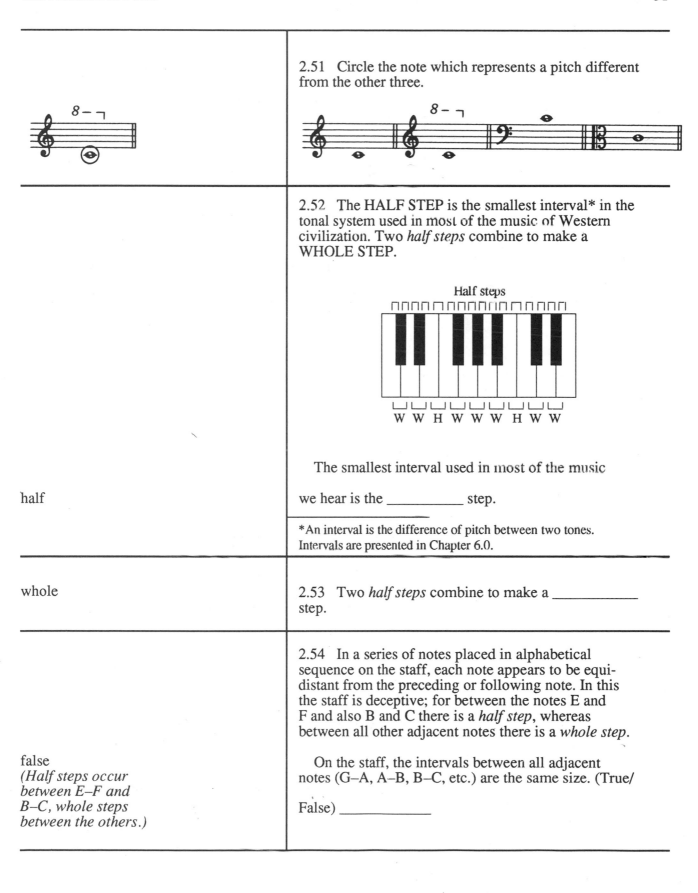

2.51 Circle the note which represents a pitch different from the other three.

2.52 The HALF STEP is the smallest interval* in the tonal system used in most of the music of Western civilization. Two *half steps* combine to make a WHOLE STEP.

Half steps

W H W W W H W

The smallest interval used in most of the music

half

we hear is the _____ step.

*An interval is the difference of pitch between two tones. Intervals are presented in Chapter 6.0.

---

whole

2.53 Two *half steps* combine to make a _____ step.

2.54 In a series of notes placed in alphabetical sequence on the staff, each note appears to be equidistant from the preceding or following note. In this the staff is deceptive; for between the notes E and F and also B and C there is a *half step*, whereas between all other adjacent notes there is a *whole step*.

false
(*Half steps occur between E–F and B–C, whole steps between the others.*)

On the staff, the intervals between all adjacent notes (G–A, A–B, B–C, etc.) are the same size. (True/

False) _____

E–F, B–C	2.55 On the staff, half steps occur between the notes _____ and _____, and the notes _____ and_____.
whole	2.56 When notes are placed on the staff in alphabetical sequence (either ascending or descending), the succession is said to be STEPWISE or DIATONIC. In a *stepwise* (or *diatonic*) succession of notes [with no accidentals (alterations)], some intervals will be half steps and some will be _____ steps.
half	2.57 The interval between E and F is a _____ step.
whole	2.58 The interval between A and B is a _____ step.
half	2.59 The interval between B and C is a _____ step.
whole	2.60 The interval between F and G is a _____ step.
whole	2.61 The interval between G and A is a _____ step.
false *(It is a whole step.)*	2.62 The interval between C and D is a half step. (True/False) _____
true	2.63 The interval between D and E is a whole step. (True/False) _____

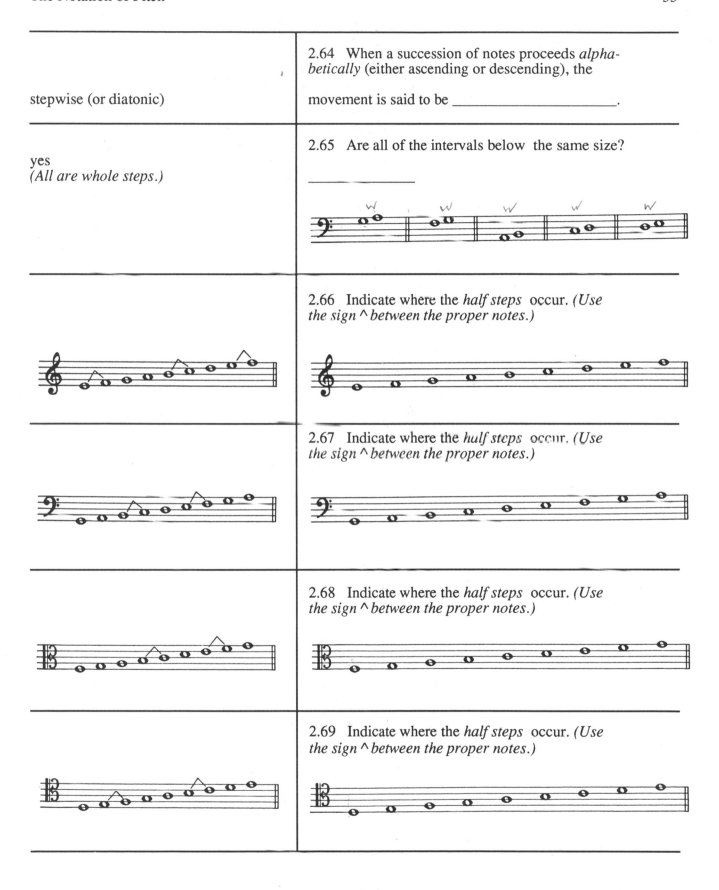

stepwise (or diatonic)

2.64 When a succession of notes proceeds *alpha-betically* (either ascending or descending), the

movement is said to be _____.

yes
(All are whole steps.)

2.65 Are all of the intervals below the same size?

_____

2.66 Indicate where the *half steps* occur. *(Use the sign ^ between the proper notes.)*

2.67 Indicate where the *half steps* occur. *(Use the sign ^ between the proper notes.)*

2.68 Indicate where the *half steps* occur. *(Use the sign ^ between the proper notes.)*

2.69 Indicate where the *half steps* occur. *(Use the sign ^ between the proper notes.)*

2.70   All notes to this point have been BASIC NOTES. The term _basic_ is used in this book to refer to notes which are not affected by certain signs called ACCIDENTALS. _Basic notes_ occur as white notes on the piano keyboard.

How many _basic notes_ occur in our system of

seven
(These are: A, B, C, D, E, F, and G.)

notation?_____

*The term _basic_ will be used later in connection with scales, intervals, and triads consisting of basic (unaltered) notes.

---

basic

2.71   The notes A, B, C, D, E, F, and G are called

_____ notes.

2.72   Basic notes may be altered by the use of signs called _accidentals_, which are shown below.

Sharp   ♯   Double-sharp   ×

Flat   ♭   Double-flat   ♭♭

Natural   ♮

The SHARP (♯) raises the pitch of a note a half step.

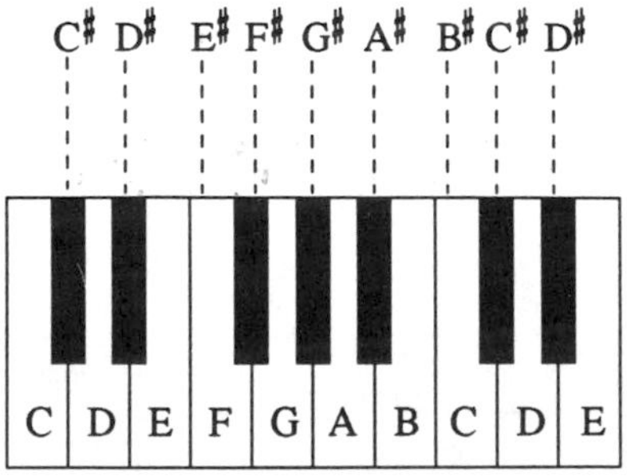

Apply a _sharp_ to each note below.
(All accidentals are placed to the left of the note and on the same line or space of the note they are to affect.)

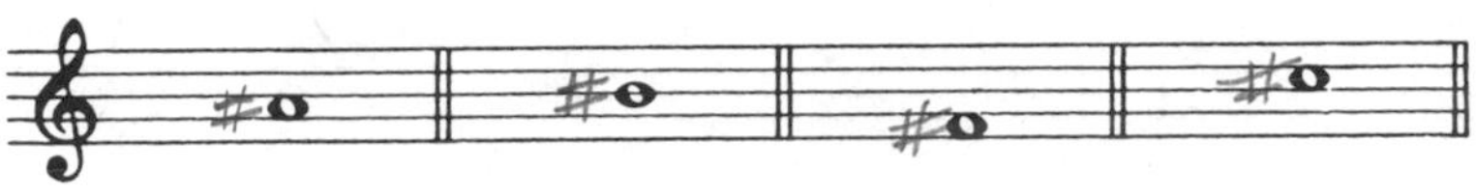

2.73 The DOUBLE-SHARP (✗) raises a *basic note* *two* half steps.

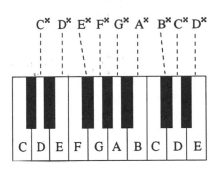

Apply a *double-sharp* to each note.

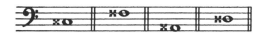

2.74 The FLAT (♭) lowers the pitch of a *basic note* *one* half step.

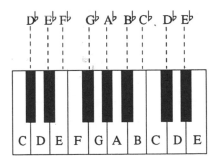

Apply a *flat* to each note.

2.75 The DOUBLE-FLAT ($\flat\flat$) lowers the pitch of a *basic note **two half steps**.*

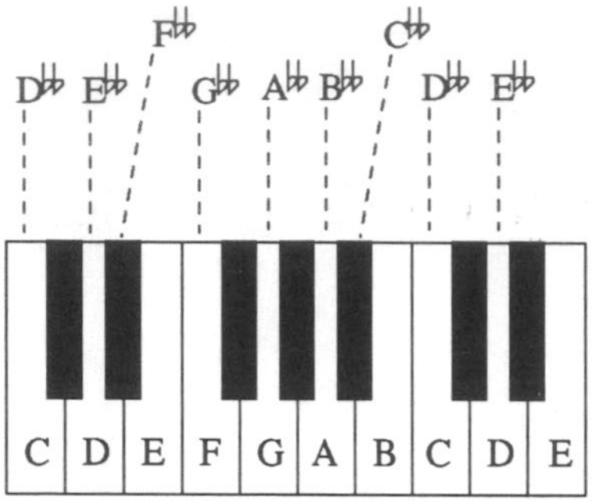

Apply a *double-flat* to each note.

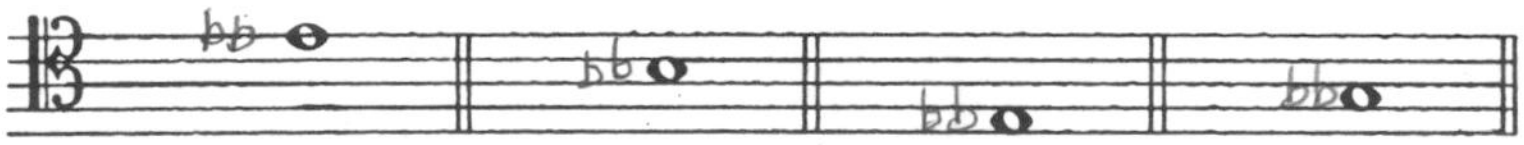

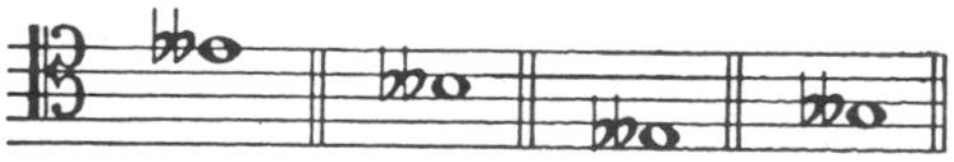

2.76 The NATURAL ($\natural$) cancels a previous accidental. (The result is a basic note.)

Apply a *natural* to the *second* note in each case.

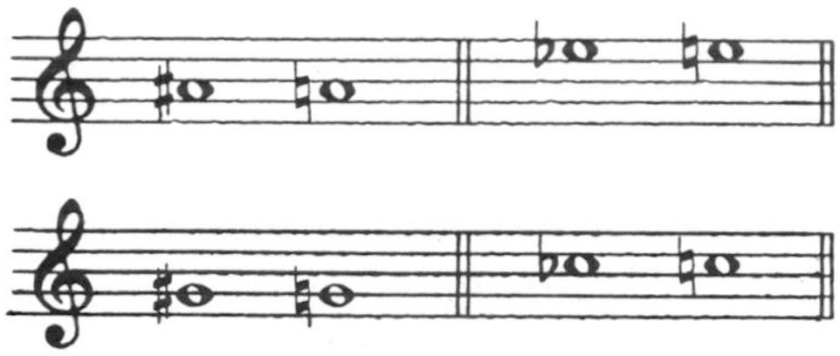

---

half

2.77 The *sharp* ($\sharp$) raises the pitch of a basic note by the interval of a _____ step.

---

half

2.78 The *flat* ($\flat$) lowers the pitch of a basic note by the interval of a _____ step.

---

true

2.79 The *natural* ($\natural$) has no effect upon a basic note unless it previously has been affected by another accidental or by a sharp or flat in the key signature.

(True/False) _____

(In all answers such as this the note may be written an octave higher or lower than shown.)

the natural (♮)

2.80 Notes affected by accidentals are called A-*flat*, D-*sharp*, D-*double-flat*, G-*sharp*, E-*natural*, and so on.
 Write the notes as directed. **Remember: the accidental is placed to the *left* of the note it is to affect.**

D♯   A♭   E♮   G𝄪   B♭♭

2.81 Vertical lines drawn through the five lines of the staff are called BAR LINES. These lines divide the music into MEASURES.

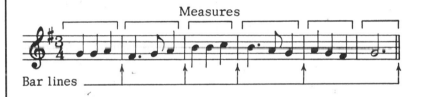

Accidentals remain in effect throughout the *measure* in which they occur; but they are cancelled by a *bar line*.

(F♯)   (F♮)

If an accidental is to be cancelled *within* a

measure, what sign is used? _____

2.82 The TIE is a curved line which connects two notes of the same pitch. It is used to prolong the duration of a note.

When a note which has been affected by an accidental is *tied* across a bar line, the accidental remains in effect for the duration of the *tied* note.

(Bb) ——————— (B♮)

Accidentals remain in effect during the measure in which they occur, or when the altered note is

tied   _____ across a bar line.

2.83 Accidentals other than the sharps or flats of the key signature* are cancelled automatically by

bar   the _____ line.

*The key signature consists of a group of sharps or flats placed immediately after the clef sign on each line of music. A B-flat in the key signature causes all Bs in the composition to be lowered to B-flat. Key signatures are studied in detail in Chapter 10.0.

2.84 An altered note may be prolonged into the next

tie   measure by means of the _____.

2.85 If a *double-sharp* is to be converted later in the same measure to a sharp, the desired accidental is then applied.*

This practice also applies to the *double-flat*.

If a natural plus a sharp appears before a note, which accidental actually applies? (The first/The

the second   second) _____

* Older printed music may differ with this practice in that a natural sign may be used to cancel a double sharp, with the desired accidental (sharp signs only, not flats) then applied.

2.86 Although some composers and arrangers are not consistent, accidentals are most commonly interpreted as affecting only notes on the particular line or space on which they are written, not notes in other octaves.

Since no sharp appears on the fourth line in the example above, the third note should be played as a D-*natural*.

What is the pitch of the fifth note? _____

G-natural

2.87   Write the name of each note. *(Use the proper accidental sign in responding.)*

Eb, C#, G♮, B♭♭, D#

— — — — —

2.88   When accidentals are applied so two or more basic notes represent the same pitch, these notes are said to be ENHARMONIC (or enharmonically related). *Enharmonic* notes are written differently but

have the same_____.

pitch

2.89   Examples of *enharmonic* notes are shown below:

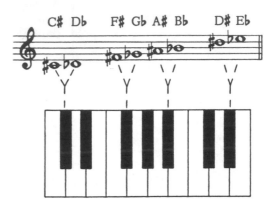

Two basic notes a whole step apart can be made *enharmonic* by applying a flat to the upper note and a

sharp

_____ to the lower note.

2.90   Other examples of *enharmonic* notes are shown below.

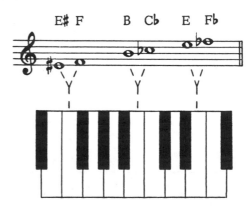

Two basic notes separated by a half step can be made *enharmonic* either by raising the lower note a half step

lowering

or by _____ the upper note a half step.

2.91   Still other examples of enharmonic notes are shown below.

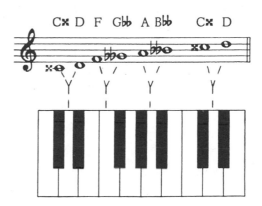

Write the two accidentals which are capable of altering the pitch of a tone by the interval of a whole

step. _____   _____

× ♭♭

2.92   Three basic notes can be made enharmonically related, as written below.

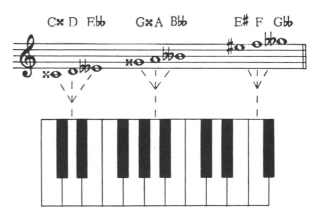

Notes which sound the same but are written

differently are said to be _____.

enharmonic

(1) B♯ or D♭♭
(2) D✕ or F♭
(3) A♭

2.93 Write an enharmonic equivalent for each note.

(1) C♯ or B✕
(2) C♭ or A✕
(3) A♭♭ or F✕

2.94 Write an enharmonic equivalent for each note.

2.95 Half steps occur between the notes E and F and the notes B and C. By the use of accidentals, half steps can be written between other notes as well.

Successions of notes moving exclusively in half steps are said to be CHROMATIC. A *chromatic* succession of

notes moves entirely in _____ steps.

half

2.96   There is a difference between DIATONIC and CHROMATIC half steps.
   A *diatonic* half step uses **two** basic notes (notes appearing on a consecutive line and space).
   A *chromatic* half step uses only **one** basic note (notes appearing on the same line or space).

DIATONIC HALF STEPS   CHROMATIC HALF STEPS

   Is the interval D up to D-sharp a *diatonic* or a

chromatic half step? _____

chromatic

2.97   Is the interval D up to E-flat a *diatonic* or a

chromatic half step? _____

diatonic

2.98   Write a *diatonic* half step above F.

2.99   Write a *chromatic* half step above F.

2.100   Do *diatonic* and *chromatic* half steps have the

same difference in size? _____

yes
(They are all half steps.)

2.101 Below is an example of a CHROMATIC SCALE.*

The notation of *chromatic scales* may vary according to the keys in which they occur. The simplest notation, however, results if sharps are used for notes inflected upward and flats are used for notes inflected downward. Observe in the example above that E and B are the only basic notes which are unaffected by accidentals. This is because the intervals between E and F and between B and

half

C are _____ steps.

*A scale consists of the tones contained in one octave arranged in consecutive series. Scales are studied in detail in Chapters 7.0, 8.0, and 9.0.

2.102 Below is another example of a *chromatic scale.*

Flats are usually used for notes inflected downward. Observe that F and C are the only basic notes unaffected by accidentals. This is due to the fact that there is a

B–C

half step between the notes _____ and _____,

E–F

and the notes _____ and _____.

2.103 Write a *chromatic scale* ascending from C to C. *(Use only sharps.)*

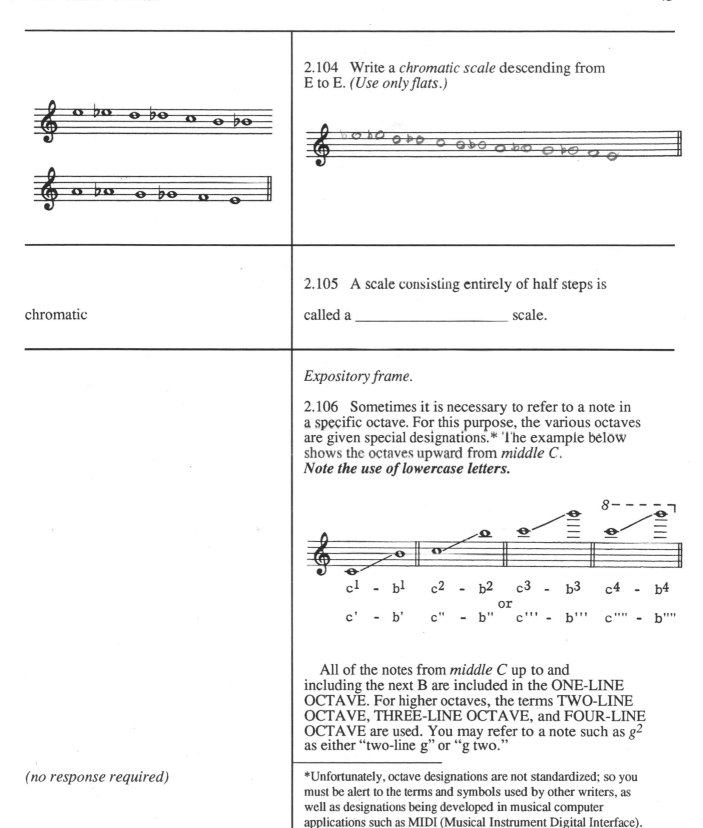

2.104   Write a *chromatic scale* descending from E to E. *(Use only flats.)*

chromatic

2.105   A scale consisting entirely of half steps is called a _____ scale.

Expository frame.

2.106   Sometimes it is necessary to refer to a note in a specific octave. For this purpose, the various octaves are given special designations.* The example below shows the octaves upward from *middle C*.
Note the use of lowercase letters.

$$c^1 - b^1 \quad c^2 - b^2 \quad c^3 - b^3 \quad c^4 - b^4$$
or
$$c' - b' \quad c'' - b'' \quad c''' - b''' \quad c'''' - b''''$$

   All of the notes from *middle C* up to and including the next B are included in the ONE-LINE OCTAVE. For higher octaves, the terms TWO-LINE OCTAVE, THREE-LINE OCTAVE, and FOUR-LINE OCTAVE are used. You may refer to a note such as g^2 as either "two-line g" or "g two."

(no response required)

*Unfortunately, octave designations are not standardized; so you must be alert to the terms and symbols used by other writers, as well as designations being developed in musical computer applications such as MIDI (Musical Instrument Digital Interface).

2.107 Indicate the octave into which each note falls. *(Use the terms one-line, two-line, etc.)*

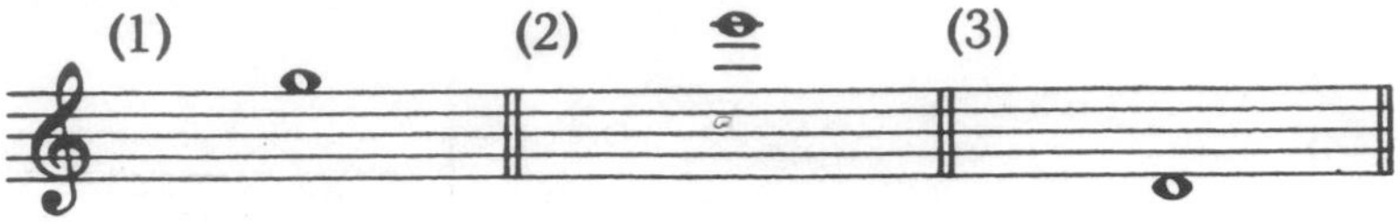

(1)   (2)   (3)

(1) _____ octave

(2) _____ octave

(3) _____ octave

(1) two-line

(2) three-line

(3) one-line

---

(1) 8⁻ ⌐   (2)   (3)

2.108 Write the notes as indicated. *(Use the ottava sign to avoid excessive ledger lines.)*

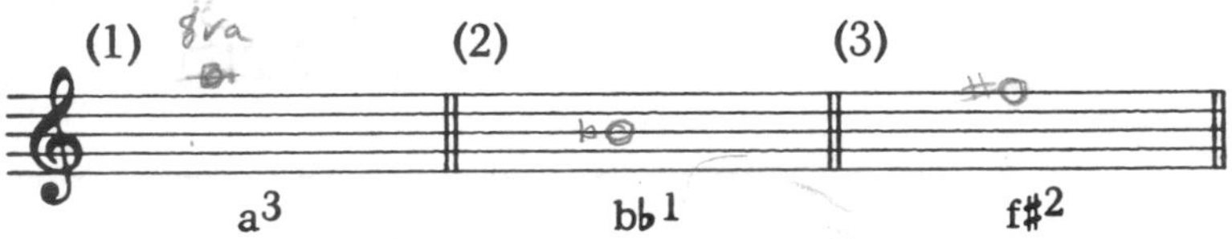

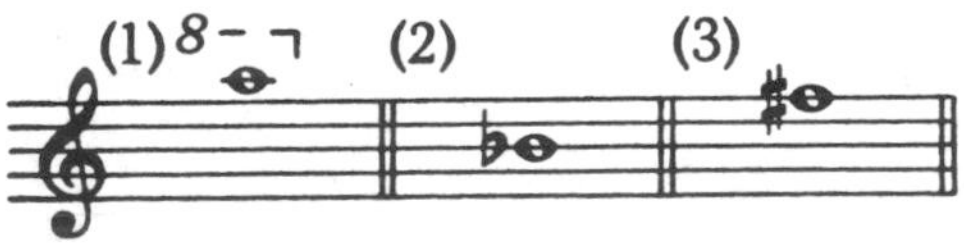

(1) *8va*   (2)   (3)

a³   bb¹   f#²

---

(1) 8⁻ ⌐   (2)   (3)

2.109 Continue as in the preceding frame.

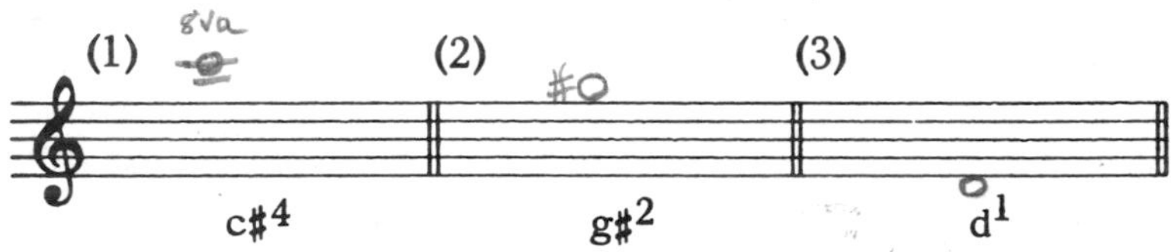

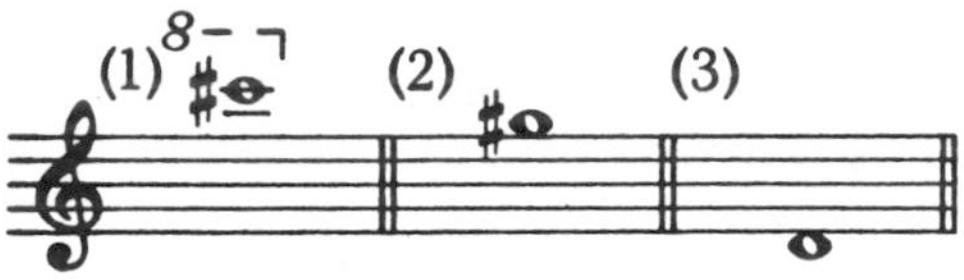

(1) *8va*   (2)   (3)

c#⁴   g#²   d¹

2.110 The one-line octave begins on middle C.

(True/False) _____

true

2.111 The first two octaves below middle C are shown below:

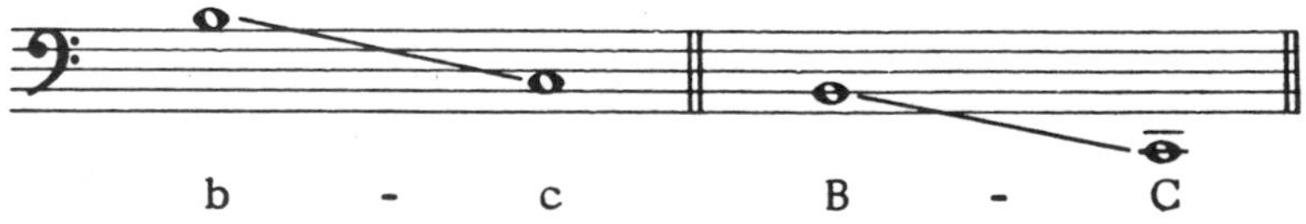

b   -   c   B   -   C

The first octave below middle C is called the SMALL OCTAVE, and lowercase letters are used; the second is called the GREAT OCTAVE, and capital letters are used.

The note *great A* is _____ octaves below *a¹*.

two

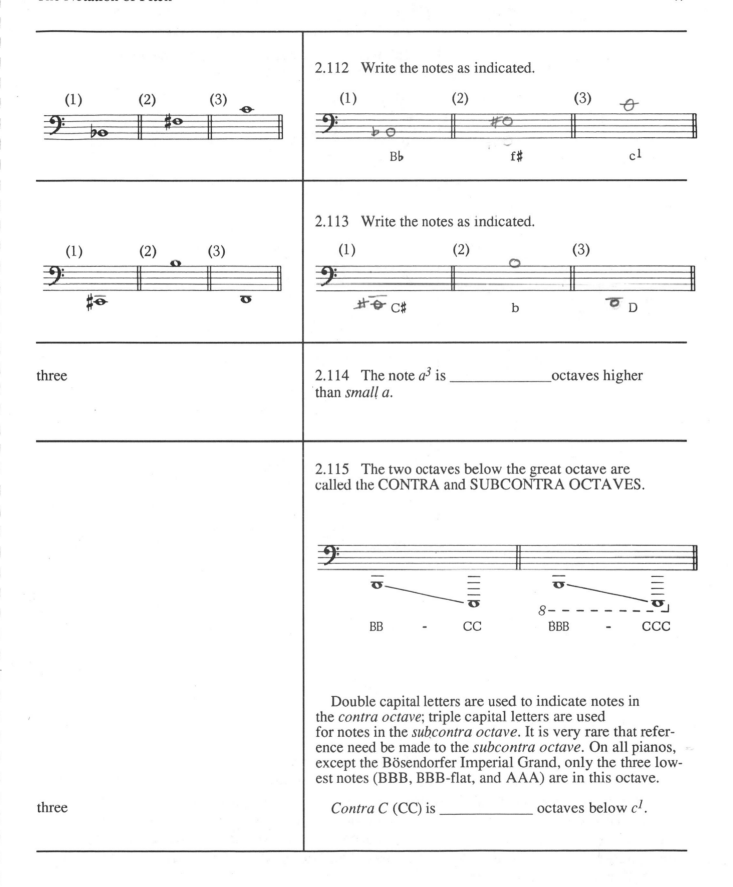

2.112 Write the notes as indicated.

(1)   (2)   (3)

Bb   f#   c¹

2.113 Write the notes as indicated.

(1)   (2)   (3)

C#   b   D

three

2.114 The note a^3 is _____ octaves higher than *small a*.

2.115 The two octaves below the great octave are called the CONTRA and SUBCONTRA OCTAVES.

BB - CC   BBB - CCC

Double capital letters are used to indicate notes in the *contra octave*; triple capital letters are used for notes in the *subcontra octave*. It is very rare that reference need be made to the *subcontra octave*. On all pianos, except the Bösendorfer Imperial Grand, only the three lowest notes (BBB, BBB-flat, and AAA) are in this octave.

Contra C (CC) is _____ octaves below c^1.

three

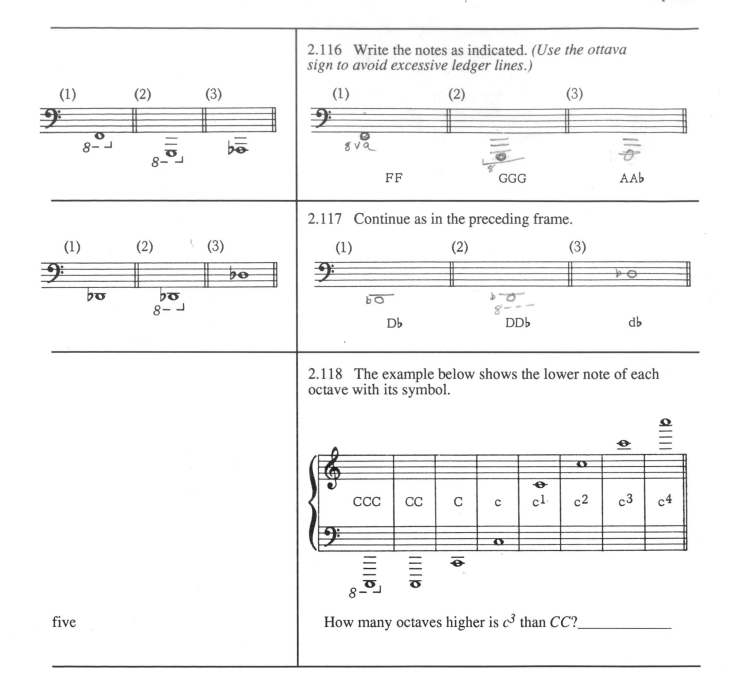

2.116   Write the notes as indicated. *(Use the ottava sign to avoid excessive ledger lines.)*

(1)   (2)   (3)

FF   GGG   AAb

2.117   Continue as in the preceding frame.

(1)   (2)   (3)

Db   DDb   db

2.118   The example below shows the lower note of each octave with its symbol.

five

How many octaves higher is c^3 than *CC*?_____

Summary

Many special symbols are required for the specific representation of pitches. Not only is the meaning of the *staff* modified by the use of various *clef* signs, but also the *basic notes* are inflected either upward or downward a *half step* by the use of *sharps* and *flats*. In addition to these, *double-sharps* and *double-flats*, which alter the pitch of a *basic note* a *whole step*, as well as *natural* signs, are necessary for correct notation. *Ledger lines* extend the range of the *staff* both upward and downward. The *ottava* sign is used to avoid excessive *ledger lines*.

Mastery Frames

(1) treble

(Frame 2.7)

(2) bass

(2.11)

(3) alto

(2.18–2.20)

(4) tenor

(2.18–2.20)

2–1   Indicate the proper name for each clef sign.

(1)

_____

(2)

_____

(3)

_____

(4)

_____

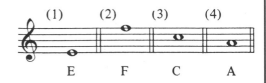

(1)   (2)   (3)   (4)

E   F   C   A

(2.6–2.10)

2–2   Identify each note.

(1)   (2)   (3)   (4)

___   ___   ___   ___

(1)   (2)   (3)   (4)

C   G   F   E

(2.19–2.22)

2–3 Identify each note.

(1)   (2)   (3)   (4)

___   ___   ___   ___

(1)   (2)   (3)   (4)

B   A   D   E

(2.11–2.15)

2–4 Identify each note.

(1)   (2)   (3)   (4)

___   ___   ___   ___

false

(2.19–2.22)

2–5 No matter what clef sign is used, whole steps occur between all adjacent basic notes (C–D, D–E, E–F, etc.)

(True/False) _____

(1)   (2)   (3)   (4)

G♯   B♭   E♭   C♮

(2.72–2.80)

2–6 Write notes on the staff as directed.

(1)   (2)   (3)   (4)

G♯   B♭   E♭   C♮

(1) *(incorrect)*   (2.73)

(2) ✓   (2.79)

(3) ✓   (2.74)

(4) *(incorrect)*   (2.86)

2–7   Check the correct statements.

   (1) A double-sharp lowers the pitch of a basic note

     by a whole step. _____

   (2) The natural always produces a basic note. _____

   (3) A flat lowers a basic note by a half step. _____

   (4) An accidental within a measure affects all such

     notes regardless of the octave. _____

---

false *(The notes in (3) are not enharmonic.)*

               (2.88–2.94)

2–8   Enharmonic equivalents are shown in each

example. (True/False) _____

               (2.42–2.51)

2–9   Write notes on the vacant staff to show the actual sounding pitch.

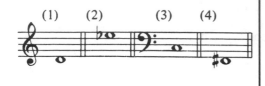

(2.111–2.118)

2–10   Write the precise pitches that are indicated. *(Do not use the **ottava** sign.)*

Supplementary Assignments

Assignment 2–1   Name: _____

1. The lines and spaces of the staff are numbered with the (highest/lowest)

    _____ in each case being given the number one.

2. Name the specific note that each clef identifies.

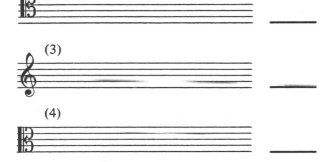

3. Name the notes on the lines and spaces of the treble clef.

4. Name the notes on the lines and spaces of the bass clef.

5. Name the notes on the lines and spaces of the tenor clef.

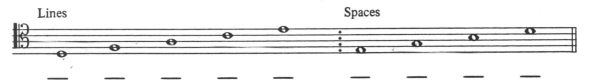

6. Name the notes on the lines and spaces of the alto clef.

7. Write "middle" C on each clef.

8. Rewrite the notes on the treble clef so they will sound the same (ledger lines are needed in some cases).

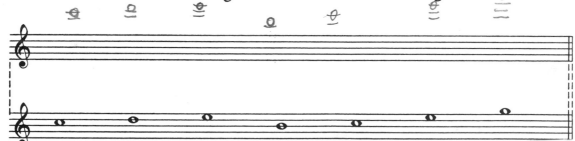

9. Rewrite the notes an octave higher. Do not use the *ottava* sign.

10. Use the *ottava* sign to indicate that the notes are to sound one octave higher.

Assignment 2–2   Name: _____

1. Use the sign ⌃ to show where half steps occur in each example.

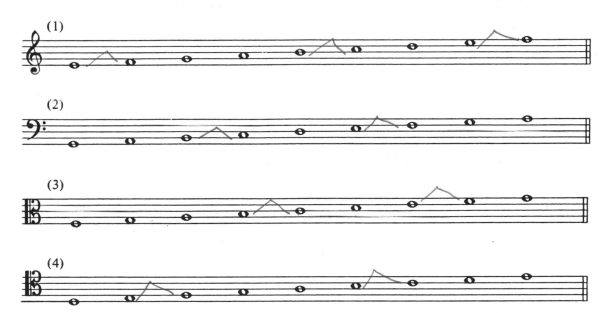

2. Draw lines to connect each accidental with the proper explanation.

(1) ♯   • Cancels a previous accidental.
(2) ♭   • Raises a basic note a whole step.
(3) ♮   • Lowers a basic note a whole step.
(4) ♭♭   • Raises a basic note a half step.
(5) ×   • Lowers a basic note a half step.

3. Write an enharmonic equivalent for each note.

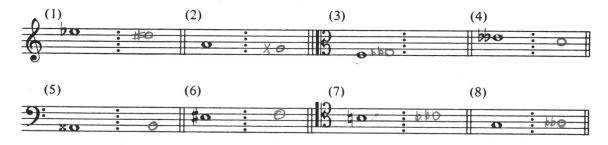

4. Write a *chromatic* half-step above each note.

5. Write a *diatonic* half step below each note.

6. Write chromatic scales as indicated.

7. Write notes in designated octaves on the grand staff as directed.

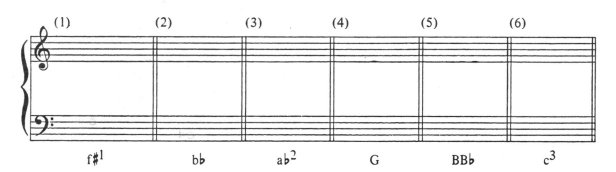

Eartraining Activities

1. Notes written on the staff in alphabetical sequence (A–G) produce a series of half or whole steps. It is essential that you recognize the difference between these two intervals. The staff produces two half steps and five whole steps. The clef sign determines where the half steps occur.

   Sing the notes below using each of the clefs indicated in turn. *(Check pitches at a keyboard.)*

2. Sing the following exercises noting the differences between half and whole steps.

   (Sing with *la*)

   The above exercises may be sung on any pitch provided the half and whole step relationships are the same.

3. Sing chromatic intervals as in the following:

4. Sing, whistle, or "think" half and whole steps in various patterns of your own invention.

3.0
Time Classification

Music is a temporal art, that is, it takes place over a period of time. In addition to sound, music is composed of various patterns of duration that combine and interact to create a unified structure in time. The various aspects of the organization of time comprise the element of music called rhythm. The basis for rhythm is the beat — a regular series of pulsations (periodic repetitions) that divide a period of time into equal parts. Beats of unequal duration are possible, and such beats are often exploited by twentieth-century composers. Most music of the eighteenth and nineteenth centuries, however, utilizes regular beats. In this book, the study of rhythm is limited to the practices of traditional music.

stress	3.1 In most music, pulsations called BEATS divide time into regular units of duration. *Beats* themselves have little expressive value, but additional interest results if some are stressed more strongly than others. *Beats* may show different degrees of _____.
no	3.2 The principle of tension and relaxation is brought into play when *beats* are given different degrees of stress. Does the degree of stress affect the duration of the *beat*? _____
stress	3.3 Patterns of stress are known as METER. *Meter* is the pattern produced by beats of varying degrees of _____
meter	3.4 The pattern that results from beats of differing degrees of stress is called the _____.

beats

3.5   Stressed beats are called STRONG; unstressed beats are called WEAK. The *meter* results from

patterns of *strong* and *weak* _____.

3.6   The simplest pattern of stresses possible is an alternation of *strong* and *weak* beats.

STRESS PATTERNS: >   U   >   U   >   U   (continuing)

BEATS: 1   2   1   2   1   2

> =   a *strong* beat
U =   a *weak* beat

Since each pattern (> U) consists of *two* beats, the term DUPLE METER is used. In a *duple* pattern the beat is organized into a sequence of one strong

and one _____ pulsation.

Tap this pattern and stress each first beat as indicated. Notice your response to this meter.

weak

---

duple

3.7   The simplest possible pattern of stresses results from an alternation of *strong* and *weak* beats. This

pattern is called _____ meter.

triple

3.8   Another simple pattern results when every third pulse is stressed.

STRESS PATTERNS: >   U   U   >   U   U
                                                                (continuing)
BEATS: 1   2   3   1   2   3

Since each pattern (> U U) consists of *three* beats, the term TRIPLE METER is used. A *strong-weak-weak* succession of pulsations results in an

organization known as _____ meter.

Tap this pattern and stress each first beat as indicated. Compare the effect of this meter with that of the meter discussed in Frame 3.6.

---

two

3.9   In *triple meter* the beat is organized into a

sequence of one strong and _____ weak beats.

Duple: > U (etc.)

Triple: > U U (etc.)

3.10   Indicate the patterns of pulsations for *duple* and *triple* meter. *(Use the signs > and U .)*

Duple meter: _____

Triple meter: _____

strong-weak-weak

3.11 *Duple meter* and *triple meter* are the two fundamental patterns produced by beats of varying degrees of stress. *Duple meter* is a succession of strong-weak beats; *Triple meter* is a series

of _____ - _____ - _____ beats.

3.12 Other more complex patterns result from combinations of duple and triple patterns. QUADRUPLE METER is a combination of two duple patterns in which the first beat is stressed more strongly than the third.

| QUADRUPLE METER |
Duple	Duple
>	U	>	U
1	2	3	4

A four-beat pattern results from a combination

duple

of two _____ patterns.

3.13 In *quadruple meter* both the first and third beats are strong. Which, however, is the stronger?

the first

_____

3.14 A combination of two duple patterns results in

quadruple

_____ meter.

3.15 Which are the weak beats in quadruple meter?

two (and) four

_____ and _____.

3.16 Which are the weak beats in triple meter?

two (and) three

_____ and _____.

3.17 A five-beat pattern is called QUINTUPLE METER. This results from a combination of a *duple* and a *triple* pattern.

```
┌─────────────────── QUINTUPLE METER ───────────────────┐
┌──────── Duple ────────┐ ┌─────────── Triple ───────────┐
>          U          >          U          U
1          2          3          4          5
```

or

```
┌─────────────────── QUINTUPLE METER ───────────────────┐
┌──────────── Triple ────────────┐ ┌──────── Duple ───────┐
>          U          U          >          U
1          2          3          4          5
```

Either the duple or the triple pattern may come first; but in either case, the first stressed beat (1) is the strongest.

A five-beat pattern results when a duple and

a _____ pattern are combined.

triple

3.18 A pattern of > U > U U or > U U > U is

called _____ meter.

quintuple

3.19 There are three strong beats in quintuple

meter. (True/False) _____

false
(*There are two strong beats.*)

3.20 How many weak beats occur in *quintuple meter*?

_____

three

3.21 *Quintuple meter* is a combination of a

triple pattern and a _____ pattern.

duple

> U > U U or
> U U > U

3.22 Indicate the pattern of beats known as quintuple meter. *(Use the signs > and U .)*

_____

3.23 The process of combining duple and triple stress patterns can be carried on to include six-beat* patterns, seven-beat patterns, and so forth; but in actual musical experiences, the ear tends to reject the larger patterns and focus instead upon smaller, repeated organizations. Thus a six-beat pattern would probably be heard as a combination of two three-beat patterns, and a seven-beat pattern as a combination of a four-beat plus a three-beat pattern (or the reverse).

(1) duple

(2) triple
(any order)

What are the two basic meters which are com-

bined to produce more complex ones? (1) _____;

and (2) _____.

_____

*Although not very common, musical situations involving these patterns may be found, in which case the terms SEXTUPLE and SEPTUPLE are appropriate.

quadruple

3.24 The stress pattern (> U > U) is called

_____ meter.

duple

3.25 The stress pattern (> U) is called _____ meter.

triple

3.26 The stress pattern (> U U) is called _____ meter.

beats	3.27 The terms *duple, triple, quadruple,* and *quintuple* refer to the number of _____ in each stress pattern.
three	3.28 Each stress pattern constitutes a MEASURE. A *measure* in triple meter consists of how many beats? _____
beats	3.29 *Measures* vary in length according to the number of _____ in each stress pattern.
subdivided	3.30 The rhythmic interest of a composition would be slight indeed if the duration of all tones should coincide with the beat. Actually, a single beat may contain two, three, four, five, or more tones. Usually beats are *divided* normally into two or three parts, or *subdivided* normally into four or six parts.* The beat itself is the most elementary organization of time possible. By establishing a meter through patterns of stress, the musical value of the beat is increased. A higher level of rhythmic complexity results from dividing the beat into two or three equal parts. Still greater rhythmic interest is obtained if the beat is _____ into four or six parts.** --- *Irregular groups of notes are presented in Chapter 4.0, Frames 4.60–.64. **You will probably tend to hear smaller groups of twos or threes first, but it is also possible to perceive larger successions of the smaller groups, depending on stress patterns emphasized by the composer. In this way rhythm and rhythmic patterns become multi-dimensional. This concept may suggest of further study later on in your music studies.

	3.31 We shall now concentrate on two basic types of rhythmic division which are determined by how beats are normally divided. If beats are divided consistently into *two* equal parts, the term SIMPLE TIME is used; if beats are divided consistently into *three* equal parts, the term COMPOUND TIME is used. The terms *simple time* and *compound time* refer to the manner in which _____ are divided.
beats	
	3.32 In *simple time* beats are divided normally into how many equal parts? _____
two	
	3.33 If beats are divided consistently into *three* equal parts, the term _____ time is used.
compound	
two (or) three	3.34 Beats may be divided into either _____ or _____ equal parts.
divided	3.35 The terms *duple, triple, quadruple,* and *quintuple* refer to the number of beats per measure, whereas the terms *simple* and *compound* refer to the manner in which beats normally are _____.

3.36   A TIME CLASSIFICATION identifies the organization of the meter and indicates the *normal division of the beat*.

   In *duple meter* the stress pattern consists of two beats (> U). If each beat is divided into *two* equal parts, the time classification is DUPLE-SIMPLE.

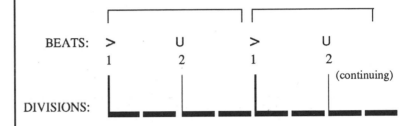

   The term *duple-simple* means there are *two* beats per measure, and each *beat* is divided into

_____ equal parts.

two

3.37   If the *beats* in duple meter are divided into *three* equal parts, the time classification is DUPLE-COMPOUND.

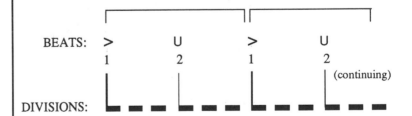

   The term *duple-compound* means there are *two* beats per measure, and each *beat* is divided

into _____ equal parts.

three

two

3.38   The term *simple time* means that beats are

normally divided into _____ equal parts.

three

3.39   The term *compound time* means that beats are

normally divided into _____ equal parts.

3.40   Music in simple time affects us quite differently
than does music in compound time.

  Sing the song *Yankee Doodle* as notated below:

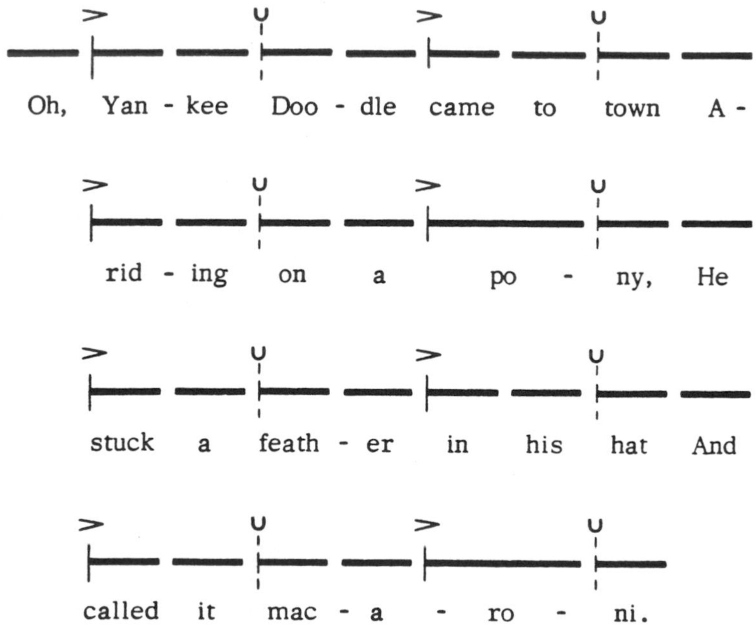

Oh,   Yan - kee   Doo - dle   came   to   town   A -

rid - ing   on   a   po   -   ny,   He

stuck   a   feath - er   in   his   hat   And

called   it   mac - a   -   ro   -   ni.

  Since the beats are divided consistently into *two* equal parts,

simple

this is an example of duple- _____ time.

3.41   Sing the song *Three Blind Mice* as notated below:

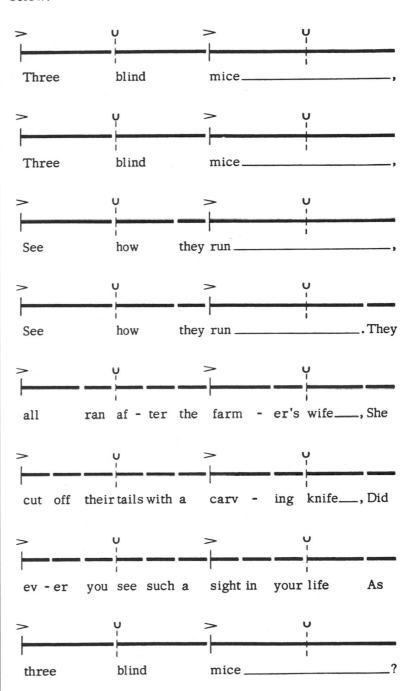

compound

This song is an example of duple-_____ time.

3.42 Composers often use simple time to express musical ideas which are "strong," "straightforward,"or "positive." Compound time is often used for ideas of a more "flowing" or "swaying" nature. Do you think the songs in Frames 3.40 and 3.41 demonstrate

your opinion

these characteristics? _____

3.43 Do you think simple and compound time need *always* give rise to emotional responses such as

your opinion

these? _____

3.44 Time classifications are interpreted as follows: The *first* part of the classification refers to the *number* of beats per measures; the *second* part indicates the *manner* in which beats are normally divided.

Thus the time classification *duple-simple* means that there are *two* beats per measure and the *normal division* of the beat is into *two* equal parts.

Time classifications indicate not only the *number* of *beats* per measure, but also the *normal division* of

beat

the _____.

3.45 Duple-simple and duple-compound time both have *two* beats per measure; but in duple-*simple* time the beat is divided into *two* equal parts, while in duple-*compound* time the *beat* is divided into

three

_____ equal parts.

the number of beats per measure	3.46 What does the *first* part of a time classification indicate? _____
the normal division of the beat	3.47 What does the *second* part of a time classification indicate? _____
two	3.48 *Triple-simple* indicates: (1) *three* beats per measure; and (2) the *division* of each beat into_____ equal parts.
four	3.49 *Quadruple-compound* indicates: (1) _____beats per measure; and (2) the *division* of each beat into *three* equal parts.
three	3.50 *Triple-compound* indicates: (1) *three* beats per measure; and (2) the *division* of each beat into_____ equal parts.
two	3.51 *Quadruple-simple* indicates: (1) *four* beats per measure; and (2) the *division* of each beat into_____ equal parts.
five	3.52 *Quintuple-simple* indicates: (1) _____beats per measure; and (2) the *division* of each beat into *two* equal parts.

three	3.53 *Duple-compound* indicates: (1) *two* beats per measure; and (2) the *division* of each beat into_____ equal parts.
two	3.54 *Duple-simple* indicates: (1) *two* beats per measure; and (2) the *division* of each beat into _____equal parts.
three	3.55 *Quintuple-compound* indicates: (1) *five* beats per measure; and (2) the *division* of each beat into _____ equal parts.
duple-simple	3.56 If there are *two* beats per measure and each beat is divided into *two* equal parts, the time classification is _____ - _____.
triple-simple	3.57 If there are *three* beats per measure and each beat is divided into *two* equal parts, the time classification is _____ - _____.
quadruple-compound	3.58 If there are *four* beats per measure and each beat is divided into *three* equal parts, the time classification is _____ - _____.

quintuple-simple	3.59 If there are *five* beats per measure and each beat is divided into *two* equal parts, the time classification is _____ - _____.
quintuple-compound	3.60 If there are *five* beats per measure and each beat is divided into *three* equal parts, the time classification is _____ - _____.
quadruple-simple	3.61 If there are *four* beats per measure and each beat is divided into *two* equal parts, the time classification is _____ - _____.
triple-compound	3.62 If there are *three* beats per measure and each beat is divided into *three* equal parts, the time classification is _____ - _____.
duple-compound	3.63 If there are *two* beats per measure and each beat is divided into *three* equal parts, the time classification is _____ - _____.
true	3.64 The terms *duple, triple, quadruple,* and *quintuple* refer to the number of beats per measure. (True/False) _____
how each beat is divided	3.65 To what do the terms *simple* and *compound* refer? _____

beat	3.66 The regularly recurring pulse of music is called the _____.
first	3.67 The number of beats per measure is expressed by the (first/second) _____ part of the time classification.
simple (and) compound	3.68 The beat can be divided into *two* or *three* equal parts. This *division* is expressed by the terms _____ and _____.

triplet	3.69 The natural division of the beat in *simple* time is into *two* equal parts. The division of the beat into *three* equal parts in simple time is called a BORROWED DIVISION (or *triplet*).
	   Tap (or say with the syllable **ta***) the divisions expressed in the line notation below:*
	
	SIMPLE TIME
	
	BEAT: 1 2
	DIVISION:
	BORROWED DIVISION:
	
	   The *borrowed division* in *simple* time is sometimes called a _____.

borrowed	3.70 *"Triplet"* is another name for a _____ division.

3.71 The natural division of the beat in *compound* time is into *three* equal parts. The division of the beat into *two* equal parts in *compound* time is called a BORROWED DIVISION (or *duplet*).
Tap (or say with the syllable* ta) *the divisions expressed in line notation below:

COMPOUND TIME

The *borrowed division* in *compound* time is

two | a division of the beat into _____ equal parts.

3.72 The term *borrowed division* refers to the use of a division in *simple* time which is normal in *compound* time or vice versa. The division is literally "borrowed" from one for use in the other.

The borrowed division in *simple* time is a

three | division of the beat into _____ equal parts.

3.73 Is the division of the beat into *two* equal parts

yes | a natural division in *simple* time? _____

3.74 Is the division of the beat into *two* equal parts

no
(This is a borrowed division or duplet.) | a natural division in *compound* time? _____

3.75 Is the division of the beat into *three* equal parts

no
(This is a borrowed division or triplet.) | a natural division in *simple* time? _____

simple	3.76 In *simple time* the beat *sub*divides into *four* equal parts. Four is the normal subdivision of the beat in _____ time.
compound	3.77 In *compound time* the beat *sub*divides into *six* equal parts. Six is the normal subdivision of the beat in _____ time.
four	3.78 What is the natural subdivision of the beat in simple time? _____
six	3.79 What is the natural subdivision of the beat in compound time? _____
false *(The term compound time refers to the division of the beat into three equal parts, not to the number of beats per measure.)*	3.80 The term *compound time* means there are three beats per measure. (True/False) _____
true	3.81 The term *duple* refers to a meter which has two beats per measure. (True/False) _____

2	3.82 What is the natural division of the beat in simple time? (2, 3, 4, 6) _____
3	3.83 What is the natural division of the beat in compound time? (2, 3, 4, 6) _____
4	3.84 What is the natural subdivision of the beat in simple time? (2, 3, 4, 6) _____
6	3.85 What is the natural subdivision of the beat in compound time? (2, 3, 4, 6) _____
3	3.86 In simple time a borrowed division divides the beat into how many parts? (2, 3, 4, 6) _____
2	3.87 In compound time a borrowed division divides the beat into how many parts? (2, 3, 4, 6) _____
true	3.88 The triplet is the same as a borrowed division in simple time. (True/False) _____
true	3.89 The duplet is the same as a borrowed division in compound time. (True/False) _____

Summary

Time is organized on various levels of complexity. The simplest is the series of pulsations called the *beat*. Next is *meter*, which results from *patterns of stress* imposed on the *beat*. The more common meters are *duple, triple, quadruple,* and *quintuple,* depending on the number of beats between each primary stress. The next level of rhythmic organization is the result of dividing beats into either *two* or *three* parts. The term *simple time* refers to the *division* of the *beat* into *two* equal parts; the term *compound time* refers to the *division* of the *beat* into *three* equal parts. *Borrowed divisions* occur when the *normal division* in *compound* time is used in *simple* time, or vice versa. Beats *subdivide* normally into *four* parts in *simple* time, and *six* parts in *compound* time.

Mastery Frames

beat (Frame 3.1)	3–1 The pulse that divides time into equal durations is called the _____.
true (3.3–3.5)	3–2 Meter is the term that refers to patterns of stress applied to beats. (True/False) _____
duple (3.6–3.7)	3–3 When the first of each group of two beats is stressed, the result is _____ meter.
triple (3.8–3.11)	3–4 When the first of each group of three beats is stressed, the result is _____ meter.
divided (3.31–3.35)	3–5 The terms simple and compound refer to how beats are normally _____.

(1) 2
(2) 3
 	
(3.31–3.35)
	3–6 Indicate the number of divisions in each case.
	
	    (1) Simple time _____
	    (2) Compound time _____

two (3.36)	3–7 The time classification duple-simple means that there are _____ beats per measure, and the beat is normally divided into two equal parts.

	Beats	Divisions
(1)	3	3
(2)	4	2
(3)	5	3

(3.44–3.68)

3–8   Supply the missing information.

Time Classification	Beats per Measure	Number of Divisions
(1) Triple-compound	_____	_____
(2) Quadruple-simple	_____	_____
(3) Quintuple-compound	_____	_____

---

compound

(3.69–3.70)

3–9   The triplet is a division of the beat that is borrowed from (simple/compound) _____time.

---

true

(3.69–3.75)

3–10   Borrowed divisions occur in both simple and compound meters. (True/False) _____

Supplementary Assignments

Assignment 3–1   Name: _____

1. Use the signs > and ∪ to indicate the stress patterns indicated below. *(Sufficient beats are marked off to show recurring patterns.)*

    (1) Duple |__|__|__|__|__|__|__|__|__|__|__|__|__|__|__|__|__|__|__|

    (2) Triple |__|__|__|__|__|__|__|__|__|__|__|__|__|__|__|__|__|__|__|

    (3) Quadruple |__|__|__|__|__|__|__|__|__|__|__|__|__|__|__|__|__|__|

    (4) Quintuple |__|__|__|__|__|__|__|__|__|__|__|__|__|__|__|__|__|__|

2. Triple meter has _____ beats per measure.

3. How many strong beats are contained in one measure of quadruple meter?

    _____

4. In simple time the beat is normally divided into _____ equal parts.

5. In compound time the beat is normally divided into _____ equal parts.

6. The first part of the time classification below indicates that there are _____ beats per measure; the second part indicates that the beat is normally divided into

    _____ equal parts.

Time classification: triple-simple

7. Provide the appropriate time classification in each case.

	Beats per Measure	Number of Divisions	Time Classification
(1)	2	2	_____ - _____
(2)	2	3	_____ - _____
(3)	3	2	_____ - _____
(4)	3	3	_____ - _____
(5)	4	2	_____ - _____
(6)	4	3	_____ - _____
(7)	5	2	_____ - _____
(8)	5	3	_____ - _____

8. Borrowed divisions in simple time are called _____.

9. Borrowed divisions in compound time are called _____.

10. In simple time the beat normally subdivides into _____parts.

11. In compound time the beat normally subdivides into _____parts.

Assignment 3–2   Name: _____

    Scan and sing the songs below and determine whether they are in simple or compound time:

Row, Row, Your Boat

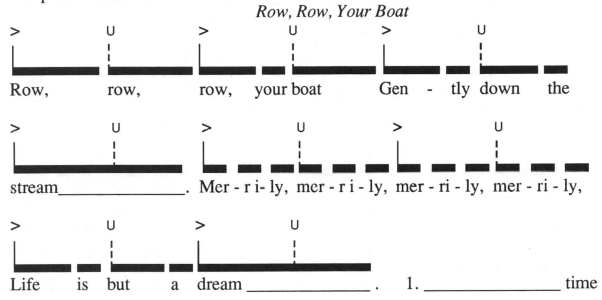

1. _____ time

Skip to My Lou

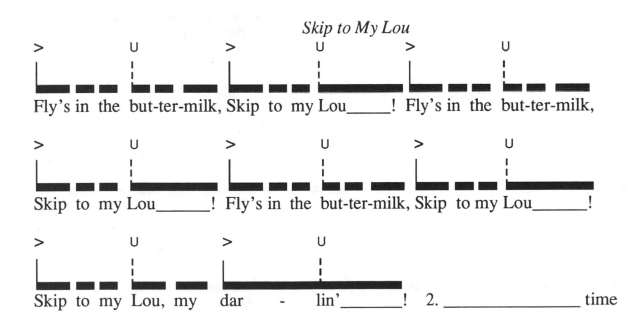

2. _____ time

She'll Be Comin' 'Round the Mountain

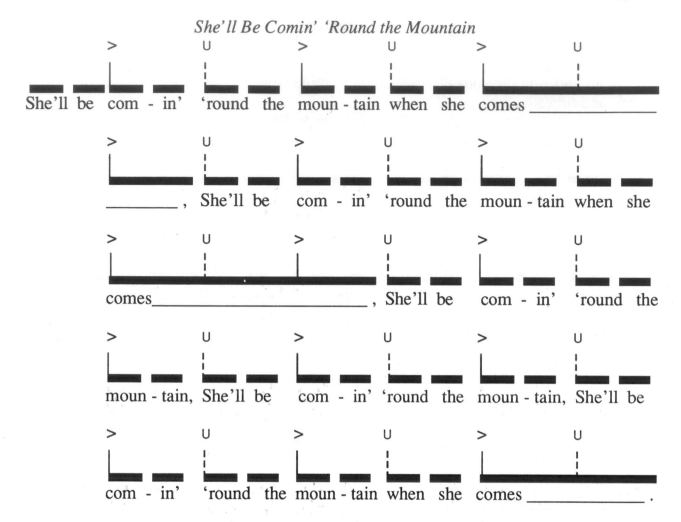

3. _____ time

For He's a Jolly Good Fellow

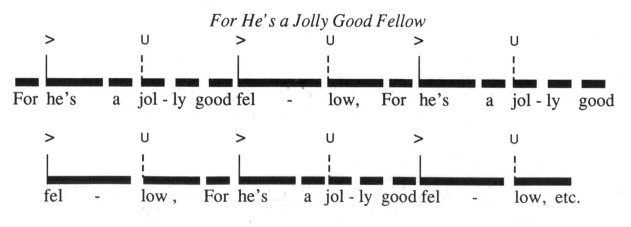

4. _____ time

Eartraining Activities

Musicians must develop a keen sense of time passing and the various ways time is organized for musical purposes. There are three basic levels of rhythmic organization: (1) the beat; (2) meter; and (3) the division and subdivision of the beat.

The rhythm of most traditional music is based on beats of equal duration; the ability to maintain a steady beat is fundamental to effective performance. Perhaps the best and most accessible resource available to help you develop a feeling for a steady beat is the naturally regular gait of normal walking. Walking also serves as an ideal background for thinking or humming rhythmic patterns.

1.   While walking (or marking time), form a mental image that suggests steady movement of a point through space. Then imagine that your steps mark off segments of the line created by the moving point. Create your own image, but the mental association of time and space is useful within many musical contexts, tonal as well as rhythmic.

2.   Experience the various meters by thinking, clapping, or humming accents as in the following:

  a. duple meter   >   U   >   U

  b. triple meter   >   U   U   >   U   U

  c. quadruple meter   >   U   >   U   >   U   >   U

  d. quintuple meter   >   U   U   >   U or >   U   >   U   U

3.   By thinking, saying "ta," clapping, or by any other means, divide beats into two or three equal parts to produce simple or compound time as in the following:

  a. duple simple

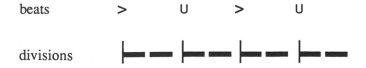

  beats   >   U   >   U

  divisions

  b. duple compound

  beats   >   U   >   U

  divisions

4.   Sing songs such as those in Frames 3.40 and 3.41 and in Assignment 3–2 in the text, focusing your attention on the rhythmic structure.

4.0

Note and Rest Values

The symbols used to represent tones are called *notes*. In Chapter 2.0 you learned that the pitch of tones is indicated by placing notes on the staff. Notes also indicate relative duration. The rhythmic element of music is often complex, but, fortunately, there are only a few basic types of notes. Also, notes bear a simple relationship to one another; each represents a duration twice as long as the next-smaller note. For each type of note there is a corresponding symbol called a *rest*, which indicates an equivalent duration of silence.

4.1 The types of notes which are used to indicate the relative duration of tones are shown below:

𝅜	double whole note (or *breve*)*	♬	sixteenth note
𝅝	whole note	♬	thirty-second note
𝅗𝅥	half note	♬	sixty-fourth note*
♩	quarter note	♬	128th note*
♪	eighth note		

Write several whole notes on various lines and spaces.

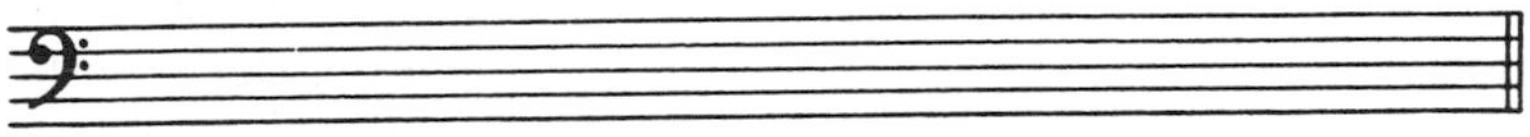

---

*The double whole note, the sixty-fourth note, and the 128th note are used so rarely that they need not be stressed here. For the remainder of this book these notes will not be used.

(etc.)

4.2 Observe the name given to each part of the note.

QUARTER NOTE   EIGHTH NOTE

Head→ ♩ ←Stem   ♪←Flag

The eighth note consists of three parts: the flag, the stem, and the _____.

head

87

4.3   Stems are one octave in length. They are placed on the *right* side of the head and extend upward if the note is *below* the third (middle) line of the staff.

If the note is *below* the third line of the staff, the stem is placed on the _____ side of the head.

right

4.4   If the note is *above* the third line of the staff, the stem is placed on the *left* side of the head and extends downward.

Stems are placed on the left side of the head and extend downward if the note is *above* the _____ line of the staff.

third (or middle)

4.5   If the note is on the third (middle) line of the staff, the stem may extend either upward or downward.* If the stem extends downward, it is placed on the *left* side of the head; if it extends upward it is placed on the *right* side of the head.

All stems which extend downward are placed on the left side of the head. All stems which extend upward are placed on the _____ side of the head.

right

*Most printed music shows a preference for the downward stem when notes are on the third line.

4.6 The flag appears on the right side of the stem in all cases.

Add a stem and one flag to each note head.

4.7 Add a stem and two flags to each note head.

4.8 The notes in the preceding frame are (half/quarter/

eighth/sixteenth) _____ notes.

sixteenth

4.9 Circle the notes that are *not* correctly written.

4.10 Write several half notes on various lines and spaces. *(Observe correct placement of stems.)*

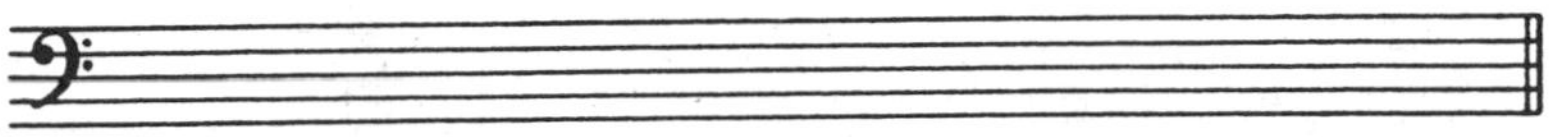

(etc.)

4.11   Write several quarter notes on various lines and spaces. *(Observe correct placement of stems.)*

4.12   Write several eighth notes on various lines and spaces. *(Observe correct placement of stems and flags.)*

4.13   Write several sixteenth notes on various lines and spaces. *(Continue to observe correct placement of stems and flags in this and the following frames.)*

4.14   Write several thirty-second notes on various lines and spaces.

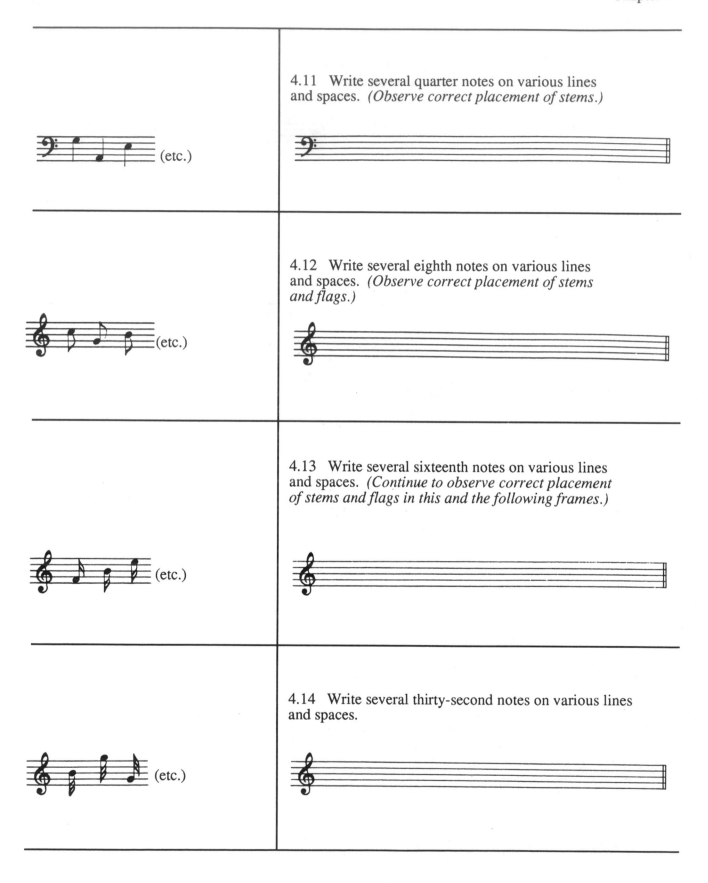

4.15 Instead of a separate flag for each note, BEAMS are often used to join several notes together.

Beam

Beams

Beams generally connect notes which are to sound within the same metrical unit (the beat or measure).

Beams take the place of _____.

flags

Note: Examples here are *not* to be interpreted within any meter. They are meant to show some generalized situations of how to handle beaming. The examples are *not* meant to be all-inclusive.

4.16 The use of beams often causes one or more of the stems to be placed differently than would be the case if a flag were used. If most of the notes are above the third (middle) line of the staff, stems extend *downward;* if most of the notes are below the third line, the stems extend *upward*.

Note that beams are always *straight* lines.

Connect the notes in each group with beams as directed.

(1) EIGHTH NOTES   (2) SIXTEENTH NOTES

(1)

(2)

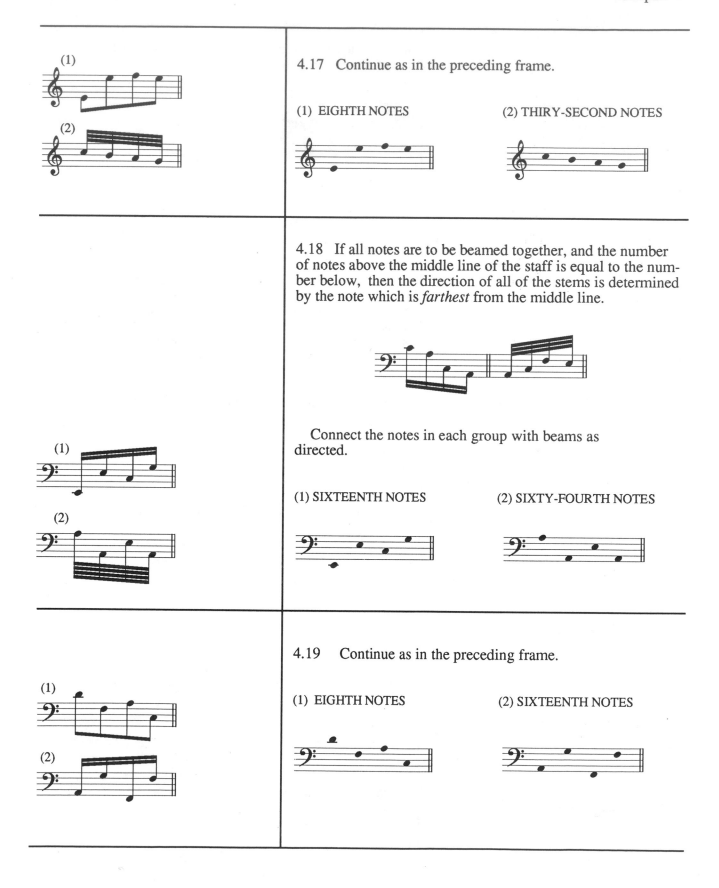

(1)

(2)

4.17 Continue as in the preceding frame.

(1) EIGHTH NOTES   (2) THIRY-SECOND NOTES

4.18 If all notes are to be beamed together, and the number of notes above the middle line of the staff is equal to the number below, then the direction of all of the stems is determined by the note which is *farthest* from the middle line.

Connect the notes in each group with beams as directed.

(1) SIXTEENTH NOTES   (2) SIXTY-FOURTH NOTES

(1)

(2)

4.19 Continue as in the preceding frame.

(1) EIGHTH NOTES   (2) SIXTEENTH NOTES

(1)

(2)

	4.20 Notes do not, in themselves, indicate duration precisely, but their values are related in the manner indicated by the name of each note.
	A whole note = 2 half notes.
	A whole note = 4 quarter notes.
	A whole note = 8 eighth notes. (etc.)
	A whole note equals how many sixteenth notes?
16	_____
four	4.21 Whereas two quarter notes equal one half note, it requires _____ eighth notes to equal one half note.
	4.22 A quarter note equals how many eighth notes?
2	_____
	4.23 A quarter note equals how many sixteenth notes?
4	_____
	4.24 An eighth note equals how many sixteenth notes?
2	_____
	4.25 Supply the answer in each case.
(1) 2	(1) A o note = _____ ♩ notes.
(2) 2	(2) A ♩ note = _____ ♩ notes.
(3) 2	(3) A ♩ note = _____ ♪ notes.

(1) 4

(2) 8

(3) 8

4.26 Continue as in the preceding frame.

(1) A o note = _____ ♩ notes.

(2) A ♩ note = _____ ♪ notes.

(3) A ♩ note = _____ ♬ notes.

(1) 2

(2) 2

(3) 4

4.27 Continue as in the preceding frame.

(1) An ♪ note = _____ ♪ notes.

(2) A ♬ note = _____ ♬ notes.

(3) A ♩ note = _____ ♪ notes.

(1) 4

(2) 4

(3) 1

4.28 Continue as in the preceding frame.

(1) An ♪ note = _____ ♬ notes.

(2) A ♩ note = _____ ♪ notes.

(3) A ♩ note = _____ ♩ notes.

4.29 RESTS are symbols which represent periods of silence. There is a rest sign that corresponds to each of the basic note values.

	double whole rest*
	whole rest
	half rest
	quarter rest
	eighth rest
	sixteenth rest
	thirty-second rest
	sixty-fourth rest*
	128th rest*

Care must be taken not to confuse the whole rest with the half rest. The whole rest hangs from the fourth line of the staff.

Write several whole rests.

(etc.)

*The double whole, sixty-fourth, and 128th rests are rarely used. They will not appear in the remainder of this book.

Expository frame.

4.30   There is now a general tradition to use the whole rest "to represent as *entire* measure of rest, [and] it must not ordinarily be employed for *less* than a measure."* While there might be exceptions to this in a 4/2, 8/4, or even a rare 3/1, 2/1 meter, "a whole rest must not be used to indicate a fractional portion of a measure."*

(no response required)

*Gardner Read, *Music Notation*, p. 98.

4.31   The half rest sits on the third line of the staff.
            Write several half rests.

4.32   Write several quarter rests.

4.33   Write several eighth rests.

4.34   Write several sixteenth rests.

4.35   Write several thirty-second rests.

4.36 Rests are related to one another in the same way as notes.

    A whole rest = 2 half rests.

    A whole rest = 4 quarter rests.

    A whole rest = 8 eighth rests.

    A whole rest equals how many thirty-second

32

rests? _____

4.37 Supply the answer in each case.

(1) 4   (1) A   ⎯   rest = _____ ⁊ rests.

(2) 2   (2) A   ⎯   rest = _____ ⁊ rests.

(3) 4   (3) A   ⎯   rest = _____ ⁊ rests.

4.38 Supply the answer in each case.

(1) 2   (1) An ⁊ rest = _____ ⁊ rests.

(2) 2   (2) A ⁊ rest = _____ ⁊ rests.

(3) 4   (3) An ⁊ rest = _____ ⁊ rests.

4.39 Supply the answer in each case.

(1) 8   (1) A   ⎯   rest = _____ ⁊ rests.

(2) 4   (2) A ⁊ rest = _____ ⁊ rests.

(3) 1   (3) An ⁊ rest = _____ ⁊ rests.

4.40 A DOT may be added to both notes and rests.*

𝆹·, 𝅗𝅥·, ♩·, ♪·, etc.

▬·, ▬·, 𝄽·, 𝄾·, etc.

The dot increases the value of a note or rest by one-half of its original value.

$$\text{♩·} = \text{♩} \smile \text{♩} \qquad \text{▬·} = \text{▬} + \text{𝄽}$$

$$\text{♩·} = \text{♩} \smile \text{♪} \qquad \text{𝄽·} = \text{𝄽} + \text{𝄾}$$

The duration of a dotted note is (longer/shorter)

longer

_____ than the same note without the dot.

*Printed music issued by some publishers reveals a tendency not to dot rests, but rather to write separate rests to represent the value desired (𝄽𝄾 instead of 𝄽· , 𝄾𝄾 instead of 𝄾· , etc.). However, it is correct to dot rests if you wish. Many examples of dotted rests can be found in published music.

4.41 Complete each problem as in the preceding frame.

(1) 𝅝 ⌣ 𝅗𝅥

(2) ♪ ⌣ 𝅘𝅥𝅯

(3) 𝅘𝅥𝅯 ⌣ 𝅘𝅥𝅰

(1) 𝅝· = _____ _____.
                    (⌣)

(2) ♪· = _____ _____.
                   (⌣)

(3 𝅘𝅥𝅯· = _____ _____.
                   (⌣)

4.42 Rewrite using dots.

(1) 𝅗𝅥·

(2) ♪·

(3) 𝅝·

(1) 𝅗𝅥 ⌣ ♩ = _____.

(2) ♪ ⌣ 𝅘𝅥𝅯 = _____.

(3) 𝅝 ⌣ 𝅗𝅥 = _____.

(1) ⊤ + ⊤	4.43 Complete each problem. *(Refer to Frame 4.40)* (1) ⊤· = _____ + _____ . (2) ɔ· = _____ + _____ . (3) ɣ· = _____ + _____ .
(1) ɔ· (2) ξ. (3) ⊤·	4.44 Rewrite using dots. (1) ɔ + ɣ = _____ . (2) ξ + ɔ = _____ . (3) ⊤ + ξ = _____ .
1/2	4.45 An additional dot may be applied to a dotted note or rest. 𝅘𝅥.. , 𝅘𝅥.. , 𝅘𝅥𝅮.. , etc. ⊤·· , ξ.. , ɔ·· , etc. The second dot increases the value of the note or rest by one-half of the value represented by the first dot. 𝅘𝅥.. = 𝅘𝅥 ⌣ 𝅘𝅥 ⌣ 𝅘𝅥𝅮 ⊤·· = ⊤ + ξ + ɔ Each successive dot increases the value of the note by (1/8, 1/4, 1/2) _____ the value of the preceding dot.

(1) 𝄽 + 𝄾 + 𝄿

(2) 𝄾 + 𝄿 + 𝅘

(3) ▬ + 𝄽 + 𝄾

4.46 Complete each problem as in the preceding frame.

(1) 𝄽..   = _____ + _____ + _____.

(2) 𝄾··   = _____ + _____ + _____.

(3) ▬··   = _____ + _____ + _____.

---

(1) ♩ ⌣ ♪ ⌣ ♬

(2) ♪ ⌣ ♬ ⌣ ♬

(3) ♩ ⌣ ♩ ⌣ ♪

4.47 Complete each problem.

(1) ♩.. = _____
                (‿)(‿)

(2) ♪.. = _____
                (‿)(‿)

(3 ♩.. = _____
                (‿)(‿)

4.48 An undotted note divides naturally into *two* equal parts.

𝅝 = ♩ ♩

♩ = ♩ ♩

♩ = ♫

Show the natural division of an eighth note.

♪ = _____

♬

𝅘𝅥𝅯𝅘𝅥𝅯𝅘𝅥𝅯

4.49 A dotted note, representing half again as long a duration as the same note without a dot, divides naturally into *three* equal parts.

$$\text{♩.} = \text{♪♪♪}$$
$$\text{♩.} = \text{♬♩}$$
$$\text{♪.} = \text{♬♬}$$

Show the natural division of a dotted sixteenth note.

$$\text{♪.} = \underline{\hspace{2cm}}$$

---

(1) ♩ ♩

(2) ♬

4.50 Show (with notes) the division of each note below.

(1) 𝅗𝅥 divides into _____.

(2) ♩ divides into _____.

---

(1) ♩ ♩ ♩

(2) 𝅘𝅥𝅮𝅘𝅥𝅮𝅘𝅥𝅮

4.51 Continue as in the preceding frame.

(1) 𝅗𝅥. divides into _____.

(2) ♩. divides into _____.

---

(1) 𝅗𝅥 𝅗𝅥

(2) 𝅘𝅥𝅯𝅘𝅥𝅯𝅘𝅥𝅯

4.52 Continue as in the preceding frame.

(1) 𝅝 divides into _____.

(2) ♪. divides into _____.

---

(1) ♩ ♩

(2) ♩ ♩ ♩

4.53 Continue as in the preceding frame.

(1) 𝅗𝅥 divides into _____.

(2) 𝅗𝅥. divides into _____.

(1) ♫	**4.54** Continue as in the preceding frame.
(2) ♫♪	(1) ♪ divides into _____.
	(2) ♩. divides into _____.
	4.55 An undotted note subdivides naturally into *four* equal parts.
	♩ subdivides into ♫♫
	♩ subdivides into ♫♫
	♪ subdivides into ♫♫
	The normal subdivision of an undotted note is
four	into _____ equal parts.
(1) ♫♫	**4.56** Show how each note naturally subdivides.
	(1) ♩ subdivides into _____.
(2) ♫♫	(2) ♪ subdivides into _____.
	4.57 A dotted note subdivides naturally into *six* equal parts.
	♩. subdivides into ♫♫♫
	♩. subdivides into ♫♫♫
	♪. subdivides into ♫♫♫
	The normal subdivision of a dotted note is into
six	_____ equal parts.

(1)  ♫♫♫♫

(2)  ♫♫♫♫

4.58 Show how each note naturally subdivides.

(1) ♩. subdivides into _____.

(2) ♪. subdivides into _____.

---

(1)  ♫♫

(2)  ♬♬♬

4.59 Show how each note naturally subdivides.

(1) ♩ subdivides into _____.

(2) ♪. subdivides into _____.

4.60 By using the proper indication, notes may be sub-divided into four, five, six, seven, or more parts.

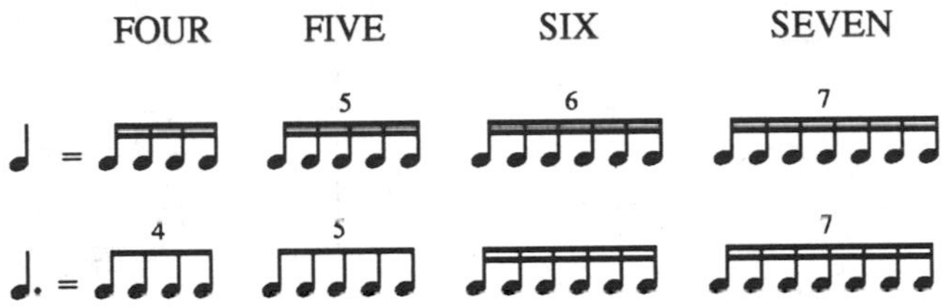

FOUR	FIVE	SIX	SEVEN

♩ = ♬♬   ♬♬⁵   ♬♬♬⁶   ♬♬♬⁷

♩. = ♬♩⁴   ♬♬⁵   ♬♬♬   ♬♬♬♬⁷

Subdivision of an undotted note into five, six, or seven parts, or the subdivision of a dotted note into four, five, or seven parts results in IRREGULAR GROUPS.* Such groups are not the result of a natural division or subdivision and thus may be regarded as "artificial." As shown above, a number is used to indicate how many notes are included in the group.

Is six a natural subdivision of an undotted note?

_____

*The terms "foreign" and "mixed" groups are also used.

---

no
(An undotted note subdivides natu-rally into four equal parts.)

Expository frame.

4.61   There is a lack of standardization regarding the note values used to indicate irregular groups.* A simple and practical principle to follow is to use the note value of the division until the subdivision is reached, and to continue to use the value of the subdivision until the natural division of the subdivision is reached.

*For further information regarding the notation of irregular divisions see Gardner Read, "Some Problems of Rhythmic Notation," *Journal of Music Theory,* 9/1 (1965), pp. 153–62, or Gardner Read, Chapter 11, "Barlines and Rhythms," *Music Notation,* Boston: Taplinger, pp. 182-222.

(1) ♩♩♩♩♩ (5)	4.62 Supply the correct notation.
	
	(1) A ♩ note subdivided into five parts is
	
	  notated _____.
	
	(2) A ♩ note subdivided into seven parts is
	
	    notated _____.

(2) ♩♩♩♩♩♩♩ (7)	

(1) ♫♫♫♫♫ (5)	4.63 Continue as in the preceding frame.
	
	(1) A ♪ note subdivided into five parts is
	
	  notated _____.
	
	(2) A ♩. note subdivided into seven parts is
	
	    notated _____.

(2) ♩♩♩♩♩♩ (7)	

(1) ♩♩♩♩ (4)	4.64 Continue as in the preceding frame.
	
	(1) A ♩. note subdivided into four parts is
	
	  notated _____.
	
	(2) A ♪. note subdivided into five parts is
	
	    notated _____.

(2) ♩♩♩♩♩ (5)	
three	4.65 The note that represents the duration of the beat is called the UNIT. How many *units* are there in one measure of triple meter? _____
two	4.66 How many *units* are there in one measure of duple meter? _____
four	4.67 How many *units* are there in one measure of quadruple meter? _____

simple	4.68 The unit in simple time is always an undotted note, since this type of note divides naturally into *two* equal parts. Any note may be the unit, but the most usual values are the half note, the quarter note, and the eighth note. The unit is always an undotted note in _____ time.
three	4.69 The unit in compound time is always a dotted note, since this type of note divides naturally into *three* equal parts. The most common units in compound time are the dotted half note, the dotted quarter note, and the dotted eighth note. The dotted note divides naturally into _____ equal parts.
unit	4.70 The note which represents the duration of the beat is called the _____.
two	4.71 The undotted note divides naturally into _____ equal parts.
compound	4.72 The unit is always a dotted note in _____ time.
(2) ♩ (4) ♪	4.73 Which of the notes below could represent the beat in simple time? _____ (1) ♩.　(2) ♩　(3) ♪.　(4) ♪

(1) 𝅗𝅥.

(3) ♪.

(4) 𝅗𝅥.

4.74 Which of the notes below could be the unit in compound time? _____

(1) 𝅗𝅥.   (2) 𝅝   (3) ♪.   (4) 𝅗𝅥.

Division: ♫

Subdivision: ♬♬

4.75 Show the division and subdivision of the unit.

Unit	Division	Subdivision
♩	_____	_____

Division: ♫

Subdivision: ♬♬

4.76 Continue as in the preceding frame.

Unit	Division	Subdivision
♪	_____	_____

Division: ♩ ♩ ♩

Subdivision: ♫ ♫ ♫

4.77 Continue as in the preceding frame.

Unit	Division	Subdivision
𝅗𝅥.	_____	_____

Division: ♩♫ Subdivision: ♪♫♫♫ (sixteenth notes beamed)	**4.78** Continue as in the preceding frame. *Unit* *Division* *Subdivision* ♩. _____ _____
Division: ♫♫ (eighth triplet grouping) Subdivision: (sixteenth notes beamed)	**4.79** Continue as in the preceding frame. *Unit* *Division* *Subdivision* ♪. _____ _____
Division: ♩ ♩ Subdivision: ♫♫	**4.80** Continue as in the preceding frame. *Unit* *Division* *Subdivision* ♩ _____ _____
♩ ♩ ♪	**4.81** Indicate the most common units in simple time: (1) _____ (2) _____ (3) _____
♩. ♩. ♪.	**4.82** Indicate the most common units in compound time: (1) _____ (2) _____ (3) _____

	4.83 Notes, in themselves, represent only relative duration. Exact duration can be indicated by establishing the rate of the unit. A sign at the beginning of a composition such as M.M. ♩ = 60* (or simply ♩ = 60), indicates that the quarter note is to progress at the rate of 60 per minute. With the same indication (♩ = 60), what is the rate of the eighth note? _____ per minute.
120	
	*The two M's stand for Mälzel Metronome. In 1816 Mälzel invented an instrument based upon the principle of the double pendulum which could be set to indicate a given number of beats per minute. Beethoven was one of the first composers to make use of metronome indications in his music.
144	4.84 If the indication is ♩ = 72, what is the rate of the quarter note? _____ per minute.
180	4.85 If the indication is ♩. = 60, what is the rate of the eighth note? _____ per minute.
60	4.86 If the indication is ♩ = 120, what is the rate of the whole note? _____ per minute.
48	4.87 If the indication is ♪. = 96, what is the rate of the dotted quarter note? _____ per minute.

Expository frame.

4.88   Composers often use Italian (sometimes English, German, or French) terms to indicate the approximate speed and character of their music. Some of the most common terms are listed below:*

Prestissimo	Extremely fast
Presto	Very fast
Allegro	Fast
Allegretto	Fast, but slower than *allegro*
Moderato	Moderate
Andante	Moderately slow
Adagio	Slow
Largo	Extremely slow

Terms such as these do not indicate the precise speed of a composition; this can be done only by making use of the metronome.

*Consult the *Glossary of Musical Terms* in the Appendix, p. 349, for other tempo and phrasing indications commonly found in music.

(no response required)

4.89   The basic rhythmic organization of *simple time* is shown below:

UNIT:

DIVISION:

BORROWED DIVISION:

SUBDIVISION:

The note which represents the duration of the beat is called the *unit*. The quarter note is often used as the unit, but we should not think of the quarter note as always "getting the beat." The eighth note and the half note are also used as units in _____ time.

simple

4.90   The basic rhythmic organization of *compound time* is shown below:

UNIT: 𝅗𝅥.   𝅘𝅥.   𝅘𝅥𝅮.

DIVISION: ♩ ♩ ♩   𝅘𝅥𝅮 𝅘𝅥𝅮 𝅘𝅥𝅮   𝅘𝅥𝅯 𝅘𝅥𝅯 𝅘𝅥𝅯

BORROWED DIVISION: ♩ ♩ (2)   𝅘𝅥𝅮 𝅘𝅥𝅮 (2)   𝅘𝅥𝅯 𝅘𝅥𝅯 (2)

SUBDIVISION: 𝅘𝅥𝅮𝅘𝅥𝅮𝅘𝅥𝅮𝅘𝅥𝅮𝅘𝅥𝅮𝅘𝅥𝅮   𝅘𝅥𝅯𝅘𝅥𝅯𝅘𝅥𝅯𝅘𝅥𝅯𝅘𝅥𝅯𝅘𝅥𝅯   𝅘𝅥𝅰𝅘𝅥𝅰𝅘𝅥𝅰𝅘𝅥𝅰𝅘𝅥𝅰𝅘𝅥𝅰

The unit in compound time is always a(n) (dotted/undotted) _____ note.

dotted

Summary

Notes and *rests* are the two basic symbols used to notate rhythm. Accurate interpretation of these symbols is necessary for correct performance. Notes represent durations of sound; rests represent durations of silence. For each type of note there is a corresponding rest.

Notes may be either *dotted* or *undotted*. *Dotted notes* divide naturally into *three* equal parts, while *undotted notes* divide naturally into *two* equal parts. In *simple time* the *unit* of the beat is an undotted note; in *compound time* the *unit* of the beat is a dotted note.

The *division* of the beat into *three* equal parts in simple time is a *borrowed division* (or triplet); the *division* of the beat into *two* equal parts in compound time is called a *borrowed division* (or duplet). The normal *subdivision* of the beat in simple time is into four parts; in compound time it is into six equal parts. *Subdivisions* of five, seven, eleven, or more in simple time are called *irregular groups*; in compound time *subdivisions* of four five, seven, eight, nine, ten, and eleven are *also* called *irregular groups*.

Mastery Frames

(1) eighth	4–1 Provide the name of each note in the example below:
(2) whole	(1) _____ (4) _____
(3) sixteenth	(2) _____ (5) _____
(4) quarter	(3) _____ (6) _____
(5) thirty-second	(1) (2) (3) (4) (5) (6)
(6) half	♪ o ♪ ♩ ♪ ♩
(Frame 4.1)	
	4–2 Supply the answer in each case.
(1) 2	(1) An eighth note = _____ sixteenth notes.
(2) 4	(2) A whole note = _____ quarter notes.
(3) 2	(3) A quarter note = _____ eighth notes.
(4.20–4.28)	
	4–3 Provide the name of each rest in the example below:
(1) sixteenth	(1) _____ (4) _____
(2) quarter	(2) _____ (5) _____
(3) half	(3) _____ (6) _____
(4) eighth	(1) (2) (3) (4) (5) (6)
(5) whole	
(6) thirty-second	
(4.29)	

(1) 4 (2) 2 (3) 4 (4.36–4.39)	**4–4** Supply the answer in each case. (1) A half rest = _____ eighth rests. (2) A sixteenth rest = _____ thirty-second rests. (3) A quarter rest = _____ sixteenth rests.

(1) ♩‿♩
 	
 (2) ♩‿♪
 	
 (4.40–4.42)
	4–5 Show with tied notes the total value of the dotted note in each case.
	
	 (1) ♩. = _____.
	              (‿)
	
	 (2) ♩. = _____.
	              (‿)

(1) ♪‿♪‿♪
 	
 (2) o‿♩‿♩
 	
 (4.45–4.47)
	4–6 Show with tied notes the total value of the doubly dotted note in each case.
	
	 (1) ♪.. = _____.
	               (‿)(‿)
	
	 (2) o.. = _____.
	               (‿)(‿)

(1) ♫ (2) ♫♪ (4.48–4.53)	**4–7** Show how each note normally divides. (1) ♩ _____. (2) ♩. _____.
(1) ♬♪ (2) ♬♬ (4.55–4.59)	**4–8** Show how each note normally subdivides. (1) ♩ _____. (2) ♩. _____.

(1) 𝅗𝅥   (4)   ♪

(4.68–4.73)

4–9 Which of the notes below could be the unit in

simple time? _____

(1) 𝅗𝅥   (2) 𝅗𝅥.   (3) ♪.   (4) ♪

192   (4.83–4.87)

4–10 If the metronome indication is 𝅗𝅥 = 96, how
many quarter notes will occur per minute?

_____

Supplementary Assignments

Assignment 4–1   Name: _____

1. Draw lines to connect each note with the correct name.

   (1)   o   • Quarter note

   (2)   ♪   • Half note

   (3)   ♪   • Whole note

   (4)   ♩   • Sixteenth note

   (5)   ♩   • Eighth note

2. Draw lines to connect each note with its corresponding rest.

   (1)   ♪   𝄽

   (2)   ♩   𝄾

   (3)   ♪   ▬

   (4)   ♩   𝄿

   (5)   o   ▬

3. Supply the information required.

    (1) A 𝅗𝅥. note = _____ ♪ notes.

    (2) A ♪ note = _____ 𝅘𝅥𝅰 notes.

    (3) A ♪. note = _____ ♪ notes.

    (4) A o note = _____ 𝅘𝅥 notes.

4. Supply the information required.

    (1) A 𝄽 rest = _____ 𝄾 rests.

    (2) A ⁻: rest = _____ ⁻ rests.

    (3) __ 𝄾 rests = 2 𝄽 rests.

    (4) __ 𝄾 rests = 1 ⁻· rest.

5. Show with tied notes the value of each note.

    (1) o· = _____

    (2) 𝅗𝅥.. = _____

    (3) ♪. = _____

    (4) 𝅗𝅥.. = _____

Assignment 4–2   Name: _____

1. Write four notes that can serve as the unit of the beat in simple time.

    _____   _____   _____   _____

2. Write four notes that can serve as the unit of the beat in compound time.

    _____   _____   _____   _____

3. Show how each note normally divides and subdivides, as well as borrowed division.

		Division	*Borrowed Division*	*Subdivision*
(1)	♩.	_____	_____	_____
(2)	♩	_____	_____	_____
(3)	♪	_____	_____	_____
(4)	♪.	_____	_____	_____

4. Show the proper notation for the various divisions and subdivisions of the quarter note.

                                        ♩

    Two parts   _____

    Three parts   _____

    Four parts   _____

    Five parts   _____

    Six parts   _____

    Seven parts   _____

5. Show the proper notation for the various divisions and subdivisions of the dotted quarter note.

$\quad\quad\quad\quad\quad\quad\quad\quad\quad\quad\quad\quad$ 𝅗𝅥.

Two parts $\quad\quad\quad\quad$ _____

Three parts $\quad\quad\quad$ _____

Four parts $\quad\quad\quad$ _____

Five parts $\quad\quad\quad$ _____

Six parts $\quad\quad\quad$ _____

Seven parts $\quad\quad$ _____

6. Indicate the number of notes that would occur per minute in each case with the given metronome indication.

$\quad\quad\quad\quad\quad\quad\quad\quad\quad\quad\quad\quad\quad\quad\quad$ *Number per*
$\quad\quad\quad\quad\quad\quad\quad\quad\quad\quad\quad\quad\quad\quad\quad\quad$ *Minute*

(1) ♩ = 80 $\quad\quad\quad\quad\quad$ o $\quad\quad$ _____

$\quad\quad\quad\quad\quad\quad\quad\quad\quad\quad$ 𝅗𝅥 $\quad\quad$ _____

$\quad\quad\quad\quad\quad\quad\quad\quad\quad\quad$ ♩ $\quad\quad$ _____

$\quad\quad\quad\quad\quad\quad\quad\quad\quad\quad$ ♪ $\quad\quad$ _____

$\quad\quad\quad\quad\quad\quad\quad\quad\quad\quad$ 𝅘𝅥𝅯 $\quad\quad$ _____

(2) 𝅗𝅥. = 60 $\quad\quad\quad\quad$ o. $\quad\quad$ _____

$\quad\quad\quad\quad\quad\quad\quad\quad\quad\quad$ 𝅗𝅥. $\quad\quad$ _____

$\quad\quad\quad\quad\quad\quad\quad\quad\quad\quad$ 𝅗𝅥. $\quad\quad$ _____

$\quad\quad\quad\quad\quad\quad\quad\quad\quad\quad$ 𝅗𝅥 $\quad\quad$ _____

$\quad\quad\quad\quad\quad\quad\quad\quad\quad\quad$ ♪ $\quad\quad$ _____

Eartraining Activities for Chapters 4.0 and 5.0

Music, the most abstract of all the arts, is often difficult to approach in a concrete way. Sometimes, mental imagery or analogy can assist us in comprehending and effectively interpreting a musical figure or phrase. This is true, not only of subtle nuances of phrasing, but also of basics such as note values and rhythmic patterns. The notation of music itself causes us to think in this way. Graphically, the time (rhythmic) element of music is represented on a horizontal plane; the sound (pitch) element is represented on a vertical plane.

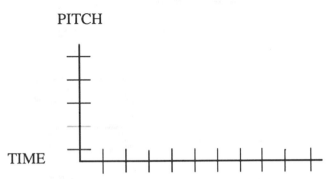

The ability to form musical images mentally varies. Even though few of us are endowed with photographic memories for images we have seen, less literal images can also be helpful. Thus, you should devise your own mental associations and form images which help you.

Visualize as vividly as you can what music notation looks like. Because printed notes are spaced approximately proportionate to their duration, mental pictures of rhythmic patterns can help you to perform figures properly.

1. The basic rhythmic patterns which occur in *simple time* are notated as follows:

UNIT	DIVISION	BORROWED DIVISION	SUBDIVISION	SUBDIVISION PATTERNS

Against a steady beat (supplied by walking, or by a metronome), practice each of these patterns separately and in combinations of your own invention. Imagine (write out, if necessary) the patterns with the eighth note and the half note as the unit.

It is within the context of these simple exercises that your ability to make mental associations will grow. Do not neglect this type of drill.

2. Apply the methods described in number 1 to the following rhythmic patterns which occur in *compound time*.

UNIT   DIVISION   BORROWED DIVISION   SUBDIVISION   SUBDIVISION PATTERNS

5.0

Time Signatures

Time signatures indicate the metrical organization of a composition. In the preceding chapter you learned that there are two types of meter: simple and compound. In simple time, beats divide naturally into two equal parts; in compound time, beats divide naturally into three equal parts. Time signatures fall into two groups: one to represent simple time, and the second to represent compound time. In this chapter you will learn how to interpret the time signatures of each group.

5.1 The metrical organization of a musical composition is indicated by a TIME SIGNATURE.* A time signature consists of two numbers placed on the staff one above the other at the beginning of the composition. There are two types of time signatures: those which indicate *simple* time, and those which indicate *compound* time.

This is how you can distinguish between simple and compound time signatures: *If the upper number is 6, 9, 12, or 15, the time signature represents COMPOUND time. Any number other than these means that the signature represents SIMPLE time, including the number 3.*

If the upper number of the time signature is 6, 9,12, or 15, the signature represents _____ time.

_____

*Time signatures are also called meter signatures.

compound

---

(1) $\frac{6}{2}$

(4) $\frac{9}{4}$

5.2 Which of the following time signatures indicate *compound* time? _____

(1) $\frac{6}{2}$ (2) $\frac{5}{4}$ (3) $\frac{3}{8}$ (4) $\frac{9}{4}$

(2) $\frac{2}{4}$

(3) $\frac{4}{8}$

5.3 Which of the following time signatures indicate *simple* time? _____

    (1) $\frac{12}{8}$ (2) $\frac{2}{4}$ (3) $\frac{4}{8}$ (4) $\frac{6}{4}$

6, 9, 12, 15, 18

5.4 What numbers are found in the upper part of *compound* time signatures?

_____

1, 2, 3, 4, 5, 7, 8
(*Others are possible,
but not practical.*)

5.5 Write some of the numbers which could be found in the upper part of *simple* time signatures.

_____

---

upper number

5.6 The upper number of the time signature tells us the number of beats per measure. Whether the meter is *duple, triple, quadruple,* or *quintuple* is

shown by the _____ _____ of the time signature.

---

(1) 3

(2) 4

(3) 5

5.7 The upper number of *simple* time signatures directly indicates the number of beats per measure.

    $\frac{2}{4}$ = 2 beats per measure

  Show the number of beats per measure indicated by each of the simple time signatures below:

    (1) $\frac{3}{2}$ = _____ beats per measure.

    (2) $\frac{4}{4}$ = _____ beats per measure.

    (3) $\frac{5}{4}$ = _____ beats per measure.

5.8 The upper number of *compound* time signatures does not directly indicate the number of beats per measure as was the case in simple time. In order to determine the number of beats per measure, the upper number of compound time signatures must be divisible by three.

$$\frac{6}{4} \div 3 = 2 \text{ beats per measure}$$

Show the number of beats per measure indicated by each of the compound time signatures below:

(1) 3

         (1) $\frac{9}{8}$ = _____ beats per measure.

(2) 4

         (2) $\frac{12}{8}$ = _____ beats per measure.

(3) 5

         (3) $\frac{15}{8}$ = _____ beats per measure.

Note: There are musical examples where a 6/4 meter may be notated to imply three beat units, i.e., a 3/2 meter, but it is still classified as compound time because of the six.

5.9 The upper number of the time signature directly indicates the number of beats per measure in

simple

_____ time.

5.10 In order to determine the number of beats per measure in compound time the upper number of the

three

time signature must be divisible by _____.

(This assumes the division of the divisible beat unit is three in number.)

5.11 Show the number of beats per measure indicated by each of the time signatures below. *Determine first whether each is a simple or compound signature*:

(1) 2

         (1) $\frac{2}{8}$ = _____ beats per measure.

(2) 2

         (2) $\frac{6}{4}$ = _____ beats per measure.

(3) 4

         (3) $\frac{4}{2}$ = _____ beats per measure.

(1) 5

5.12 Continue as in the preceding frame.

(1) $\frac{5}{8}$ = _____ beats per measure.

(2) 3

(2) $\frac{9}{4}$ = _____ beats per measure.

(3) 4

(3) $\frac{12}{16}$ = _____ beats per measure.

5.13 Continue as in the preceding frame.

(1) 3

(1) $\frac{3}{2}$ = _____ beats per measure.

(2) 7

(2) $\frac{7}{8}$ = _____ beats per measure.

(3) 5

(3) $\frac{15}{8}$ = _____ beats per measure.

5.14 What does each pair of time signatures below have in common?

(1) $\frac{2}{4}$ & $\frac{6}{8}$ (2) $\frac{3}{8}$ & $\frac{9}{4}$ (3) $\frac{4}{4}$ & $\frac{12}{8}$

Each pair
indicates the same
number of beats
per measure:
(1) two beats
(2) three beats
(3) four beats

_____

_____

5.15 From the upper number of the time signature we deduce the meter (the number of beats per measure).
The UNIT is indicated by the lower number, but simple and compound time signatures must be interpreted differently.

The kind of note which represents the beat is deduced

lower

from the (upper/lower) _____ number of the time signature.

(1) 𝅗𝅥

(2) ♪

(3) ♩

5.16 The lower number of *simple* time signatures directly indicates the *unit.**

$$\frac{2}{4} \quad \text{Unit:} = \text{♩}$$

(The number 4 represents a quarter note.)

Show the *unit* indicated by each of the simple time signatures below:

(1) $\frac{5}{2}$ unit = _____

(2) $\frac{3}{8}$ unit = _____

(3) $\frac{4}{4}$ unit = _____

*The type of note that receives one beat.

---

(1) ♪

(2) ♪

(3) ♩

5.17 The lower number of *compound* time signatures represents the DIVISION of the *unit.**

$$\frac{6}{8} \quad \text{Division:} = \text{♪}$$

(The number 8 represents an eighth note.)

Show the *division* indicated by each of the compound time signatures below:

(1) $\frac{12}{16}$ division = _____

(2) $\frac{6}{8}$ division = _____

(3) $\frac{9}{4}$ division = _____

*The type of note that is the *division* of the (beat) unit.

---

division

5.18 The lower number of *simple* time signatures indicates the *unit*.

The lower number of *compound* time signatures

indicates the _____.

5.19 The *unit* in *compound* time consists of three *divisions*. Thus, three *divisions* combine to make the *unit*.

$$\frac{6}{8} \quad \text{Division:} \; = \; \eighthnote$$

$$\eighthnote \; \eighthnote \; \eighthnote \; = \; \dottedquarter \quad \text{(the unit)}$$

In compound, time a note that is equal in value

unit

to three divisions is called the _____.

5.20 The unit in compound time is equal in value to

divisions

three _____.

5.21 The unit in compound time is always a DOTTED note.*

Show the unit indicated by each of the compound time signatures below :

(1) $\dottedquarter$

(1) $\frac{9}{8}$ unit = _____

(2) $\dottedhalf$

(2) $\frac{6}{4}$ unit = _____

(3) $\dottedquarter$

(3) $\frac{12}{8}$ unit = _____

*In a very slow tempo it may be more convenient to assign the beat to the division rather than the unit. Duple-compound meter, for example, might be counted as a six-beat measure. However, chord changes, rhythmic patterns, phrase structure, and the location of cadences will usually give evidence to the underlying duple organization.

(1) ♩.

(2) ♪.

(3) 𝅗𝅥.

5.22 Continue as in the preceding frame.

(1) $\frac{15}{8}$ unit = _____

(2) $\frac{6}{16}$ unit = _____

(3) $\frac{9}{4}$ unit = _____

---

dotted

5.23 In compound time the lower number of the time signature indicates the division. Three divisions combine to make the unit. The unit in compound time

is always a(n) (dotted/undotted) _____ note.

---

undotted

5.24 In simple time the lower number of the time signature directly indicates the unit. The unit in simple time is always a(n) (dotted/undotted)

_____ note.

---

(1) ♩.

(2) ♩

(3) 𝅗𝅥.

5.25 Show the unit indicated by each of the time signatures below. *Determine first whether each is a simple or compound signature:*

(1) $\frac{9}{8}$ Unit = _____

(2) $\frac{2}{4}$ Unit = _____

(3) $\frac{12}{4}$ Unit = _____

(1) 𝅗𝅥.

(2) 𝅗𝅥

(3) ♪

5.26 Continue as in the preceding frame.

(1) $\frac{15}{8}$ unit = _____

(2) $\frac{3}{2}$ unit = _____

(3) $\frac{4}{8}$ unit = _____

---

(1) 𝅗𝅥.

(2) 𝅘𝅥.

(3) 𝅘𝅥

5.27 Continue as in the preceding frame.

(1) $\frac{9}{8}$ unit = _____

(2) $\frac{12}{8}$ unit = _____

(3) $\frac{5}{4}$ unit = _____

5.28 TIME CLASSIFICATION is expressed by terms such as duple-simple, duple-compound, triple-simple, quadruple-simple, and quintuple-simple.

The first part of the classification refers to the number of beats per measure.

Duple	= 2 beats per measure.
Triple	= 3 beats per measure.
Quadruple	= 4 beats per measure.
Quintuple	= 5 beats per measure.

Indicate the *first* part of the time classification for each signature.

(1) triple

(2) triple

(3) duple

(1) $\frac{3}{4}$ _____

(2) $\frac{9}{8}$ _____

(3) $\frac{2}{4}$ _____

(1) duple

(2) quadruple

(3) quadruple

5.29 Continue as in the preceding frame.

(1) $\frac{6}{8}$ _____

(2) $\frac{4}{4}$ _____

(3) $\frac{12}{8}$ _____

---

(1) quintuple

(2) triple

(3) quintuple

5.30 Continue as in the preceding frame.

(1) $\frac{5}{4}$ _____

(2) $\frac{3}{2}$ _____

(3) $\frac{15}{8}$ _____

---

(1) triple

(2) duple

(3) quadruple

5.31 Continue as in the preceding frame.

(1) $\frac{3}{8}$ _____

(2) $\frac{6}{4}$ _____

(3) $\frac{4}{8}$ _____

---

(1) simple

(2) simple

(3) compound

5.32 The second part of the time classification tells whether the beat is divided into *two* parts (simple time), or *three* parts (compound time). It also tells whether the unit is an undotted or a dotted note.

Indicate the *second* part of the time classification for each time signature.

(1) $\frac{2}{4}$ _____

(2) $\frac{3}{8}$ _____

(3) $\frac{9}{8}$ _____

5.33 Continue as in the preceding frame.

(1) compound

(1) $\frac{12}{4}$ _____

(2) simple

(2) $\frac{5}{8}$ _____

(3) compound

(3) $\frac{6}{4}$ _____

5.34 Continue as in the preceding frame.

(1) compound

(1) $\frac{15}{8}$ _____

(2) simple

(2) $\frac{3}{4}$ _____

(3) simple

(3) $\frac{7}{8}$ _____

5.35 The time classification of simple time signatures is interpreted as below:

Time signature: $\begin{cases} \frac{3}{4} = 3 \text{ beats per measure - TRIPLE} \\ \frac{3}{4} = \text{Unit: } \quad ; \text{ Div.: } \quad \text{ - SIMPLE} \end{cases}$

Time Classification: TRIPLE-SIMPLE

Supply the time classification for each of the time signatures below:

(1) quadruple-simple

(1) $\frac{4}{4}$ _____ - _____

(2) quintuple-simple

(2) $\frac{5}{8}$ _____ - _____

(3) duple-simple

(3) $\frac{2}{2}$ _____ - _____

5.36 The time classification of compound time signatures is interpreted as below:

Time signature: $\begin{cases} \frac{9}{8} \div 3 = 3 \text{ beats per measure - TRIPLE} \\ \frac{9}{8} = \text{Div: } \flat\!\!\flat \text{ ; } \sqcup\!\!\sqcup\!\!\sqcup = \text{♩. (Unit) - COMPOUND} \end{cases}$

Time Classification: TRIPLE-COMPOUND

Supply the time classification for each of the time signatures below:

(1) $\frac{6}{2}$ _____ - _____

(2) $\frac{12}{16}$ _____ - _____

(3) $\frac{15}{16}$ _____ - _____

---

(1) duple-compound

(2) quadruple-compound

(3) quintuple-compound

5.37 Continue as in the preceding frame.

(1) $\frac{4}{8}$ _____ - _____

(2) $\frac{6}{16}$ _____ - _____

(3) $\frac{3}{2}$ _____ - _____

---

(1) quadruple-simple

(2) duple-compound

(3) triple-simple

5.38 Continue as in the preceding frame.

(1) $\frac{9}{4}$ _____ - _____

(2) $\frac{4}{2}$ _____ - _____

(3) $\frac{12}{8}$ _____ - _____

---

(1) triple-compound

(2) quadruple-simple

(3) quadruple-compound

no
(It must be divided
by three.)

5.39   In simple time, the upper number directly indicates the number of beats per measure.

Does the upper number in compound time signatures directly indicate the number of beats per measure? _____

5.40   Notice the relation of the upper number of the time signature to the number of beats per measure in compound time:

Upper Number	Beats per Measure	Meter
6	2	duple
9	3	triple
12	4	quadruple
15	5	quintuple

In simple time, duple meter is indicated by the number 2. What is the upper number of the time signature in duple-compound time? _____

6

$\frac{3}{2}$ $\frac{3}{4}$ $\frac{3}{8}$ $\frac{3}{16}$

(any three)

5.41   Supply three of the possible time signatures for the time classification below:

Triple-simple _____ _____ _____

5.42   Continue as in the preceding frame.

Duple-compound _____ _____ _____

$\frac{6}{4}$ $\frac{6}{8}$ $\frac{6}{16}$

$\frac{9}{4}$ $\frac{9}{8}$ $\frac{9}{16}$

5.43   Continue as in the preceding frame.

Triple-compound _____ _____ _____

$\frac{2}{2}$ $\frac{2}{4}$ $\frac{2}{8}$ $\frac{2}{16}$

(any three)

5.44   Continue as in the preceding frame.

Duple-simple _____ _____ _____

$\frac{4}{2}$ $\frac{4}{4}$ $\frac{4}{8}$ $\frac{4}{16}$

(any three)

5.45   Continue as in the preceding frame.

Quadruple-simple _____ _____ _____

$\frac{15}{4}$ $\frac{15}{8}$ $\frac{15}{16}$

5.46   Continue as in the preceding frame.

Quintuple-compound _____ _____ _____

$\frac{12}{4}$ $\frac{12}{8}$ $\frac{12}{16}$

5.47   Continue as in the preceding frame.

Quadruple-compound _____ _____ _____

$\frac{5}{2}$ $\frac{5}{4}$ $\frac{5}{8}$ $\frac{5}{16}$

(any three)

5.48   Continue as in the preceding frame.

Quintuple-simple _____ _____ _____

5.49 Two time signatures (**c** and **¢**) are vestiges of earlier systems of notation. The sign (**c**) stands for the signature $\frac{4}{4}$ (quadruple-simple) and is called COMMON TIME.

Common time is the same as quadruple-simple.

Write the signature for *common time*. _____

c

5.50 The signature (**¢**) is called ALLA BREVE. This indicates a quick duple-simple meter, in which the half note receives the beat. It is the equivalent of $\frac{2}{2}$ time.

The time classification of *alla breve* is _____-

_____.

duple-simple

5.51 Write the signature for *alla breve*. _____

¢

Although the terms *common time* and *alla breve* are essentially the same as the $\frac{4}{4}$ and $\frac{2}{2}$ signatures, they should be properly used only in conjunction with the signature signs of **c** and **¢**.

four

5.52   How many beats per measure are indicated by the signature **C** ?

_____

two

5.53   How many beats per measure are indicated by the signature **¢** ?

_____

♩

5.54   Write the unit in common time. _____

𝅗𝅥

5.55   Write the unit in alla breve. _____

5.56   The TIE is a curved line which connects two notes of the same pitch in order to express a longer duration.

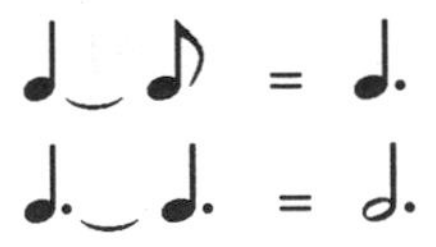

$$\text{♩ ⌣ ♪ = ♩.}$$
$$\text{𝅗𝅥. ⌣ 𝅗𝅥. = 𝅝.}$$

The duration of one note value can be added

tie

to the duration of another by the use of a _____.

5.57   Ties between units in simple time

Some typical patterns:*

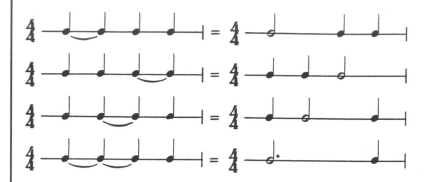

Rewrite without ties (as above) the following rhythm:

* While it is possible to show any arithmetically correct groups of notes/rests within a measure, musicians generally expect notes/rhythms to be consistently grouped according to the time signature.

5.58   Ties between units in compound time

Some typical patterns:

Rewrite without ties (as above) the following rhythm:

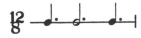

5.59 Ties between divisions in simple time

Some typical patterns:

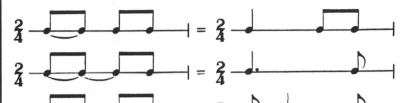

Borrowed division:

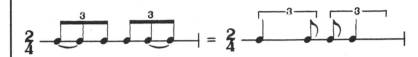

Rewrite without ties (as above) the following rhythm:

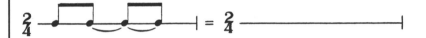

5.60 Rewrite without ties the following rhythm:

5.61 Continue as in the preceding frame.

5.62 Continue as in the preceding frame.

5.63 Ties between divisions in compound time

Some typical patterns:

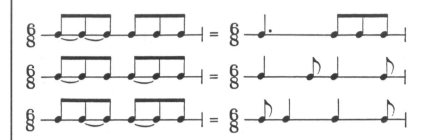

Rewrite the rhythm below without ties:

5.64 Rewrite the rhythm below without ties:

5.65 Continue as in the preceding frame.

5.66 Continue as in the preceding frame.

5.67 Typical subdivision patterns in simple time

Unit:

Rewrite the rhythm below without ties:

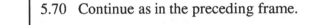

5.68 Rewrite the rhythm below without ties:

5.69 Continue as in the preceding frame.

5.70 Continue as in the preceding frame.

5.71   Typical subdivision patterns in compound time*

Unit: ♩.

Rewrite the rhythm below without ties:

* Subdivision patterns in compound time are so numerous
that only the most common are shown.

5.72   Rewrite the rhythm below without ties:

5.73   Continue as in the preceding frame.

5.74 Continue as in the preceding frame.

5.75 Continue as in the preceding frame.

5.76 When notes are tied in such a way that the
longer values do not coincide with the beat, the result
is called SYNCOPATION. *Syncopation* is demonstrated
in each case below:

Syncopation causes accents to be placed more
or less counter to the stresses of the meter, which creates
the impression that the beat (or pulse) is not where it is
expected. One way this is accomplished is through a
displacement of the notes by means of rests or by the use

ties

of _____.

5.77   Notes which occur within a beat are usually beamed together.

Notice that in each example the total value of the notes in every beat is the same. The sum of the note values must equal the value of the unit in all cases.

Group the notes by using beams instead of flags so that the meter is clearly expressed.

5.78   Group the notes by using beams instead of flags so that the meter is clearly expressed.

5.79   Continue as in the preceding frame.

$\frac{6}{8}$ ♩ 𝅘𝅥𝅯𝅘𝅥𝅯 𝅘𝅥𝅯𝅘𝅥𝅯𝅘𝅥𝅯𝅘𝅥𝅯

5.80 Continue as in the preceding frame.

$\frac{6}{8}$ ♩ 𝅘𝅥𝅯𝅘𝅥𝅯𝅘𝅥𝅮 𝅘𝅥𝅯𝅘𝅥𝅯𝅘𝅥𝅯𝅘𝅥𝅮 = $\frac{6}{8}$ ————————————————|

$\frac{3}{4}$ 𝅘𝅥𝅯𝅘𝅥𝅯 𝅘𝅥𝅯𝅘𝅥𝅯 𝅘𝅥𝅯𝅘𝅥𝅮

5.81 Continue as in the preceding frame.

$\frac{3}{4}$ 𝅘𝅥𝅮𝅘𝅥𝅮 𝅘𝅥𝅮𝅘𝅥𝅮 𝅘𝅥𝅮𝅘𝅥𝅮 𝅘𝅥𝅮 = $\frac{3}{4}$ ————————————————|

$\frac{6}{4}$ 𝅘𝅥𝅮𝅘𝅥𝅮𝅘𝅥𝅮𝅘𝅥𝅮 ♩ 𝅘𝅥𝅮

5.82 Continue as in the preceding frame.

$\frac{6}{4}$ 𝅘𝅥𝅮𝅘𝅥𝅮𝅘𝅥𝅮𝅘𝅥𝅮𝅘𝅥𝅮 𝅘𝅥𝅮𝅘𝅥𝅮 = $\frac{6}{4}$ ————————————————|

$\frac{9}{8}$ 𝅘𝅥𝅮𝅘𝅥𝅮 𝅘𝅥𝅮𝅘𝅥𝅮 𝅘𝅥𝅮𝅘𝅥𝅮

5.83 Continue as in the preceding frame.

$\frac{9}{8}$ 𝅘𝅥𝅮𝅘𝅥𝅮𝅘𝅥𝅮𝅘𝅥𝅮𝅘𝅥𝅮𝅘𝅥𝅮 = $\frac{9}{8}$ ————————————————|

5.84 Each of the examples below is a complete measure. Select the correct time signature from the alternatives supplied.

(1) $\frac{3}{8}$

(2) $\frac{6}{4}$

(3) $\mathbf{C}$

(1) $\frac{6}{8}$ $\frac{2}{4}$ $\frac{3}{8}$ $\frac{5}{16}$ ——

(2) $\frac{3}{2}$ $\frac{12}{8}$ $\frac{5}{2}$ $\frac{6}{4}$ ——

(3) $\frac{7}{8}$ $\mathbf{C}$ $\frac{6}{4}$ $\frac{2}{1}$ ——

(1) $\frac{5}{8}$

(2) $\frac{6}{8}$

(3) $\frac{2}{4}$

5.85 Continue as in the preceding frame.

(1) $\frac{2}{4}$ $\frac{3}{4}$ $\frac{5}{8}$ $\frac{2}{2}$ ___

(2) $\frac{6}{8}$ $\frac{3}{4}$ $\frac{7}{8}$ $\frac{2}{2}$ ___

(3) C $\frac{2}{4}$ $\frac{5}{8}$ $\frac{3}{8}$ ___

(1) $\frac{12}{8}$

(2) $\frac{4}{4}$

(3) $\frac{3}{8}$

5.86 Continue as in the preceding frame.

(1) $\frac{4}{4}$ $\frac{2}{2}$ $\frac{6}{4}$ $\frac{12}{8}$ ___

(2) $\frac{4}{4}$ $\frac{3}{2}$ $\frac{7}{8}$ $\frac{5}{4}$ ___

(3) C $\frac{6}{8}$ $\frac{3}{8}$ $\frac{9}{16}$ ___

(1) $\frac{2}{2}$

(2) $\frac{9}{4}$

(3) $\frac{3}{4}$

5.87 Continue as in the preceding frame.

(1) $\frac{5}{4}$ $\frac{2}{2}$ $\frac{3}{4}$ $\frac{6}{4}$ ___

(2) $\frac{3}{2}$ $\frac{9}{4}$ $\frac{5}{2}$ $\frac{3}{1}$ ___

(3) $\frac{3}{4}$ $\frac{7}{8}$ $\frac{4}{4}$ $\frac{5}{8}$ ___

(1) $\frac{5}{4}$	5.88 Continue as in the preceding frame. (1) $\frac{4}{4}$ $\frac{9}{8}$ $\frac{5}{4}$ $\frac{12}{8}$ ___ 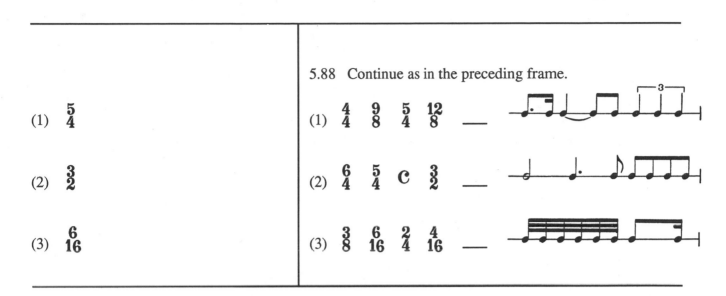
(2) $\frac{3}{2}$	(2) $\frac{6}{4}$ $\frac{5}{4}$ **C** $\frac{3}{2}$ ___
(3) $\frac{6}{16}$	(3) $\frac{3}{8}$ $\frac{6}{16}$ $\frac{2}{4}$ $\frac{4}{16}$ ___

Summary

   Time signatures are interpreted differently, depending on whether they represent *simple* or *compound* time. *The upper number of simple time signatures indicates the number of beats per measure (meter), and the lower number represents the unit. In the case of compound time signatures, however, the upper number must be divided by three to ascertain the number of beats per measure, and since the lower number represents the division rather than the unit, three of the notes represented by this number must be combined to produce the unit.* Notes that occur in a single beat, or some other metric unit such as the measure, are usually beamed together whenever possible. This is to facilitate the interpretation of rhythmic patterns by making a graphic representation of the pulse.

Mastery Frames

6, 9, 12, 15 (Frames 5.1–5.4)	5–1 Write four numbers that, when they appear in the upper part of a time signature, represent compound time. _____
false (5.7–5.8)	5–2 The upper number of both simple and compound time signatures directly indicates the number of beats per measure. (True/False) _____
(1) 2 (2) 4 (3) 3 (5.7–5.14)	5–3 Show the number of beats per measure in each case. (1) $\frac{6}{8}$ = _____ beats per measure. (2) $\frac{4}{4}$ = _____ beats per measure. (3) $\frac{3}{8}$ = _____ beats per measure.
(1) 2 (2) 3 (3) 2 (5.7–5.14)	5–4 Continue as in the preceding frame. (1) $\frac{2}{2}$ = _____ beats per measure. (2) $\frac{9}{8}$ = _____ beats per measure. (3) $\frac{6}{4}$ = _____ beats per measure.
true (5.16)	5–5 The lower number of a simple time signature directly indicates the unit of the beat. (True/False) _____

division

(5.17)

5–6 The lower number of a compound time signature represents the (unit/division/subdivision)

_____ of the beat.

(1) 𝅗𝅥

(2) ♪

(3) ♩

(5.16)

5–7 Write the note that serves as the unit of the beat in each case.

(1) $\frac{3}{2}$ Unit = _____

(2) $\frac{4}{8}$ Unit = _____

(3) $\frac{5}{4}$ Unit = _____

(1) 𝅗𝅥.

(2) ♪.

(3) 𝅗𝅥.

(5.17–5.22)

5–8 Write the note that serves as the unit of the beat in each case.

(1) $\frac{12}{8}$ Unit = _____

(2) $\frac{6}{16}$ Unit = _____

(3) $\frac{9}{4}$ Unit = _____

(1) C

(2) ¢

(5.49–5.55)

5–9 Write time signatures as directed.

(1) Common time _____

(2) Alla breve _____

Supplementary Assignments

Assignment 5–1   Name: _____

1. Explain the chief difference between simple and compound time.

    _____

    _____

    _____

2. Indicate the type of time signature in each case.

	Simple	*Compound*		*Simple*	*Compound*
$\frac{6}{4}$	_____	_____	$\frac{7}{4}$	_____	_____
$\frac{3}{2}$	_____	_____	$\frac{15}{8}$	_____	_____
$\frac{5}{4}$	_____	_____	$\frac{3}{4}$	_____	_____
$\frac{2}{2}$	_____	_____	$\frac{4}{4}$	_____	_____
$\frac{9}{8}$	_____	_____	$\frac{12}{16}$	_____	_____

3. Explain how the number of beats per measure is deduced by referring to the upper number of a time signature in each case.

    Simple time signatures:_____

    _____

    _____

    Compound time signatures:_____

    _____

    _____

4. Explain how the unit of the beat is deduced by referring to the lower number of a time signature in each case.

    Simple time signatures:_____

    _____

    _____

    Compound time signatures:_____

    _____

    _____

5. Provide information regarding the time signatures below:

	Time classification	Unit
C	_____	_____
¢	_____	_____

6. Provide information as indicated.

	Beats per measure	Unit
12/8	_____	_____
3/2	_____	_____
6/16	_____	_____
5/8	_____	_____
9/4	_____	_____

Assignment 5–2   Name: _____

1.   Explain what is meant by the term "syncopation." _____

      _____

      _____

2.   Which measures contain an example of syncopation? _____

3.   Rewrite the examples using beams to clarify the meter.

      (1)

      (2)

      (3)

      (4)

      (5)

4. Each example below represents one complete measure. Provide an appropriate time signature in each case.

An *interval* consists of the difference in pitch level between two tones. The tones may sound successively or simultaneously. Because intervals are basic building blocks for both melody and harmony, knowledge about them is essential. Your success in more advanced music study will depend on your ability to write intervals, recognize them aurally, and apply the terminology used to classify them.

melodic	6.1 Two tones sounding simultaneously produce a HARMONIC interval. A MELODIC interval occurs when two tones are sounded successively. The interval below is a (harmonic/melodic) _____ interval.
harmonic	6.2 The interval below is a (harmonic/melodic) _____ interval.
difference	6.3 Our concern now is to learn the terminology used to classify the difference in pitch between the two tones of an interval. When the difference in pitch is relatively great, the tones sound "far apart," and the interval seems "large." When the difference is relatively little, the tones sound "close together," and the interval seems "small." Intervals vary in size depending on the _____ in pitch between the two tones which constitute them.

6.4 There are various methods of classifying intervals. In the field of acoustics (the scientific study of sound), for example, intervals are classified mathematically as the ratio between the frequencies of the two tones. But this is a specialized approach seldom used in practical musical terminology. In music theory, intervals are classified numerically from 1 to 8, according to the number of basic notes encompassed by the interval.

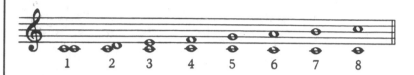

The basic classification of intervals is numerical.

1 (to) 8

The numbers _____ to _____ are used to make this classification.

6.5 The numerical classification of intervals is very easy to determine. Merely count the number of basic notes encompassed by the interval. **Remember:** *Both the lower and upper notes are part of the interval.* Call the lower note 1, and count lines and spaces to include the upper note.

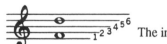 The interval is a sixth.

Indicate the numerical classification of each interval.

(1) (2) (3) (4) (5)

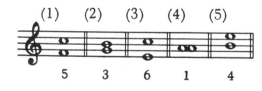

5   3   6   1   4

(1) (2) (3) (4) (5)

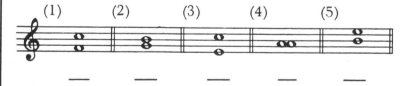

___ ___ ___ ___ ___

---

(1) (2) (3) (4) (5)

8   2   3   7   6

6.6 Indicate the numerical classification of each interval.

(1) (2) (3) (4) (5)

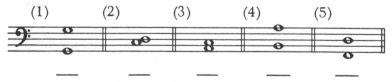

___ ___ ___ ___ ___

6.7   The intervals which have been designated 1 and 8 have special names derived from Latin numerations: 1 = unison,* 8 = octave. It is customary to use ordinal numbers when referring to the remaining intervals.

1	unison	(or prime)
2	second	(2nd)
3	third	(3rd)
4	fourth	(4th)
5	fifth	(5th)
6	sixth	(6th)
7	seventh	(7th)
8	octave	(8th)

An interval which encompasses eight lines and

octave

spaces is called a(n) _____.

---

*The term *prime* is also used.

6.8   Intervals larger than an octave are called COMPOUND INTERVALS.

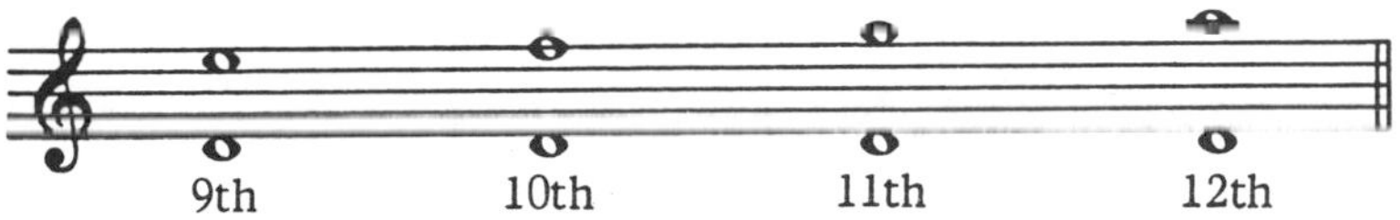

9th   10th   11th   12th

All *compound intervals* are larger than an

octave

_____.

6.9   Occasionally it is necessary to refer to *compound intervals* as 9ths, 10ths, 11ths, etc., but often they are analyzed as simple intervals (within a single octave). The relation of certain *compound intervals* to *simple intervals* is shown below:

Compound:	9th	10th	11th	12th
Simple:	2nd	3rd	4th	5th

If reduced in size by the interval of an octave, a

5th

12th becomes a _____.

3rd

6.10   The example below shows that the interval of a

10th consists of an octave plus a _____.

Note: Compound intervals are classified the same as their smaller
counterparts, so they need not be of further concern in this study.

6.11   Write intervals *above* the notes as directed.

(1)   (2)   (3)   (4)   (5)

2nd   4th   unis.   3rd   5th

6.12   Write intervals *above* the notes as directed.

(1)   (2)   (3)   (4)   (5)

8ve   2nd   7th   4th   6th

6.13   Intervals may be written below a note by counting *down* the required number of lines and spaces. To
write a 7th below C, for example, call the third space
1, and count down seven lines and spaces.

F

What note is a 5th below C? _____

(1) (2) (3) (4) (5)

8ve 6th 3rd 5th 7th

6.14 Write intervals *below* the notes as directed.

(1) (2) (3) (4) (5)

8ve 6th 3rd 5th 7th

(1) (2) (3) (4) (5)

4th 5th 2nd 6th unis.

6.15 Write intervals *below* the notes as directed.

(1) (2) (3) (4) (5)

4th 5th 2nd 6th unis.

6.16 The numerical classification of intervals is not affected by accidentals. The intervals in the example below are all 3rds.

(1) (2) (3) (4)

3rd 3rd 3rd 3rd

numerical

Accidentals do not affect the _____ classification of intervals.

6.17 Accidentals applied to a basic interval make it larger or smaller, yet no amount of alteration changes the basic (numerical) classification. Thus, additional terminology is necessary to distinguish between different types of 3rds, 6ths, etc. As the first step in learning to use the terms applied to intervals, we shall divide intervals into two groups:

GROUP I	GROUP II
unison	2nd
4th	3rd
5th	6th
octave	7th

The unison, 4th, 5th, and octave comprise one group of intervals. Name the intervals which comprise the

2nd, 3rd, 6th, 7th

second group. _____

unison, 4th, 5th, 8ve	6.18 Name the intervals of Group I. _____ _____
d	6.19 The intervals of Group I (unison, 4th, 5th, and 8ve) use the terms PERFECT, AUGMENTED, and DIMINISHED.* These terms are abbreviated as below: Perfect P Augmented A Diminished d A capital P is used to symbolize the term *perfect*; a capital A is used to symbolize the term *augmented*. What is the symbol for the term *diminished*? _____ _____ *There is one exception: the unison cannot be diminished (see Frame 6.25).
no	6.20 A PERFECT UNISON consists of two tones of the same pitch and notation. P1 P1 P1 Is there any difference in pitch between the two tones which produce a *perfect unison*? _____
  (1) (2) (3)	6.21 Write the note which will produce a perfect unison in each case. Write here (1) (2) (3)

6.22   The unison is augmented if one tone is a half step higher or lower than the other.

The two notes which comprise the augmented unison must have the same letter name. (True/False)_____

true

6.23   Write the note which will produce an augmented unison *above* the given note in each case. ***Remember: The augmented unison is a chromatic alteration of the same basic note.***

Write here

(1)   (2)   (3)

6.24   Write the note which will produce an augmented unison *below* the given note in each case.

Write here

(1)   (2)   (3)

6.25   The term *augmented* is used for an interval that is one half step *larger* than a perfect interval. In the case of a perfect unison, there is no difference in pitch between the two tones, whereas the difference is one half step in the case of an augmented unison.

   The term *diminished* is used for an interval that is one half step *smaller* than a perfect interval. Since the frequency of two tones cannot be less than zero (perfect unison), the diminished unison is impossible. The other intervals of Group I, however, may be diminished as well as perfect or augmented.

   Unisons may be either _____ or

_____, but not diminished.

perfect (or) augmented
(any order)

6.26 A perfect octave is the same as a perfect unison except that one note is displaced by the interval of an octave.

P8   P8   P8

Write a perfect octave *above* each note.

(1)   (2)   (3)

P8   P8   P8

(1)   (2)   (3)

P8   P8   P8

6.27 Write a perfect octave *below* each note.

(1)   (2)   (3)

P8   P8   P8

(1)   (2)   (3)

P8   P8   P8

6.28 Octaves may be perfect, augmented, or diminished.

d8   P8   A8

A diminished octave is one half step smaller than a perfect octave; an augmented octave is one

larger

half step _____ than a perfect octave.

6.29 Observe the relation between the terms *diminished, perfect,* and *augmented.*

larger ⟶

[d]   half step   [P]   half step   [A]

⟵ smaller

A diminished interval is one half step smaller than a

two

perfect interval, but _____ half steps smaller than an augmented interval.

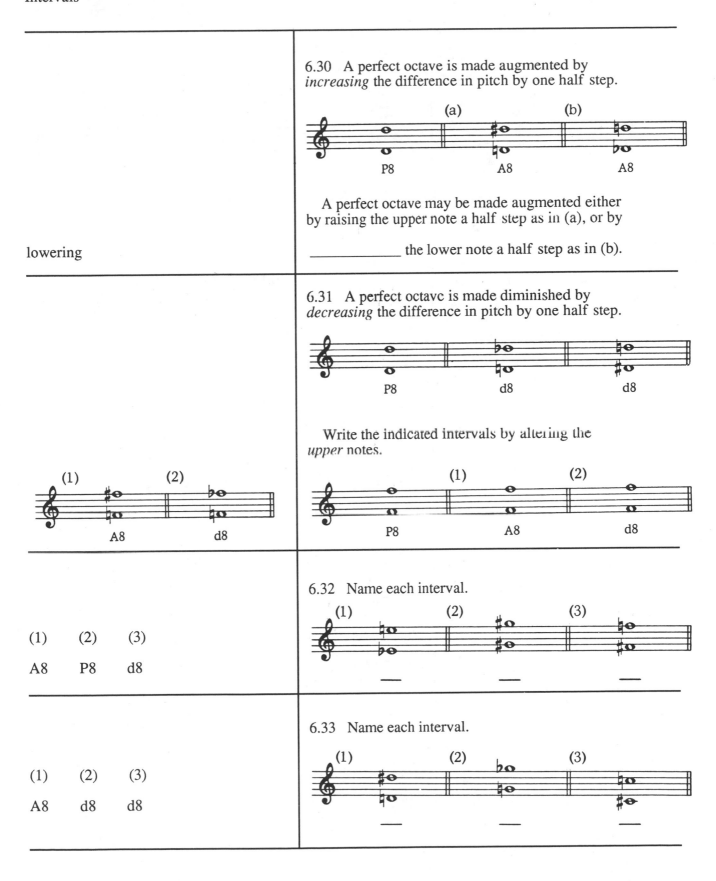

lowering

6.30 A perfect octave is made augmented by *increasing* the difference in pitch by one half step.

(a)   (b)

P8   A8   A8

A perfect octave may be made augmented either by raising the upper note a half step as in (a), or by

_____ the lower note a half step as in (b).

6.31 A perfect octave is made diminished by *decreasing* the difference in pitch by one half step.

P8   d8   d8

Write the indicated intervals by altering the *upper* notes.

(1)   (2)

P8   A8   d8

(1)   (2)

A8   d8

6.32 Name each interval.

(1)   (2)   (3)

___   ___   ___

(1)   (2)   (3)

A8   P8   d8

6.33 Name each interval.

(1)   (2)   (3)

___   ___   ___

(1)   (2)   (3)

A8   d8   d8

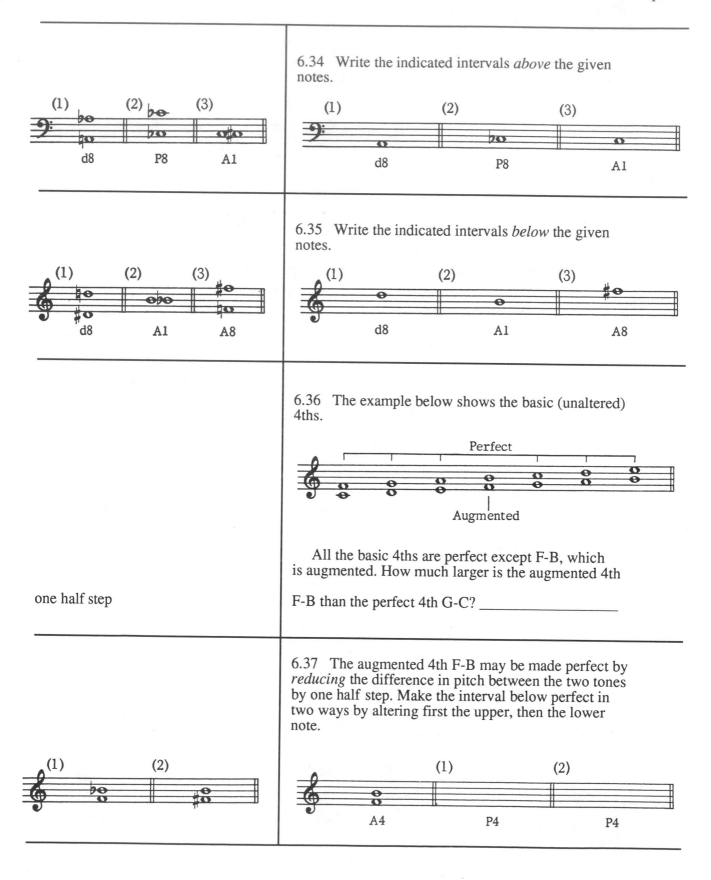

6.34 Write the indicated intervals *above* the given notes.

(1)   (2)   (3)

d8   P8   A1

6.35 Write the indicated intervals *below* the given notes.

(1)   (2)   (3)

d8   A1   A8

6.36 The example below shows the basic (unaltered) 4ths.

Perfect

Augmented

All the basic 4ths are perfect except F-B, which is augmented. How much larger is the augmented 4th

F-B than the perfect 4th G-C? _____

one half step

6.37 The augmented 4th F-B may be made perfect by *reducing* the difference in pitch between the two tones by one half step. Make the interval below perfect in two ways by altering first the upper, then the lower note.

(1)   (2)

(1)   (2)

A4   P4   P4

6.38 If the basic interval is perfect, the same accidental applied to each note will cause no change in quality.

P4   P4   P4   P4   P4

But, if the two notes are affected differently, a change of quality will occur.

P4   d4   A4   A4

false
(F-B is an augmented 4th)

All basic 4ths are perfect. (True/False)_____

6.39 By referring to the quality (perfect or augmented) of the basic interval, and taking into account the effect of accidentals (if any), you should be able to analyze any 4th. *Remember: A perfect interval made a half step smaller is diminished; a perfect interval made a half step larger is augmented.*

Name each interval.

(1)   (2)   (3)

(1)   (2)   (3)

A4   P4   d4

___   ___   ___

6.40 Name each interval.

(1)   (2)   (3)

(1)   (2)   (3)

A4   P4   A4

___   ___   ___

6.41 Write the indicated intervals *above* the given notes.

(1)   (2)   (3)

P4   d4   A4

6.42 Write the indicated intervals *below* the given notes.

(1)   (2)   (3)

A4   d4   P4

6.43 The example below shows the quality of the basic 5ths.

Perfect

Diminished

All the basic 5ths are perfect except B-F, which is diminished. The diminished 5th is one half step

true

smaller than the perfect 5th. (True/False) _____

6.44 The diminished 5th B-F may be made perfect by *increasing* the difference in pitch between the two tones by one half step. Make the interval below perfect in two ways by altering first the upper, then the lower note.

(1)   (2)

P5   P5

(1)   (2)

d5   P5   P5

6.45 Make the perfect 5th below diminished in two ways by altering first the upper, then the lower note.

6.46 Name each interval.

6.47 Name each interval.

6.48 Write the indicated intervals *above* each note.

6.49 Write the indicated intervals *below* each note.

6.50   We shall now take up the matter of INTERVAL INVERSION. Knowledge of inversion is essential for the study of both harmony and counterpoint. Besides, it is useful in spelling and analyzing intervals, especially the larger ones. Only the inversion of Group I intervals will be considered now; the others are treated in Frames 6.88–6.91.

An interval is inverted by rewriting it in such a way that the upper note becomes the lower and vice versa.

Interval inversion is the process of changing the

upper notes so that the lower becomes the _____.

6.51   Below is an example of *interval inversion*:

In (1) the original interval is inverted by writing the upper note (D) an octave lower; in (2) the lower note of the original interval is written an octave higher. The result is the same in either case.

If an interval is rewritten so that the upper note becomes the lower and vice versa, the interval is said

inverted to be _____.

6.52   In both (1) and (2) in the preceding frame the displaced note was moved the interval of an octave. This is called *inversion at the octave*. Inversion can take place at other intervals,* but here we shall deal only with octave inversion, as it is by far the most common and useful type.

The most common interval of inversion is the

octave _____.

---

*Inversion at the 10th and 12th is encountered frequently in contrapuntal music of the 16th, 17th, and 18th centuries.

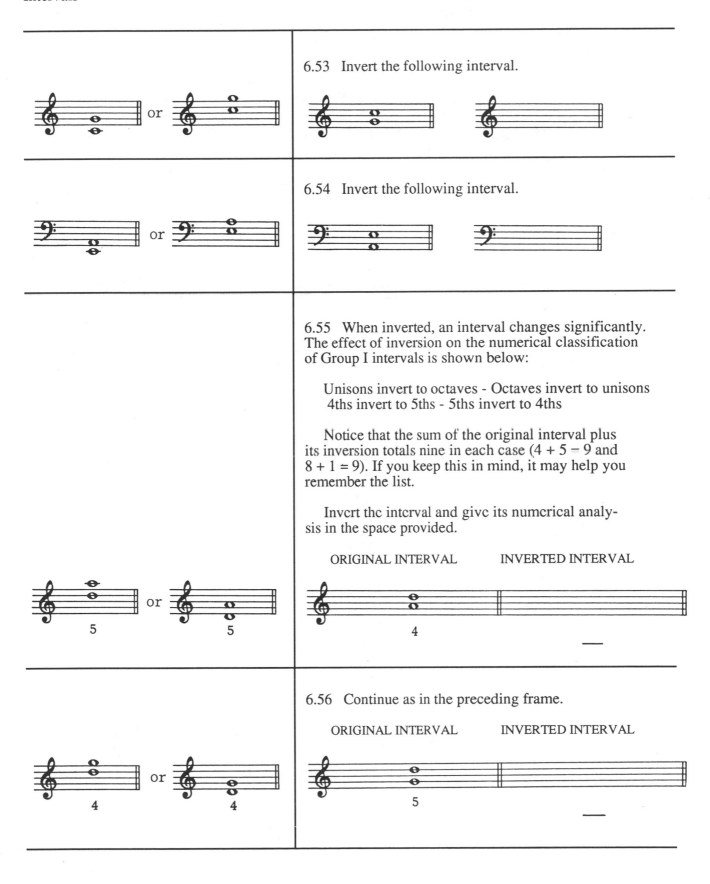

6.53 Invert the following interval.

6.54 Invert the following interval.

6.55 When inverted, an interval changes significantly. The effect of inversion on the numerical classification of Group I intervals is shown below:

   Unisons invert to octaves - Octaves invert to unisons
   4ths invert to 5ths - 5ths invert to 4ths

   Notice that the sum of the original interval plus its inversion totals nine in each case (4 + 5 = 9 and 8 + 1 = 9). If you keep this in mind, it may help you remember the list.

   Invert the interval and give its numerical analysis in the space provided.

ORIGINAL INTERVAL   INVERTED INTERVAL

4   ___

6.56 Continue as in the preceding frame.

ORIGINAL INTERVAL   INVERTED INTERVAL

5   ___

6.57 Continue as in the preceding frame.

ORIGINAL INTERVAL   INVERTED INTERVAL

8   ___

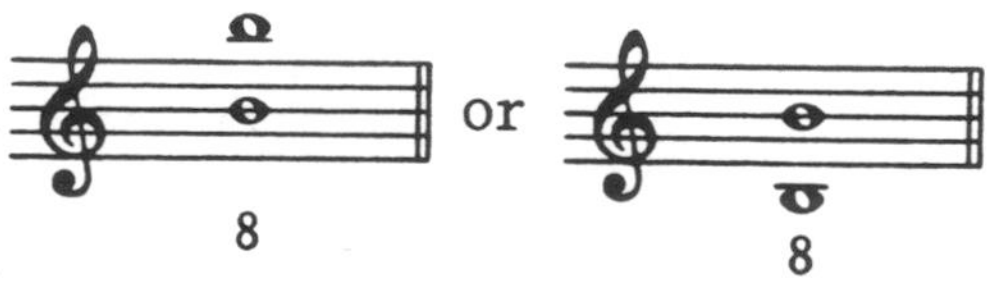

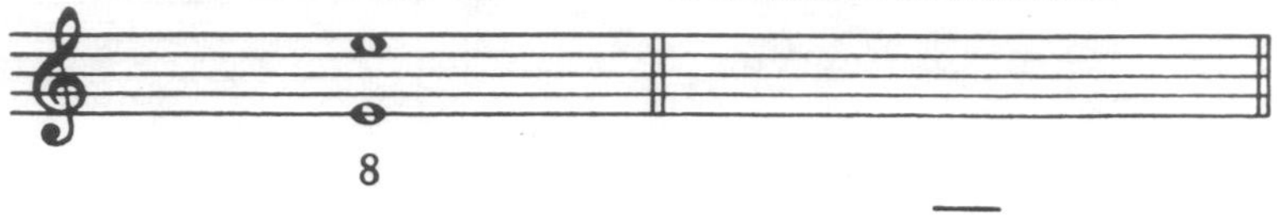

6.58 Continue as in the preceding frame.

ORIGINAL INTERVAL   INVERTED INTERVAL

1   ___

6.59 Interval inversion causes not only changes of numerical classification, but also, in some cases, changes of quality.

Study the chart below:

ORIGINAL INTERVAL	INVERTS TO
Perfect	Perfect
Diminished	Augmented
Augmented*	Diminished

Perfect intervals remain perfect when inverted. Diminished and augmented intervals, however, exchange quality.

What does a perfect 4th become when inverted?

_____

_____

*Because it is larger than the interval of inversion, the augmented octave cannot be inverted at the octave.

perfect 5th

6.60 Complete each statement (use abbreviations).

(1) A d5 inverts to a(n) _____.

(2) A P8 inverts to a(n) _____.

(3) An A1 inverts to a(n) _____.

(1) A4

(2) P1

(3) d8

(1) d5	**6.61** Continue as in the preceding frame.
(2) P4	(1) An A4 inverts to a(n) _____.
(3) A1	(2) A P5 inverts to a(n) _____.
	(3) A d8 inverts to a(n) _____.

6.62 Invert each interval, and give its correct analysis.

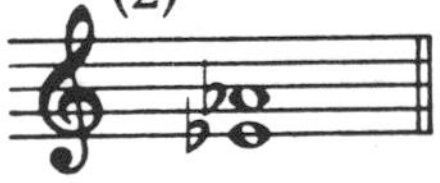

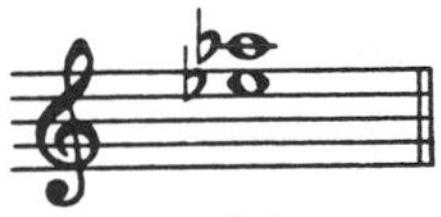

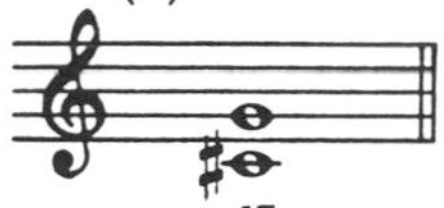

(1) d8	or	d8
(2) P4	or	P4
(3) d5	or	d5

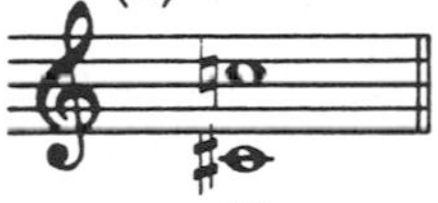

ORIGINAL   INVERTED

(1) A1 ____

(2) P5 ____

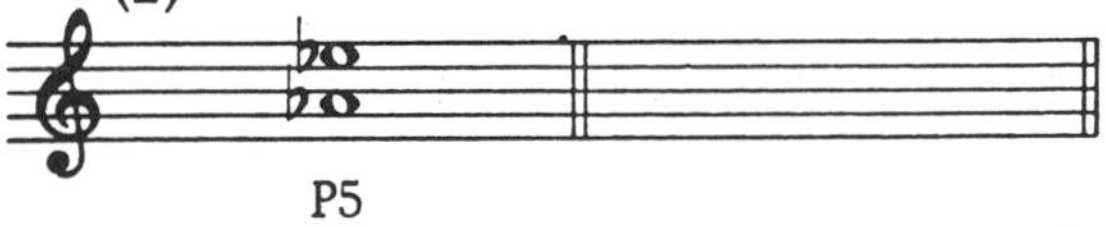

(3) A4 ____

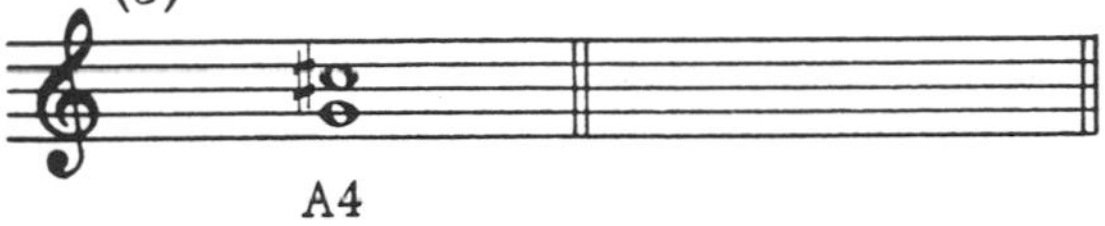

6.63 We shall now learn to use the terms applied to the intervals of Group II (2nds, 3rds, 6ths, and 7ths). These intervals use the terms MAJOR, MINOR, DIMINISHED, and AUGMENTED. The abbreviations for these terms are shown below:

Augmented	A
Major	M
Minor	m
Diminished	d

The intervals of both Group I and Group II use the terms diminished and augmented. Which term used by intervals of Group I is not used by those of

Perfect   Group II? _____

major (and) minor *(any order)*	6.64 Instead of the term perfect, the intervals ofGroup II use the terms _____ and_____.
two	6.65 Observe the relation between the terms which apply to 2nds, 3rds, 6ths, and 7ths. larger ⟶ d half step m half step M half step A ⟵ smaller The intervals of Group II have four classifications. The smallest is diminished, and the largest is augmented. A minor interval is _____ half step(s) smaller than an augmented interval.
one	6.66 A major interval is made minor by decreasing its size by _____ half step.

6.67 The interval below is a diminished 3rd. Change this interval in (1), (2), and (3) as directed. *Apply accidentals to the upper notes only.*

(1)   (2)   (3)   (1)   (2)   (3)

m3   M3   A3   d3   m3   M3   A3

6.68 The interval below is a diminished 6th. Change this interval in (1), (2), and (3) as directed. *Apply accidentals to the lower notes only.*

(1)   (2)   (3)   (1)   (2)   (3)

m6   M6   A6   d6   m6   M6   A6

6.69   The examples below shows the basic (unaltered) 2nds.

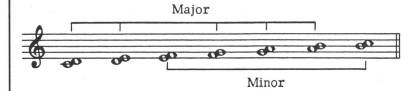

You should have little difficulty remembering the quality of basic 2nds because you have already learned that on the staff, half steps occur between the notes E-F and B-C. *(It is useful to remember that a minor 2nd consists of a half step, and a major 2nd consists of a whole step.)*

Except fo E-F and B-C, all basic 2nds are_____.

major

6.70   A minor 2nd may be made major by *increasing* the difference in pitch between the two tones by one half step. Make the interval below major in two ways by altering first the upper, then the lower note.

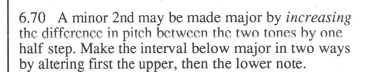

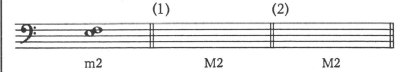

6.71   A major 2nd may be made minor by *reducing* the difference in pitch between the two tones by one half step. Make the major 2nd below minor in two ways by altering first the upper, then the lower note.

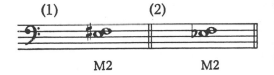

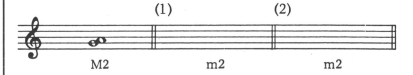

6.72   By referring to the quality of the basic interval, and taking into account the effect of accidentals (if any), you should be able to identify the quality of any 2nd. *(Be sure to keep in mind the chart in Frame 6.65.)*

Name each interval.

(1)   (2)   (3)

(1)   (2)   (3)

M2   m2   M2

6.73   Name each interval.

(1)   (2)   (3)

(1)   (2)   (3)

M2   A2   m2

6.74   Name each interval.

(1)   (2)   (3)

(1)   (2)   (3)

M2   m2   d2

6.75   If the diminished 2nd in (3) of the preceding frame had been written as either two C-sharps or D-flats,* the interval would have been analyzed as a

_____ unison.

perfect

*Intervals which sound the same but are notated differently are called *enharmonic*. (See Frames 6.102–6.106)

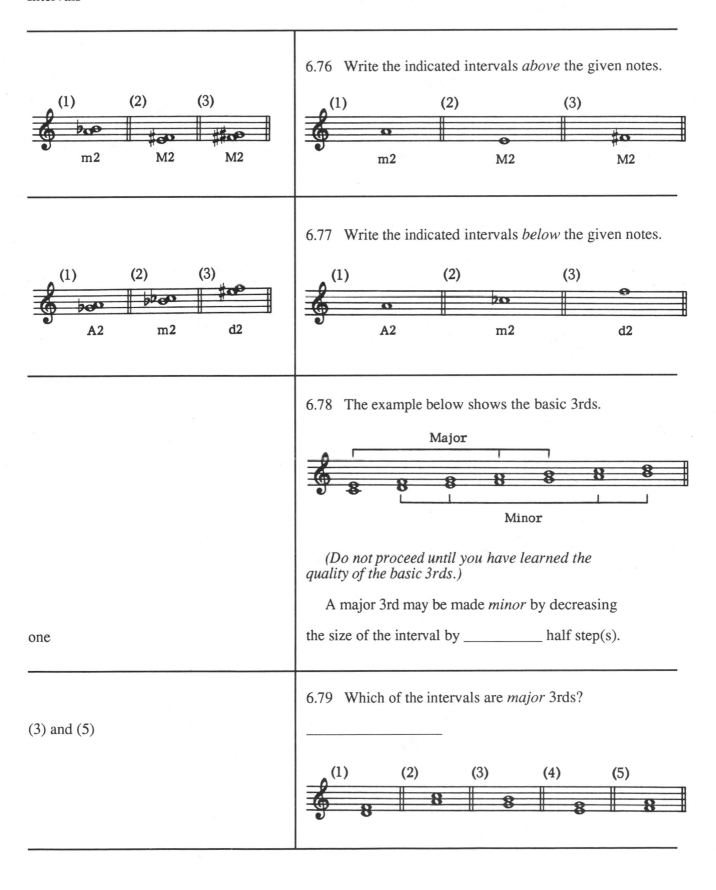

(1) (2) (3)

m2 M2 M2

6.76 Write the indicated intervals *above* the given notes.

(1) (2) (3)

m2 M2 M2

(1) (2) (3)

A2 m2 d2

6.77 Write the indicated intervals *below* the given notes.

(1) (2) (3)

A2 m2 d2

6.78 The example below shows the basic 3rds.

Major

Minor

(Do not proceed until you have learned the quality of the basic 3rds.)

A major 3rd may be made *minor* by decreasing

one

the size of the interval by _____ half step(s).

(3) and (5)

6.79 Which of the intervals are *major* 3rds?

_____

(1) (2) (3) (4) (5)

(1), (2), and (4)

6.80 Which of the intervals are *minor* 3rds?

_____

(1)   (2)   (3)   (4)   (5)

---

(1)   (2)   (3)   (4)

M3   M3   M3   M3

6.81 The intervals below are minor 3rds. Make each major by altering the *upper* note.

(1)   (2)   (3)   (4)

---

(1)   (2)   (3)

m3   m3   m3

6.82 The intervals below are major 3rds. Make each minor by altering the *lower* note.

(1)   (2)   (3)

---

(1)   (2)   (3)

m3   d3   M3

6.83 Name each interval.

(1)   (2)   (3)

___   ___   ___

(1)   (2)   (3)

M3   A3   m3

6.84 Name each interval.

(1)   (2)   (3)

(1)   (2)   (3)

m3   M3   M3

6.85 Name each interval.

(1)   (2)   (3)

(1)   (2)   (3)

M3   m3   M3

6.86 Write the indicated intervals *above* the given notes.

(1)   (2)   (3)

M3   m3   M3

(1)   (2)   (3)

M3   d3   m3

6.87 Write the indicated intervals *below* the given notes.

(1)   (2)   (3)

M3   d3   m3

6.88 We shall make use of interval inversion to spell 6ths and 7ths. When inverted, the numerical classification of Group II intervals changes as below:

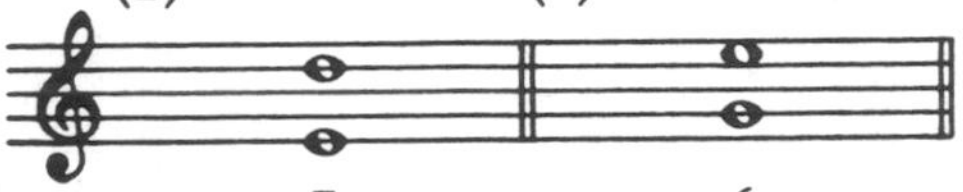

2nds invert to 7ths - 7ths invert to 2nds
3rds invert to 6ths - 6ths invert to 3rds

Invert the intervals and give their numerical classification.

(1)   (2)

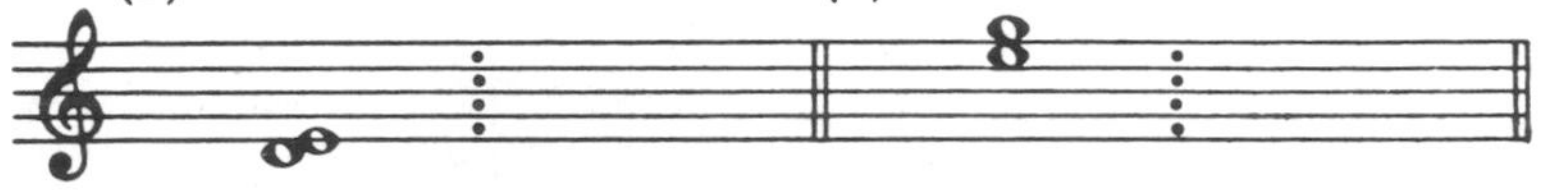

7   6

(1)   (2)

2   ___   3   ___

minor 3rd

6.89 The effect of inversion on the quality of Group II intervals is shown below:

ORIGINAL INTERVAL	INVERTS TO
Major	Minor
Minor	Major
Diminished	Augmented
Augmented	Diminished

What does a major 6th become when inverted?

_____

(1) M6

(2) A6

(3) m6

6.90 Complete each statement (use abbreviations).

(1) A m3 inverts to a(n) _____.

(2) A d3 inverts to a(n) _____.

(3) A M3 inverts to a(n) _____.

(1) d3

(2) M3

(3) A3

6.91 Complete each statement (use abbreviations).

(1) An A6 inverts to a(n) _____.

(2) A m6 inverts to a(n) _____.

(3) A d6 inverts to a(n) _____.

6.92   Now we shall see how inversions are used to spell 6ths and 7ths. The problem in this frame is to spell a major 6th *above* the note E.

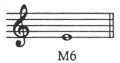

M6

The solution is reached in two steps: (1) identify the inversion of the desired interval (a major 6th inverts to a minor 3rd), (2) write a minor 3rd *below* the (higher) octave of the given note.

M6

If a minor 6th had been desired, it would have been

necessary to write a _____ 3rd below the (higher) octave of the given note.

major

6.93   Let us try another example. The problem this time is to spell a minor 7th *below* the note E.

m7

Step 1: A m7 inverts to a _____.

M2

6.94   To complete the problem of spelling a minor 7th below E, continue with step 2: write a major 2nd *above* the (lower) octave of the given note.

(M2)   └──────Write here

m7

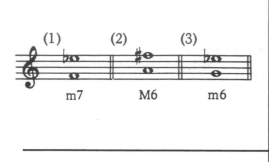

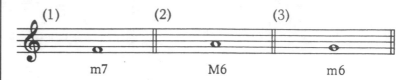

6.95 Write the indicated intervals *above* the given notes.

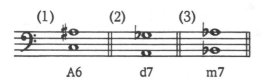

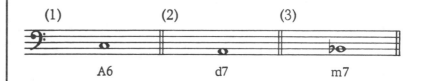

6.96 Write the indicated intervals *above* the given notes.

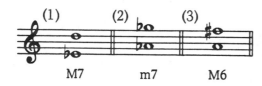

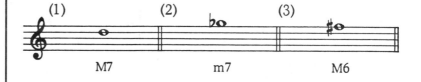

6.97 Write the indicated intervals *below* the given notes.

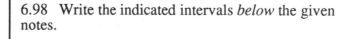

6.98 Write the indicated intervals *below* the given notes.

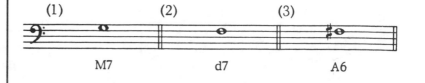

6.99 You may also use your knowledge of inversions to analyze an interval. The interval E-flat to D can be identified in two steps as shown below.

Step 1: Invert the interval

Step 2: Inverted, the interval is a minor 2nd. Thus, in its original form, it must be a _____ 7th.

major

6.100 Name each interval.

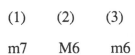

(1)   (2)   (3)
m7   M6   m6

6.101 Name each interval.

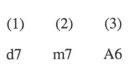

(1)   (2)   (3)
d7   m7   A6

(1) (2) A6 m7	6.102 Two intervals which sound the same but are notated differently are said to be ENHARMONIC. Name each of the intervals below: _____ _____
enharmonic	6.103 The preceding frame shows that an augmented 6th is _____ with a minor 7th.
 A2 m3	6.104 Apply accidentals to the notes of the second interval to make it *enharmonic* with the first. Also, name each interval. _____ _____
 A4 d5	6.105 Apply an accidental to one of the notes of the second interval to make it *enharmonic* with the first. Also, name each interval. _____ _____

(1) m3

(2) d5

(3) m7

6.106 The preceding few frames have shown several enharmonic intervals.* Although others are possible, the ones presented are those most frequently encountered in the study of music theory.

Complete the list below:

(1) An A2 is enharmonic with a _____.

(2) An A4 is enharmonic with a _____.

(3) An A6 is enharmonic with a _____.

* It is not general musical practice to make enharmonic substitutions when constructing intervals unless the musical context suggests it.

6.107 Occasionally an interval is altered to such an extent that the terms *diminished* and *augmented* do not suffice. In such a case the interval is referred to as *doubly diminished* or *doubly augmented*.

AA4   dd5

two

The *doubly augmented* 4th is _____ half steps larger than the perfect 4th.

6.108 Write the indicated intervals *above* the given notes.

AA5   dd6   AA4

AA5   dd6   AA4

6.109 Name each interval.

(1)   (2)   (3)

A4   d3   AA5

___   ___   ___

Summary

The terms used by the intervals of Groups I and II are shown below:

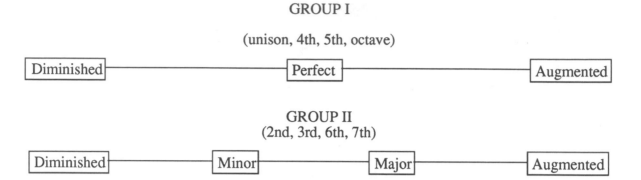

GROUP I

(unison, 4th, 5th, octave)

| Diminished | Perfect | Augmented |

GROUP II
(2nd, 3rd, 6th, 7th)

| Diminished | Minor | Major | Augmented |

Group I intervals have three possible categories, whereas Group II intervals have four. The term *diminished* represents the smallest interval. Each successive term (left to right) represents an increase in size of one half step.

In addition to its importance for more advanced theory study, knowledge of *interval inversion* may be used to spell larger intervals such as 6ths and 7ths. When inverted, the numerical classification and the quality of intervals change in the following manner:

ORIGINAL	INVERTED
Perfect	Perfect
Major	Minor
Minor	Major
Augmented	Diminished
Diminished	Augmented
Unison	Octave
2nd	7th
3rd	6th
4th	5th
5th	4th
6th	3rd
7th	2nd
Octave	Unison

Mastery Frames

(b) (Frames 6.1–6.2)	6–1 Rewrite the interval below as a harmonic interval. (a) (b)
(1) (2) (3) (4) 1 3 6 7 (6.4–6.16)	6–2 Write the numerical classification of each interval. (1) (2) (3) (4) — — — —
perfect, augmented, and diminished (6.19)	6–3 Write the terms that are used by intervals of Group I (unison, 4th, 5th, octave). _____ _____
augmented, major minor, diminished (6.63–6.66)	6–4 Write the terms that are used by intervals of Group II (2nd, 3rd, 6th, 7th). _____ _____
augmented diminished (6.29–6.31)	6–5 Write the terms that identify intervals as stated. *Original interval* *Perfect* Half step larger: _____ Half step smaller: _____

6–6 Write the terms that identify intervals as stated.

	Original interval	*Major*
augmented	Half step larger:	_____
minor	Half step smaller:	_____
diminished	Whole step smaller:	_____
(6.65–6.68)		

6–7 Provide the missing information.

(1) P8	*Original interval*	*Inverted interval*
(2) d7	(1) P1	_____
(3) M6	(2) A2	_____
(4) P5	(3) m3	_____
(5) A4	(4) P4	_____
(6) M3	(5) d5	_____
(7) M2	(6) m6	_____
(8) A1	(7) m7	_____
(6.55–6.62; 6.88–6.91)	(8) d8	_____

6–8 Which pairs of intervals are enharmonic?

(1), (3), (5)

(6.102–6.106)   _____

Supplementary Assignments

Assignment 6–1   Name: _____

1.   Indicate the numerical classification of each interval.

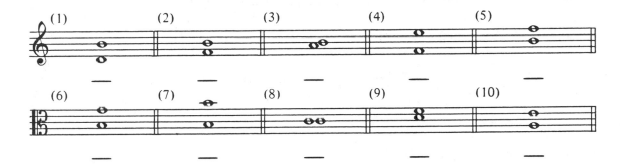

2.   List the four intervals that use the term perfect.

(1) _____ (2) _____ (3) _____ (4) _____

3.   List the four intervals that use the terms major and minor, but not the term perfect.

(1) _____ (2) _____ (3) _____ (4) _____

4.   Invert each interval at the octave, and analyze both the original and the inverted interval.

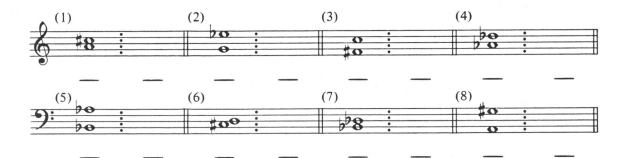

5.   When inverted at the octave:

Perfect intervals become _____ intervals.

Major intervals become _____ intervals.

Minor intervals become _____ intervals.

Diminished intervals become _____ intervals.

Augmented intervals become _____ intervals.

6.   When inverted at the octave:

Unisons become _____.

2nds become _____.

3rds become _____.

4ths become _____.

5ths become _____.

6ths become _____.

7ths become _____.

Octaves become _____.

Assignment 6–2   Name: _____

1. Provide the missing information.

    (1) All basic 2nds are major except _____ and _____, which are minor.

    (2) All basic 3rds are _____ except C-E, F-A, and G-B, which are _____.

    (3) All basic 4ths are perfect except _____, which is _____.

    (4) All basic 5ths are _____ except B-F, which is _____.

    (5) All basic 6ths are major except _____, _____, and _____, which are minor.

    (6) All basic 7ths are minor, except _____ and _____, which are _____.

2. Write intervals *above* the given notes.

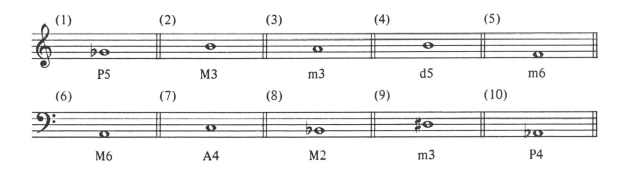

3. Write intervals *below* the given notes.

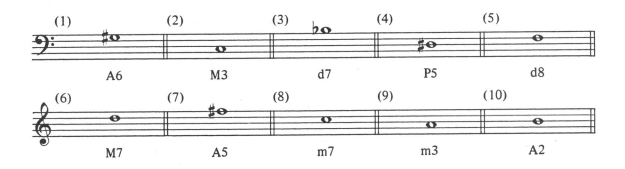

4.   Write an enharmonic equivalent for each interval.

5.   Name an enharmonic equivalent for each interval below:

	Original Interval	*Enharmonic Equivalent*
(1)	A1	_____
(2)	A2	_____
(3)	AA4	_____
(4)	d5	_____
(5)	A6	_____
(6)	d7	_____

Eartraining Activities

The following exercises are quite comprehensive and may take some time to master. You may need to keep working on them even after going ahead to other topics.

1. The numerical classification of intervals stems from the number of basic notes encompassed by the interval. The following exercise will help you to associate numbers with interval size. You may begin on any pitch, but the higher notes must be included in the major scale of the lowest note. (Major scales are presented in Chapter 8.0.)

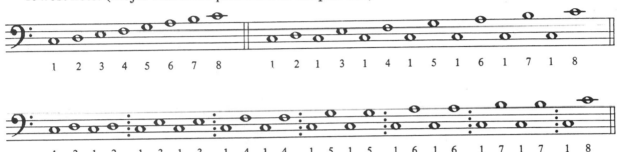

2. In the preceding exercise the intervals are sung upward from the stationary note C. The direction is reversed in the following exercise:

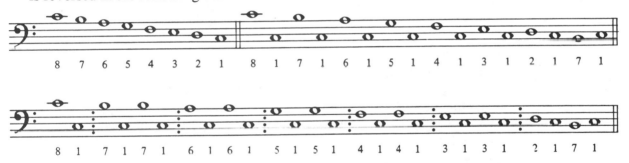

3. *Perfect intervals (unison, 4th, 5th, octave).* The perfect unison and the perfect octave are perhaps the easiest of all intervals to hear. The two notes of the unison have the same pitch and in the case of the octave, one note is virtually the replica of the other. Nevertheless, when notes lie outside our own vocal ranges, it is sometimes difficult to duplicate them by ear. It is desirable, therefore, that you practice matching pitches both within and outside your range. Play widely spaced notes at the piano in order that each will be disassociated with the preceding note.

    The following example may serve as a model. Sing after each note.

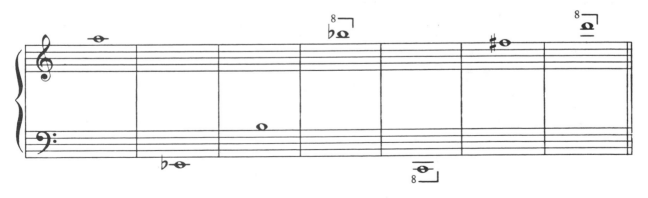

The numbers associated with the intervals in the next exercise reflect the numerical classification (5th, 4th). Play the first note at the piano; then sing the second two notes. (Check your responses, if necessary.)

4. *Augmented 4th, diminished 5th (tritones).* The tritone is easy to recognize, but sometimes difficult to sing. The peculiar effect of this interval stems from the facts that three whole tones are encompassed, and that the interval divides the octave into two equal parts. The augmented 4th and the diminished 5th are enharmonic. It is useful, however, to approach them as related to perfect 4ths and 5ths. Sing the following exercises:

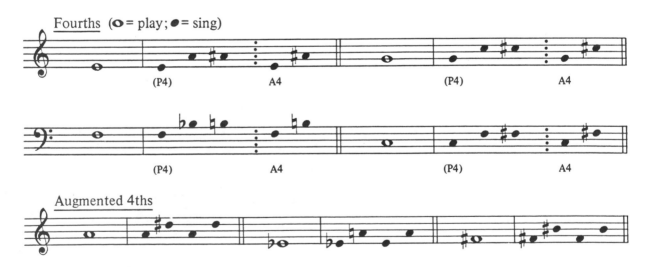

Fifths

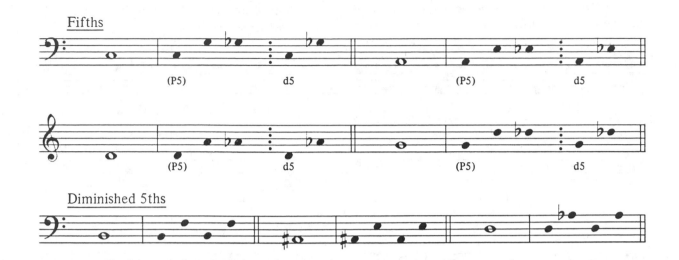

Diminished 5ths

5. *Major and minor 2nds.*

6. *Major and minor 7ths.* The octave can be helpful in learning to sing 7ths. This will be shown in the exercises that follow. (*Sing with numbers if they help, otherwise use* la.)

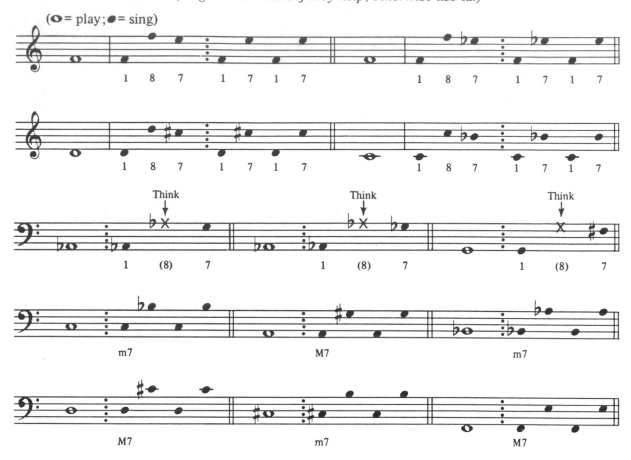

7. *Major and minor 3rds.*

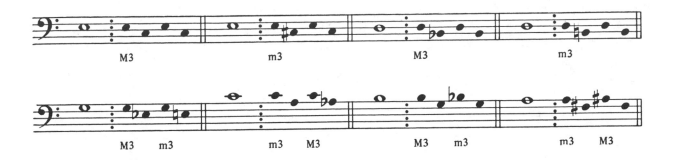

8. *Major and minor 6ths.* The first few exercises show the relationships of major and minor 3rds to their inversions (minor and major 6ths respectively).

Major 6ths

Minor 6ths

7.0
The Basic Scales

The word *scale* is derived from the Latin, *scala*, which means "ladder." It refers to an orderly ascending or descending arrangement of successive pitches within the limit of an octave. There are many kinds of scales, depending on the intervallic relation of the notes. This chapter is concerned with the scales formed by only the seven basic (unaltered) notes. Because no accidentals are used, these are called *basic scales*. Other writers may also refer to these *basic scales* as "modes."

	7.1 A STEPWISE arrangement of the tones contained in one octave is called a SCALE. *Stepwise* means an alphabetical arrangement of the letters which represent tones.
	Write the letters which produce a *stepwise* series of tones starting and ending on A.
A B C D E F G A	— — — — — — — —

	7.2 Write the letters representing a *stepwise* series of tones starting and ending on E.
E F G A B C D E	— — — — — — — —

	7.3 In a *scale* the tones contained in one octave are organized stepwise. In a stepwise series of tones, the letters representing the sounds appear in
alphabetical	_____order.

7.4   A stepwise arrangement of tones is also said to be DIATONIC. To form a *diatonic* scale, all of the seven basic notes must be present plus the octave duplication of the first note. Thus, eight notes are required to form a *diatonic scale*. Also, the notes must be stated in alphabetical order; none may be repeated (except for the octave duplication of the first note), *and none may be omitted.*

How many notes are needed to form a *diatonic*

scale? _____

eight

Note: The discussion here and in the following chapters is aimed at building elementary knowledge of basic scales (modes), diatonic/chromatic scales, and major/minor scales. Other scales such as pentatonic, octatonic, and whole tone, as well as transpositions of these and the modes presented later in this chapter, could be included at an instructor's discretion since they are outside the study intended here.

7.5   The CHROMATIC SCALE arranges *all* of the sounds contained in one octave (in the system of equal temperment), and consists of thirteen tones (including the octave duplication of the first tone).
          Other scales are limited to eight tones, including the octave duplication of the first tone. These are called *diatonic scales.*

All of the tones normally contained in one octave

are included in the _____ scale.

chromatic

Play the chromatic scale at a keyboard from C up to C. Note that all the intervals are half-steps. Sing the same scale.

7.6   Scales which utilize only basic (unaltered) notes are called BASIC SCALES.

Write the letters representing the *basic scale* starting on C.

__ __ __ __ __ __ __ __

C D E F G A B C

7.7   Write on the staff the *basic* scale starting on F.

7.8 Write on the staff the *basic scale* starting on G.

7.9 Write on the staff the *basic scale* starting on B.

7.10 Write on the staff the *basic scale* starting on C.

7.11 Since a scale may be started on any of the seven basic notes, there are how many basic scales?

seven

_____

7.12 Although all basic scales consist of only the seven basic notes, each possesses its own pattern of half and whole steps.

No two basic scales have the same pattern of

half (and) whole

_____ and _____ steps.

7.13 In all the basic scales a *half step* occurs between E and F, and between B and C. All other adjacent notes are a *whole step* apart.

Indicate where *half steps* occur in the scale below. *(Use the sign* ⌃ *between the proper notes.)*

7.14 Note in the preceding frame that the notes of the scale are numbered from 1 to 8 beginning with the lowest note. Thus we can say that, in the *basic scale* starting on F, *half steps* occur between the 4th and 5th and between the 7th and 8th degrees.

Indicate where *half steps* occur in the scale below. *(Use the sign* ⌃ *between the proper notes.)*

1st - 2nd
5th - 6th

7.15 Between which degrees do *half steps* occur in

the scale below? _____ and _____; _____ and _____.

3rd - 4th
6th - 7th

7.16 Between which degrees do *half steps* occur in

the scale below? _____ and _____; _____ and _____.

3rd - 4th
7th - 8th

7.17 Between which degrees do *half steps* occur in

the scale below? _____ and _____; _____ and _____.

seven

7.18 Due to the pattern of half and whole steps, each basic scale has its own unique intervallic structure. For this reason no two basic scales sound alike.

When tonal material is limited to the basic notes,

how many diatonic scales are possible? _____

Sing, or play at a keyboard the seven basic scales. Note the effect that each scale has because of its particular pattern of half and whole steps.

D

7.19 Each of the *basic scales* has a modal name.*

BASIC SCALE	MODAL NAME
A B C D E F G A	**AEOLIAN**
B C D E F G A B	**LOCRIAN**
C D E F G A B C	**IONIAN**
D E F G A B C D	**DORIAN**
E F G A B C D E	**PHRYGIAN**
F G A B C D E F	**LYDIAN**
G A B C D E F G	**MIXOLYDIAN**

The *Dorian mode* is the same as the basic

scale starting on the note _____.

Study the list of modal names above before continuing with the next frame.

*These names are derived from tonal structures known as the Church modes. Dorian, Phrygian, Lydian, and Mixolydian date from about the 8th century. Ionian and Aeolian were added to the system by the theorist Glareanus in his treatise *Dodekachordon* (1547). The Locrian mode existed at this time merely as a theoretical possibility. The Church modes served as the tonal basis of Western music until about 1600, after which time they were gradually modified to form the major-minor tonal system which is the basis of most music heard today.

Ionian	7.20 You must not think that *modal scales* can be written only with basic (unaltered) notes. By using accidentals, any mode can be constructed on any pitch. But learning to associate the various *modes* with their equivalent *basic scale* can serve as a useful point of reference when transposition to other pitches is desired*. Our concern here is that you appreciate the variety of scale structures available with merely the seven basic notes. What is the *modal* name of the *basic scale* starting on C? _____ --- *It is also possible to deal with transposition by relating modes to a particular scale degree of the Ionian mode (or major scale). Thus the second scale degree is Dorian mode, the third is Phrygian, etc., and any Ionian (major) scale degree can be utilized accordingly from any pitch. Please see Chapters 8.0 and 10.0 for related information.
A	7.21 The *Aeolian mode* is the same as the *basic scale* starting on the note _____.
E	7.22 The *Phrygian mode* is the same as the *basic scale* starting on the note _____.
C	7.23 The *Ionian mode* is the same as the *basic scale* starting on the note _____.
Lydian	7.24 What is the *modal* name of the *basic scale* starting on F? _____

Dorian	7.25 What is the *modal* name of the *basic scale* starting on D? _____
Mixolydian	7.26 What is the *modal* name of the *basic scale* starting on G? _____
Locrian	7.27 What is the *modal* name of the *basic scale* starting on B? _____
	7.28 Write the Dorian mode. *(Use basic notes only.)*
	7.29 Write the Mixolydian mode. *(Use basic notes only.)*
	7.30 Write the Phrygian mode. *(Use basic notes only.)*

7.31 Write the Locrian mode. *(Use basic notes only.)*

7.32 Write the Lydian mode. *(Use basic notes only.)*

7.33 Write the Ionian mode. *(Use basic notes only.)*

7.34 Write the Aeolian mode. *(Use basic notes only.)*

4th - 5th

7th - 8th

7.35 In the Lydian mode a *half step* occurs between

the _____ and _____ degrees, and between the _____

and _____ degrees. *(You may refer to the scale you have written in Frame 7.32.)*

3rd - 4th

7th - 8th

7.36 In the Ionian mode a *half step* occurs between

the _____ and _____ degrees, and between the _____

and _____ degrees. *(You may refer to the scale you have written in Frame 7.33.)*

1st - 2nd 5th - 6th	7.37 In the Phrygian mode a *half step* occurs between the _____ and _____ degrees, and between the _____ and _____ degrees. *(You may refer to the scale you have written in Frame 7.30.)*
D	7.38 The first and last note of a scale is called the KEYNOTE. The *keynote* is also called the "tonic-note," or "key-center." The *keynote* of the *Dorian mode* (as you have written it in Frame 7.28) is _____.
G	7.39 What is the *keynote* of the *Mixolydian mode* (as you have written it in Frame 7.29)? _____
G	7.40 What is the *keynote* of the *basic scale* whose 3rd degree is B? _____
E	7.41 What is the *keynote* of the *basic scale* whose 4th degree is A? _____
D	7.42 What is the *keynote* of the *basic scale* whose 7th degree is C? _____
A	7.43 What is the *keynote* of the *basic scale* whose 6th degree is F? _____

E	7.44 What is the *keynote* of the *basic scale* whose 5th degree is B? _____
keynote	7.45 The note upon which a scale begins and ends is called the _____.

Summary

A *basic scale* may be constructed on each of the seven basic notes. Thus there are seven *basic scales*. No two of these sound alike because the pattern of *half* and *whole* *steps* is different in each case. *Basic scales* are sometimes identified by their *modal* names.

These are shown below:

Basic scale starting on A - *Aeolian*

Basic scale starting on B - *Locrian*

Basic scale starting on C - *Ionian*

Basic scale starting on D - *Dorian*

Basic scale starting on E - *Phrygian*

Basic scale starting on F - *Lydian*

Basic scale starting on G - *Mixolydian*

Mastery Frames

true	(Frame 7.4)	7–1 All of the seven basic notes (A, B, C, D, E, F, G) must be present to form a diatonic scale. (True/False) _____
true	(7.6)	7–2 Basic scales are diatonic scales in which no accidentals appear. (True/False) _____
B-C (and) E-F	(7.13–7.18)	7–3 All basic scales contain two half steps. The remaining intervals are whole steps. Identify the two half steps. Half steps: _____ - _____ and _____ - _____
All signs should be between B-C and E-F on all the scale examples. (7.13–7.18)		7–4 Use the sign ⌃ to indicate where half steps occur in the basic scales below: (1) (2) (3) (4)

Aeolian

Locrian

Ionian

Dorian

Phrygian

Lydian

Mixolydian   (7.19)

A   (7.38–7.45)

7–5   Write the modal names for the basic scales that start on each note below:

A _____

B _____

C _____

D _____

E _____

F _____

G _____

7–6   What is the keynote of the Aeolian mode?

_____

Supplementary Assignments

Assignment 7–1   Name: _____

1. Show with the sign ⌃ where half steps occur in the scales below:

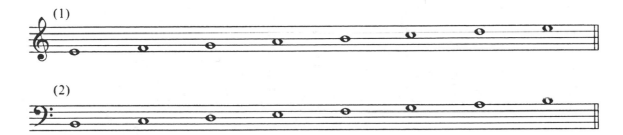

2. Write a basic scale beginning with each note, and indicate where half steps occur with the sign ⌃ .

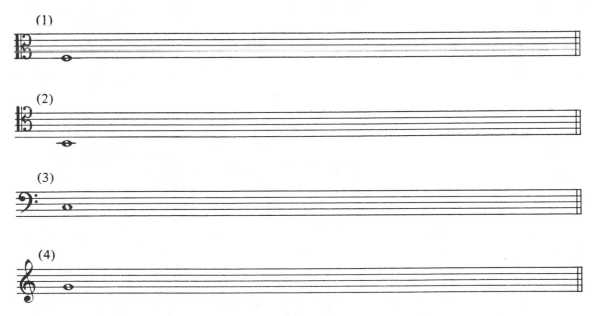

3. The first and last note of a scale is called the _____.

4. No accidentals may occur in a basic scale. (True/False) _____

5. All basic scales are diatonic scales. (True/False) _____

6. Indicate between which scale degrees half steps occur in each of the seven basic scales. *(Use the sign ⌒ .)*

    KEYNOTE   SCALE DEGREES

        A   1   2   3   4   5   6   7   8
        B   1   2   3   4   5   6   7   8
        C   1   2   3   4   5   6   7   8
        D   1   2   3   4   5   6   7   8
        E   1   2   3   4   5   6   7   8
        F   1   2   3   4   5   6   7   8
        G   1   2   3   4   5   6   7   8

7. Explain why, although the same notes occur in each basic scale, no two sound alike.

    _____

    _____

    _____

8. Complete the information below:

    MODE: BASIC SCALE ON THE NOTE:

    Lydian   =   _____

    Ionian   =   _____

    Dorian   =   _____

    Mixolydian   =   _____

    Locrian   =   _____

    Aeolian   =   _____

    Phrygian   =   _____

Eartraining Activities

By associating the numbers 1–8 with the various scale degrees, a feeling for tonal relations and for the keynote is developed. Letter names or a syllable such as *la* may also be used.

Sing the various basic scales. Be alert to the half and whole steps. (Half steps are indicated by the sign ⌃.)

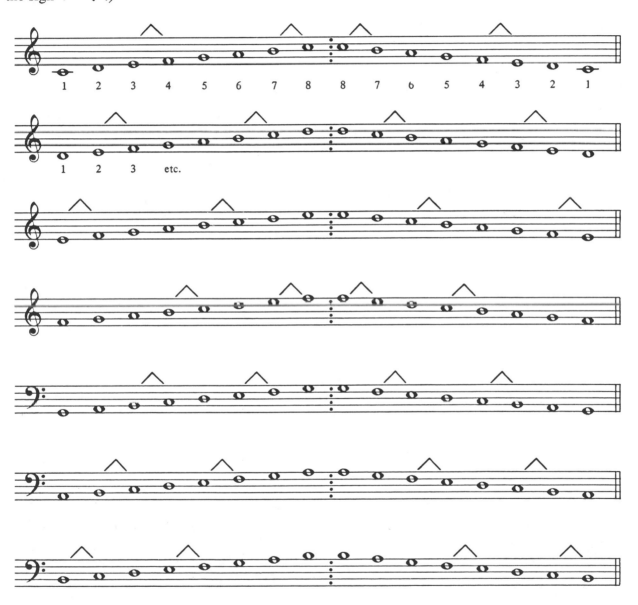

On your own, search out compositions, select from those you may be performing, or seek suggestions from your instructor for examples to visually and aurally practice (hear in your head or sing) basic scale and mode identification.

The Major Scale

The character of each type of scale is determined by the pattern of intervals that occur between the successive scale degrees. The *basic scale* on the note C is called the *C major scale*. The same pattern of intervallic relationships can be produced beginning on any note by applying the appropriate accidentals. In this chapter you will learn how this is done.

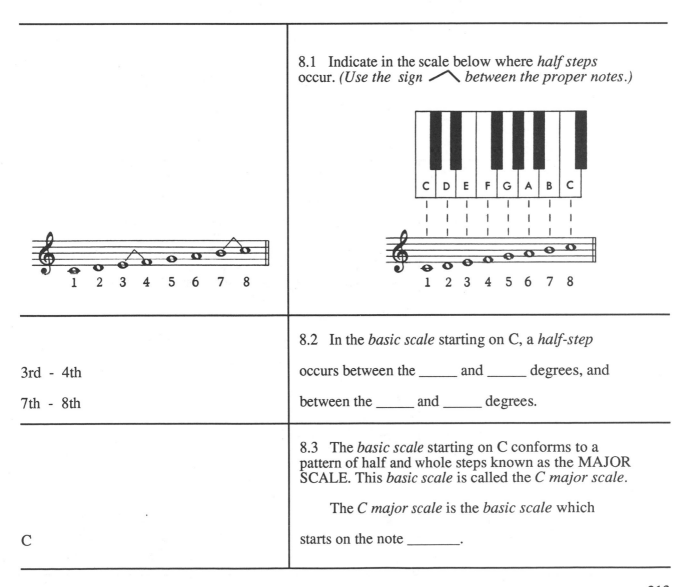

8.1 Indicate in the scale below where *half steps* occur. *(Use the sign ⌃ between the proper notes.)*

	8.2 In the *basic scale* starting on C, a *half-step*
3rd - 4th	occurs between the _____ and _____ degrees, and
7th - 8th	between the _____ and _____ degrees.

	8.3 The *basic scale* starting on C conforms to a pattern of half and whole steps known as the MAJOR SCALE. This *basic scale* is called the *C major scale*.
	The *C major scale* is the *basic scale* which
C	starts on the note _____.

8.4 The *major scale* may be represented as a series of steps, as below

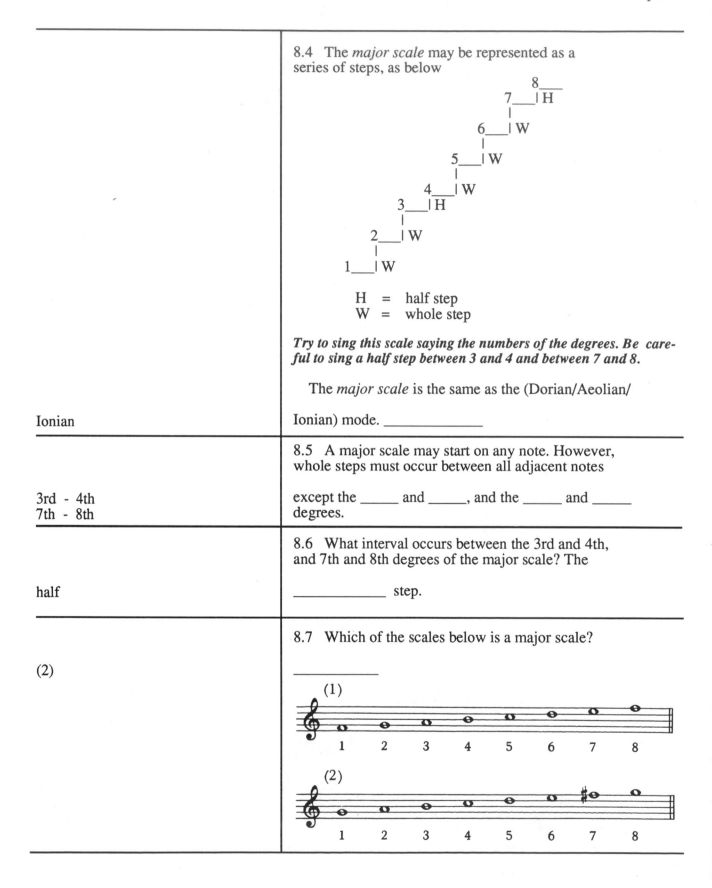

H = half step
W = whole step

Try to sing this scale saying the numbers of the degrees. Be careful to sing a half step between 3 and 4 and between 7 and 8.

The *major scale* is the same as the (Dorian/Aeolian/Ionian) mode. _____

Ionian

8.5 A major scale may start on any note. However, whole steps must occur between all adjacent notes

except the _____ and _____, and the _____ and _____ degrees.

3rd - 4th
7th - 8th

8.6 What interval occurs between the 3rd and 4th, and 7th and 8th degrees of the major scale? The

_____ step.

half

8.7 Which of the scales below is a major scale?

_____

(1)

1 2 3 4 5 6 7 8

(2)

1 2 3 4 5 6 7 8

(2)

(1)

(2)

F-sharp

8.8 Which of the scales below is a *major scale*?

_____

(1)

1 2 3 4 5 6 7 8

(2)

1 2 3 4 5 6 7 8

8.9 Which of the scales below is a *major scale*?

_____

(1)

1 2 3 4 5 6 7 8

(2)

1 2 3 4 5 6 7 8

8.10 Scale (2) in the preceding frame shows that a major scale may start on an altered note as well as a basic note. This scale is called the *G-flat major scale* because the first and last notes are G-flat and because half-steps occur B-flat to C-flat (3-4) and F to G-flat (7-8). Bear in mind that the words *sharp* and *flat* are included in the name of the scale only when the first note (keynote) is sharped or flatted.

What is the keynote of the *F-sharp major scale*?

_____

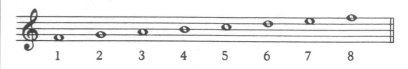

8.11   Add accidentals to form the *F major scale*.

8.12   Add accidentals to form the *G major scale*.

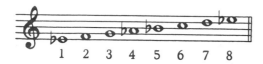

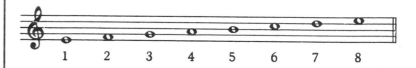

8.13   Add accidentals to form the *E-flat major scale*.

8.14   Add accidentals to form the *D major scale*.

8.15   Add accidentals to form the *B-flat major scale*.

8.16 Add accidentals to form the *A major scale*.

8.17 Add accidentals to form the *A-flat major scale*.

8.18 Write the *E major scale*.

8.19 Write the *D-flat major scale*.

8.20 Write the *F-sharp major scale*.

8.21   Write the *G-flat major scale*.

8.22   Write the *B major scale*.

8.23   Write the *C-sharp major scale*.

8.24   Write the *C-flat major scale*.

8.25   The basic scale which conforms to the pattern of half and whole steps of the major scale begins

and ends on the note _____.

C

true	8.26 All adjacent scale degrees in the major scale are separated by either a whole step or a half step. (True/False) _____
false *(Half steps occur between 3–4, and 7–8 in the major scale.)*	8.27 In the major scale a half step occurs between the 3rd and 4th, and between the 6th and 7th degrees. (True/False) _____
B-flat	8.28 What accidental must be added to the Lydian Mode (F up to F) to form a major scale? _____
F-sharp	8.29 What accidental must be added to the Mixolydian Mode (G up to G) to form a major scale? _____
E major	8.30 F-sharp is the *second* degree of what *major scale*? _____
G-flat major	8.31 B-flat is the *third* degree of what *major scale*? _____
A-flat major	8.32 D-flat is the *fourth* degree of what *major scale*? _____

E major

8.33   B is the *fifth* degree of what *major scale*?

_____

F major

8.34   D is the *sixth* degree of what *major scale*?

_____

D major

8.35   C-sharp is the *seventh* degree of what *major scale*?

_____

---

two whole steps followed

by a half step
(or equivalent)

8.36   You may find it helpful to regard the major scale as consisting of two groups of four notes each called TETRACHORDS.

D MAJOR SCALE   upper tetrachord

lower tetrachord

Examine the succession of intervals contained in each *tetrachord*. The *lower tetrachord* consists of two whole steps followed by a half step; the *upper*

tetrachord consists of _____

_____

8.37 The example in the preceding frame shows that the *upper* and *lower tetrachords* of the major scale contain the same successions of intervals (two whole steps followed by a half step). The interval separating the two *tetrachords* is a (half/whole)

whole   _____ step.

8.38 Write the *lower tetrachord* of the *A-flat major scale*.

8.39 Write the *upper tetrachord* of the *A-flat major scale*. **Remember: The first note of the upper tetrachord is a whole step above the last note of the lower.**

8.40 Any tetrachord consisting of two whole steps followed by a half step may be either the upper or lower tetrachord of a major scale. The tetrachord

Lower: C

C D E F is the lower tetrachord of the _____ major

Upper: F

scale, and also the upper tetrachord of the _____ major scale.

8.41 The tetrachord below is the lower tetrachord of

Lower: B

the _____ major scale, and also the upper tetrachord

Upper: E

of the _____ major scale.

C	8.42 The lower tetrachord of the G major scale is the same as the upper tetrachord of the _____ major scale.
A	8.43 The upper tetrachord of the D major scale is the same as the lower tetrachord of the _____ major scale.

Summary

A *tetrachord* is a four-note scale pattern. Two *tetrachords* combine to make a *scale*. For *major scales*, both the *upper* and *lower tetrachords* contain the same *intervals*: two *whole steps* followed by a *half step*. Any *tetrachord* which has this pattern may be either the *upper* or *lower tetrachord* of a *major scale*. In *major scales*, a *whole step* separates the *upper* from the *lower tetrachord*. Considered as a whole, the *major scale* consists of *whole steps*, except for *half steps* between the 3rd and 4th, and the 7th and 8th degrees. By using *accidentals* to produce this pattern, a *major scale* can be constructed on any note.

The intervallic pattern of the *major scale* is shown schematically below:

LOWER TETRACHORD   UPPER TETRACHORD

[1] W [2] W [3] H [4] W [5] W [6] W [7] H [8]

Mastery Frames

C (Frames 8.1–8.4)	8–1 Which basic scale contains the same intervallic pattern as a major scale? The scale beginning on the note _____
1 2 3̂ 4 5 6 7̂ 8 (8.1–8.6)	8–2 Use the sign ⌃ to show where half steps occur in the major scale. 1 2 3 4 5 6 7 8
(8.36)	8–3 Write the lower tetrachord of the C major scale.
(8.36–8.37)	8–4 Write the upper tetrachord of the C major scale.

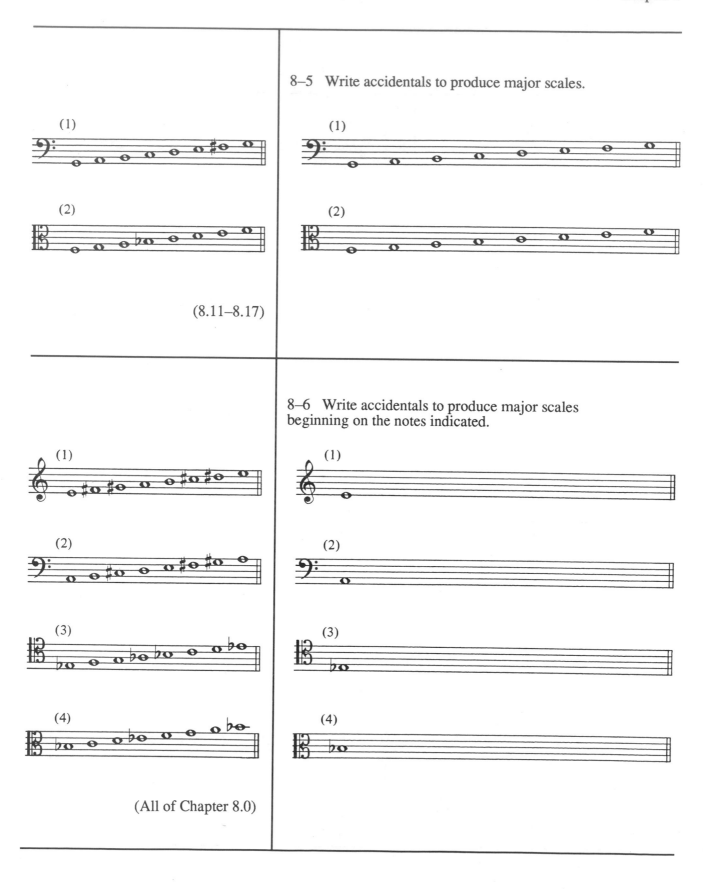

8–5 Write accidentals to produce major scales.

(1)

(2)

(8.11–8.17)

8–6 Write accidentals to produce major scales beginning on the notes indicated.

(1)

(2)

(3)

(4)

(All of Chapter 8.0)

Supplementary Assignments

Assignment 8–1   Name: _____

1. Between which scale degrees do half steps occur in the major scale?

    _____

2. Indicate the intervals that occur within the two tetrachords of the major scale.
    (Use abbreviations: W = whole steps; H = half step.)

        Lower tetrachord: 1 _____   2 _____   3 _____

        Upper tetrachord: 1 _____   2 _____   3 _____

3. What interval separates or connects the lower and upper tetrachords of a major
    scale?

    _____

4. Add two accidentals to produce the F-sharp major scale.

5. Which is a major scale? _____

    (1)

    (2)

6. Write a major scale on each note.

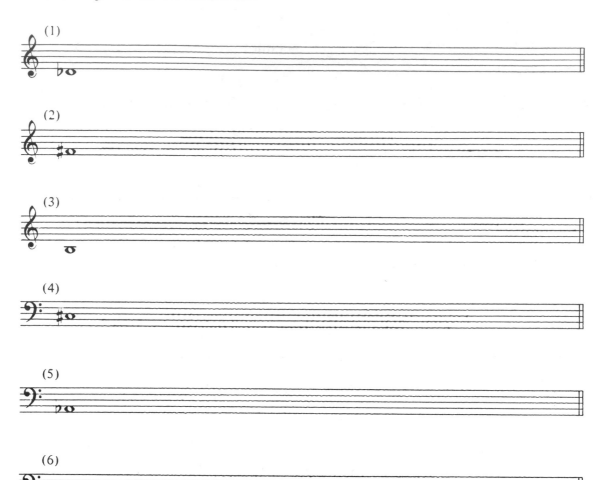

Eartraining Activities

1. Sing the following scales. Be alert to the half steps which occur between 3–4 and 7–8.

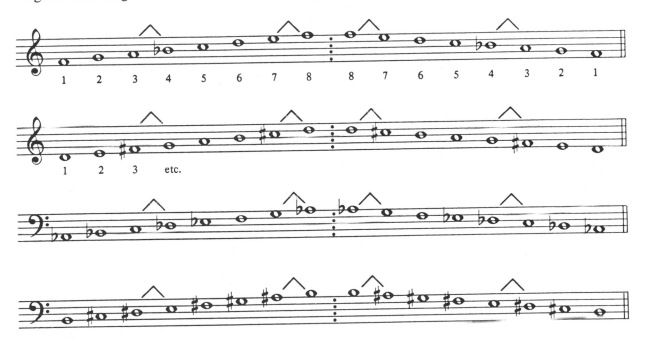

2. Use the note A as the 1st, 2nd, 3rd, and 4th degrees of a minor scale as indicated in the following exercise. Try to do this exercise by ear. Use your knowledge of the half and whole step pattern of the major scale. Resort to a keyboard for aid, if necessary.

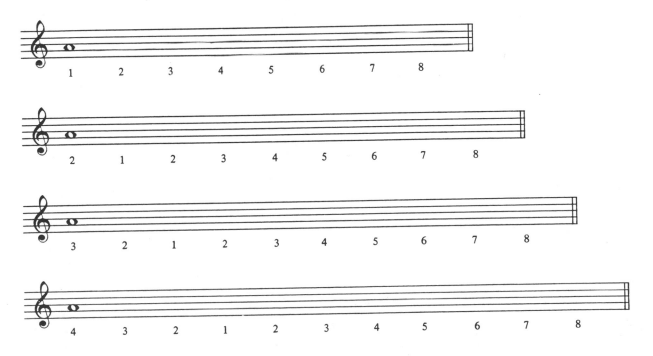

3. Use the note C as the 5th, 6th, 7th, and 8th degrees of a major scale as indicated in the following exercise. Proceed as in the last exercise.

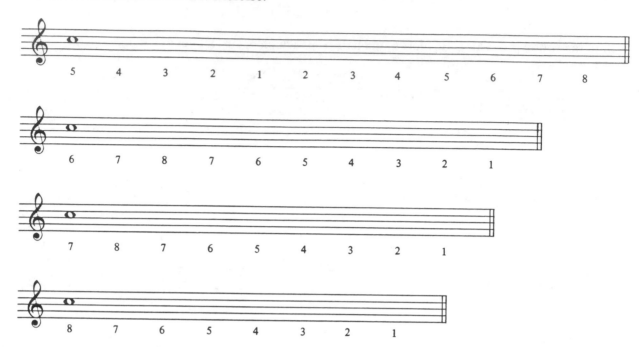

4. On your own, search out compositions, select from those you may be performing, or seek suggestions from your instructor for examples to visually and aurally practice (hear in your head or sing) major scale and mode identification.

9.0

The Minor Scales

The character of a scale results from the intervals that occur between the various scale degrees. Unlike the major scale, which has a single pattern of half and whole steps there are three types of *minor scales*. Each of these has its distinctive arrangement of intervals, as we shall learn in this chapter. The three types of minor scales are called *natural, harmonic,* and *melodic*. These scales ultimately derive from actual musical practice.

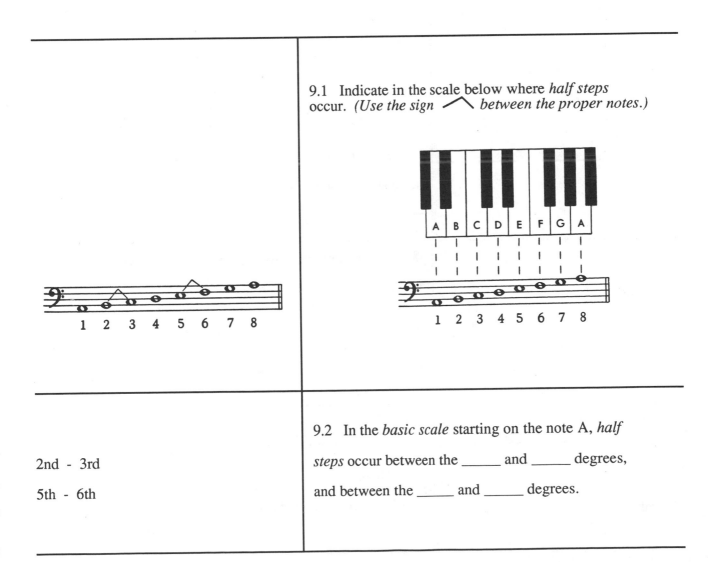

9.1 Indicate in the scale below where *half steps* occur. *(Use the sign* ⌃ *between the proper notes.)*

2nd - 3rd

5th - 6th

9.2 In the *basic scale* starting on the note A, *half steps* occur between the _____ and _____ degrees, and between the _____ and _____ degrees.

9.3   The *basic scale* starting on the note A conforms to the pattern of half and whole steps of the NATURAL MINOR SCALE.*

   The *natural minor scale* may be represented as a series of steps, as below:

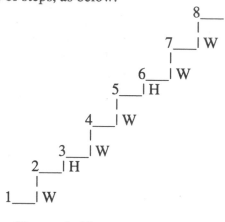

   H = half step
   W = whole step

Try to sing this natural minor scale. Be careful to observe the correct pattern of half and whole steps.

   The *natural minor scale* is the same as the basic scale starting on the note _____.

―――――――――――

*The natural minor scale is also called the *pure, normal,* or *Aeolian* minor.

A

9.4   Between which scale degrees do half steps occur in the natural minor scale? _____ and _____; _____ and _____.

2nd - 3rd

5th - 6th

9.5   The natural minor scale is the same as the _____ mode.

Aeolian

9.6   There are three types of minor scales: (1) *harmonic minor*, (2) *melodic minor*, and (3) _____ *minor*.

natural

(2)

9.7 Which of the scales below is a natural minor scale? _____

(1)

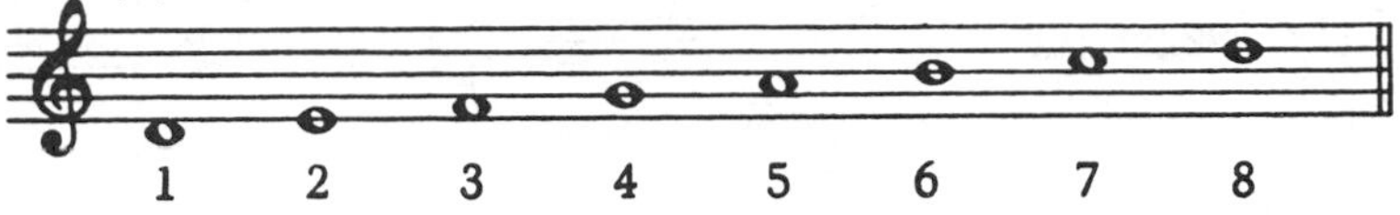

1   2   3   4   5   6   7   8

(2)

1   2   3   4   5   6   7   8

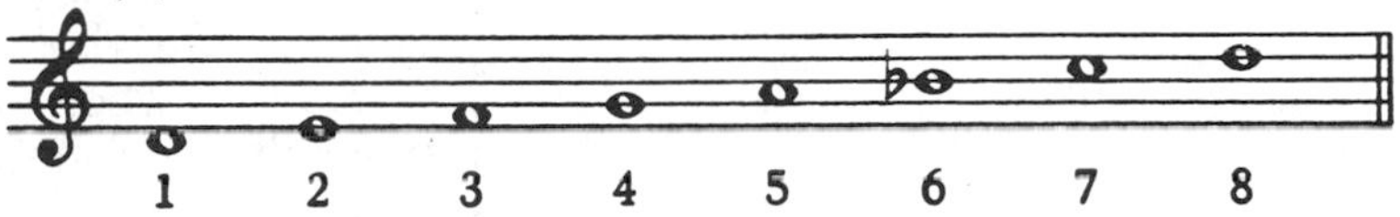

(1)

9.8 Which of the scales below is a natural minor scale? _____

(1)

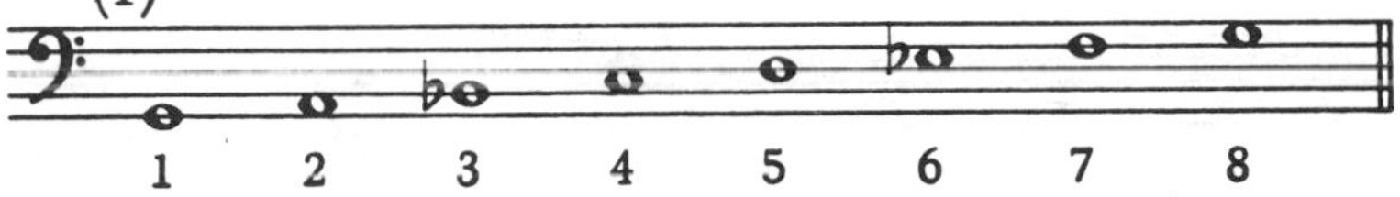

1   2   3   4   5   6   7   8

(2)

1   2   3   4   5   6   7   8

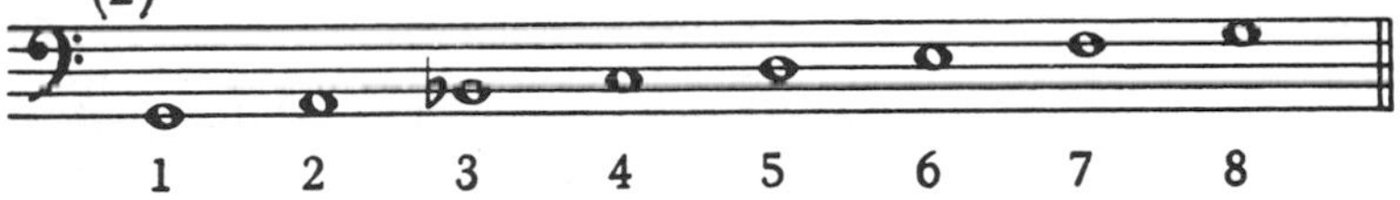

9.9 The *lower* tetrachord of the *C natural minor scale* is notated below. Analyze the intervals contained in this tetrachord as indicated.

W = whole step   H = half step

W   H   W

___   ___   ___

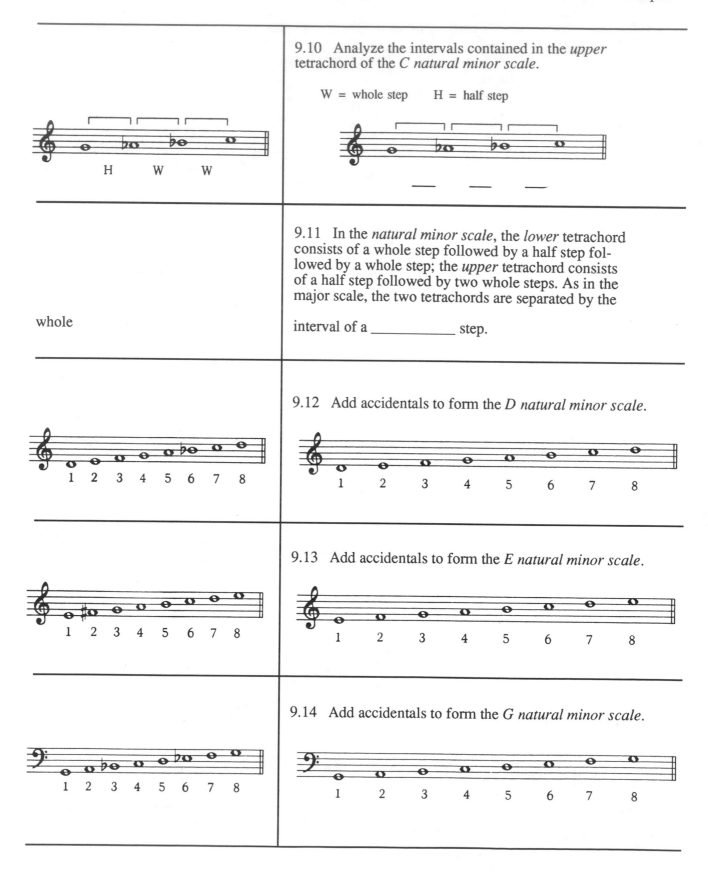

9.10 Analyze the intervals contained in the *upper tetrachord of the C natural minor scale.*

W = whole step   H = half step

9.11 In the *natural minor scale,* the *lower* tetrachord consists of a whole step followed by a half step followed by a whole step; the *upper* tetrachord consists of a half step followed by two whole steps. As in the major scale, the two tetrachords are separated by the interval of a _____ step.

whole

9.12 Add accidentals to form the *D natural minor scale.*

9.13 Add accidentals to form the *E natural minor scale.*

9.14 Add accidentals to form the *G natural minor scale.*

9.15   Add accidentals to form the *B natural minor scale.*

9.16   Write the *F-sharp natural minor scale.*

9.17   Write the *C natural minor scale.*

9.18   Write the *C-sharp natural minor scale.*

9.19   Write the *F natural minor scale.*

9.20 The HARMONIC MINOR SCALE has half steps between the 2nd and 3rd, 5th and 6th, and 7th and 8th degrees.

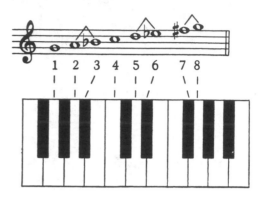

How many half steps are contained in the

harmonic minor scale? _____

three

9.21 What is the interval separating the 6th and 7th degrees of the *harmonic minor scale?*

_____

(Refer to the scale in the preceding frame.)

augmented 2nd

9.22 A unique feature of the harmonic minor scale is the *augmented 2nd* which occurs between the 6th and 7th degrees. The *augmented 2nd* is the same as a

whole step plus a _____ step.

half

9.23 Show the degrees between which half steps occur in the harmonic minor scale.

_____ and _____; _____ and _____; _____ and _____.

2nd (and) 3rd
5th (and) 6th
7th (and) 8th

9.24 The *harmonic minor scale* may be represented as a series of steps, as below:

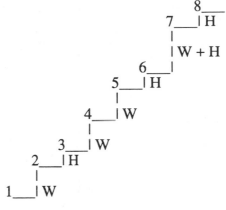

H = half step
W = whole step

Try to sing this harmonic minor scale. Be careful to observe the correct pattern of half and whole steps.

In the *harmonic minor scale*, half steps occur between the 2nd and 3rd, 5th and 6th, and 7th and 8th degrees. The interval between the 6th and 7th degrees is a *step-and-a-half*. The remaining intervals are all

whole

_____ steps.

9.25 Is the scale below a harmonic minor scale?

yes

_____

9.26 Is the scale below a harmonic minor scale?

yes

_____

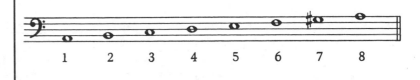

no

9.27 Is the scale below a harmonic minor scale?

_____

natural minor

9.28 What type of scale is shown in the preceding

frame? _____

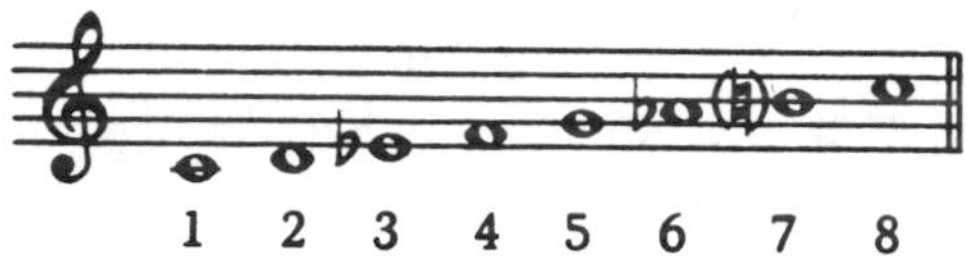

9.29 Rewrite the proper accidentals for the scale in Frame 9.27 so that it is a *C harmonic minor scale.*

the 7th scale degree

was raised a half step

9.30 As originally written, the scale in Frame 9.27 was a natural minor scale. What alteration was necessary to transform it into a harmonic minor scale?

_____

_____

half

9.31 The harmonic minor scale differs from the natural minor scale only in that the 7th degree is

raised a _____ step.

9.32 To write a harmonic minor scale: (1) write a natural minor scale; (2) raise the 7th degree a half step.

Transform the natural minor scale below into a harmonic minor scale in the manner described above.

9.33 Transform the natural minor scale below into a harmonic minor scale.

9.34 Add accidentals to form the *D harmonic minor scale. (Check all intervals.)*

9.35 Add accidentals to form the *E harmonic minor scale. (Check all intervals.)*

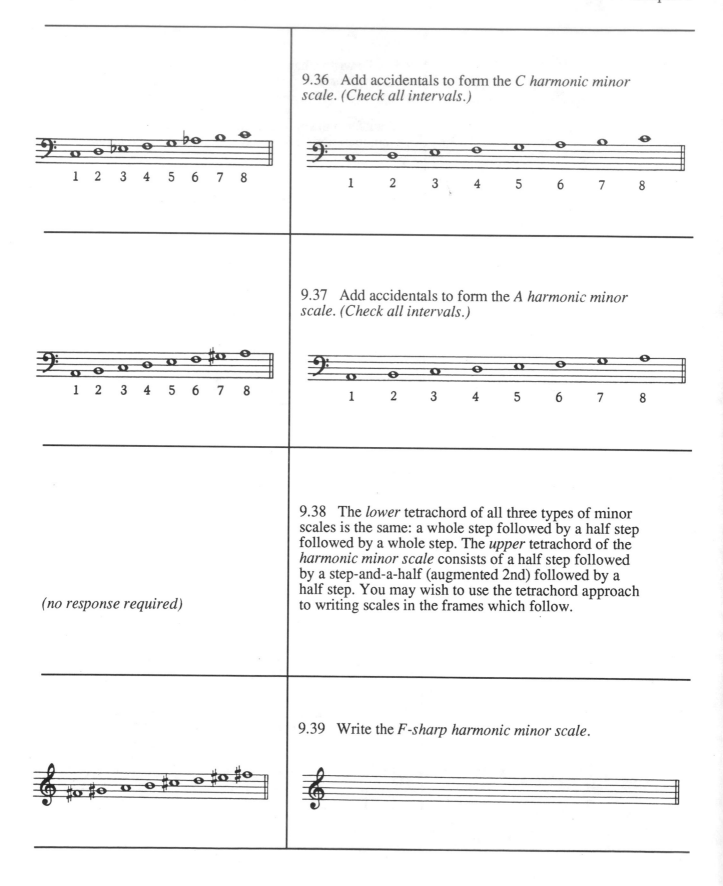

9.36 Add accidentals to form the *C harmonic minor scale. (Check all intervals.)*

1   2   3   4   5   6   7   8

1   2   3   4   5   6   7   8

9.37 Add accidentals to form the *A harmonic minor scale. (Check all intervals.)*

1   2   3   4   5   6   7   8

1   2   3   4   5   6   7   8

(no response required)

9.38 The *lower* tetrachord of all three types of minor scales is the same: a whole step followed by a half step followed by a whole step. The *upper* tetrachord of the *harmonic minor scale* consists of a half step followed by a step-and-a-half (augmented 2nd) followed by a half step. You may wish to use the tetrachord approach to writing scales in the frames which follow.

9.39 Write the *F-sharp harmonic minor scale.*

9.40 Write the *F harmonic minor scale.*

9.41 Write the *C-sharp harmonic minor scale.*

9.42 Write the *B-flat harmonic minor scale.*

9.43 Write the *G-sharp harmonic minor scale.*

9.44 Write the *E-flat harmonic minor scale.*

9.45 Write the *D-sharp harmonic minor scale.*

9.46 Write the *A-flat harmonic minor scale.*

9.47 Write the *A-sharp harmonic minor scale.*

natural

9.48 The minor scale which has half steps between the 2nd and 3rd and the 5th and 6th degrees is called

the _____ minor scale.

harmonic

9.49 The minor scale which has half steps between the 2nd and 3rd, 5th and 6th, and 7th and 8th degrees

is called the _____ minor scale.

melodic

9.50 In all the scales studied to this point the *ascending* and *descending* forms have contained the same notes. The MELODIC MINOR SCALE, however, has one pattern of half and whole steps for its *ascending* form and another for its *descending* form.

The only scale which has different patterns of half and whole steps for its *ascending* and *descending*

forms is called the _____ minor scale.

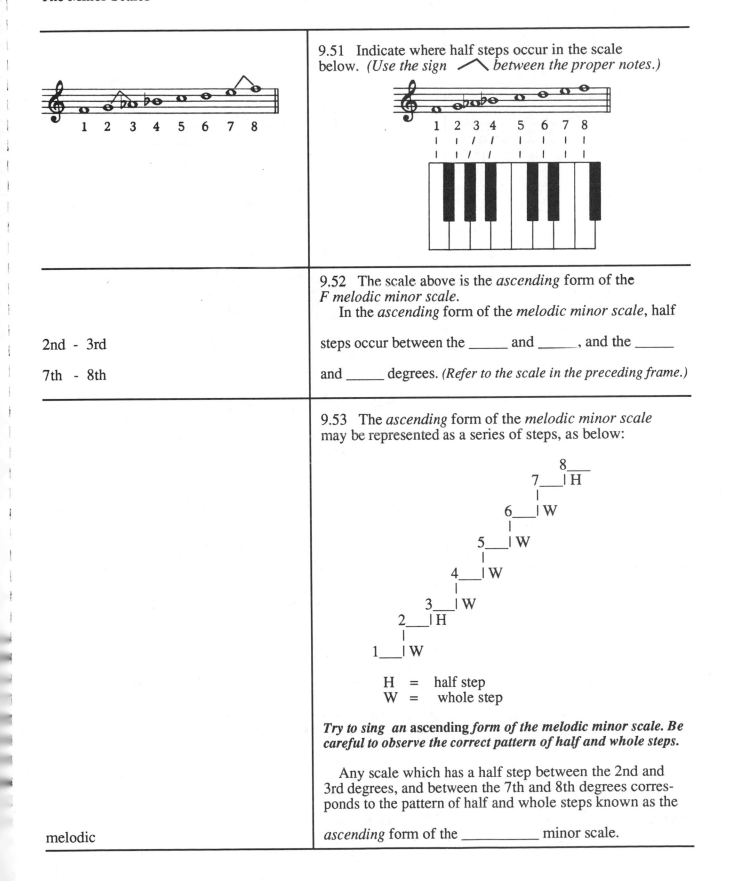

9.51 Indicate where half steps occur in the scale below. (*Use the sign* ⌃ *between the proper notes.*)

9.52 The scale above is the *ascending* form of the *F melodic minor scale*.

In the *ascending* form of the *melodic minor scale*, half

2nd - 3rd

steps occur between the _____ and _____, and the _____

7th - 8th

and _____ degrees. (*Refer to the scale in the preceding frame.*)

9.53 The *ascending* form of the *melodic minor scale* may be represented as a series of steps, as below:

```
                              8___
                          7___| H
                             |
                      6___| W
                         |
                  5___| W
                     |
              4___| W
                 |
          3___| W
      2___| H
         |
  1___| W
```

H = half step
W = whole step

Try to sing an ascending form of the melodic minor scale. Be careful to observe the correct pattern of half and whole steps.

Any scale which has a half step between the 2nd and 3rd degrees, and between the 7th and 8th degrees corresponds to the pattern of half and whole steps known as the

melodic

ascending form of the _____ minor scale.

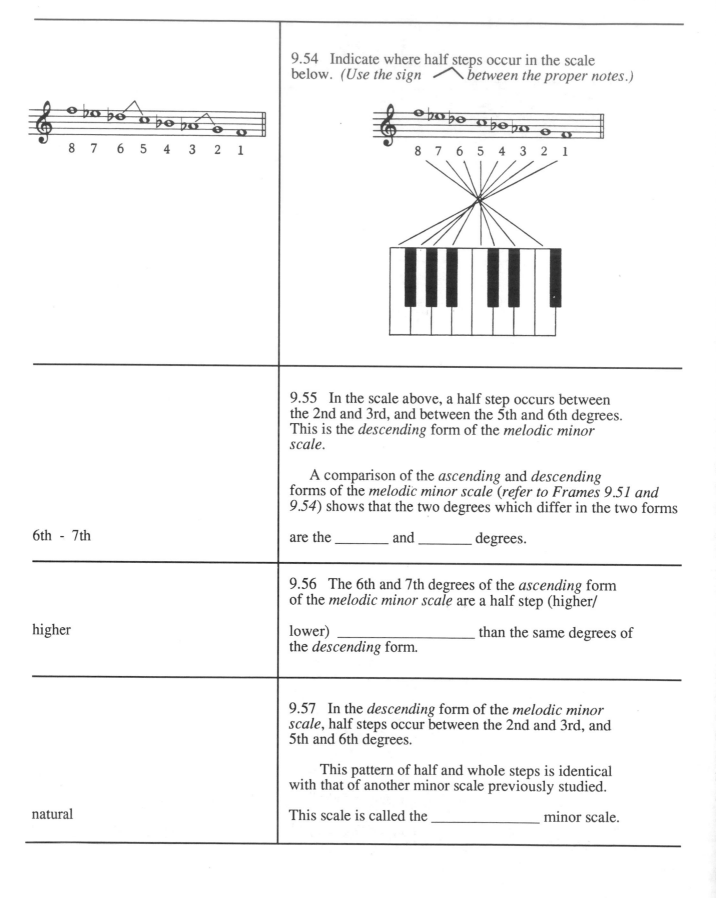

9.54 Indicate where half steps occur in the scale below. *(Use the sign* ⌃ *between the proper notes.)*

9.55 In the scale above, a half step occurs between the 2nd and 3rd, and between the 5th and 6th degrees. This is the *descending* form of the *melodic minor scale*.

A comparison of the *ascending* and *descending* forms of the *melodic minor scale (refer to Frames 9.51 and 9.54)* shows that the two degrees which differ in the two forms are the _____ and _____ degrees.

6th - 7th

9.56 The 6th and 7th degrees of the *ascending* form of the *melodic minor scale* are a half step (higher/

lower) _____ than the same degrees of the *descending* form.

higher

9.57 In the *descending* form of the *melodic minor scale*, half steps occur between the 2nd and 3rd, and 5th and 6th degrees.

This pattern of half and whole steps is identical with that of another minor scale previously studied.

This scale is called the _____ minor scale.

natural

9.58 The *descending* form of the *melodic minor scale* may be represented as a series of steps, as below:

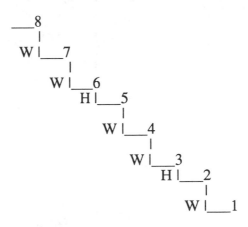

H = half step
W = whole step

Try to sing a descending form of the melodic minor scale. Be careful to observe the correct pattern of half and whole steps.

The pattern of half and whole steps in the *natural minor scale* is the same as that of the ___ _____ form of the *melodic minor scale*.

descending

---

(1)

9.59 Which of the scales below is the descending form of the D melodic minor scale? _____

(1)

(2)

(2)

9.60 Which of the scales below is the *ascending* form of the C-sharp melodic minor scale? _____

(1)

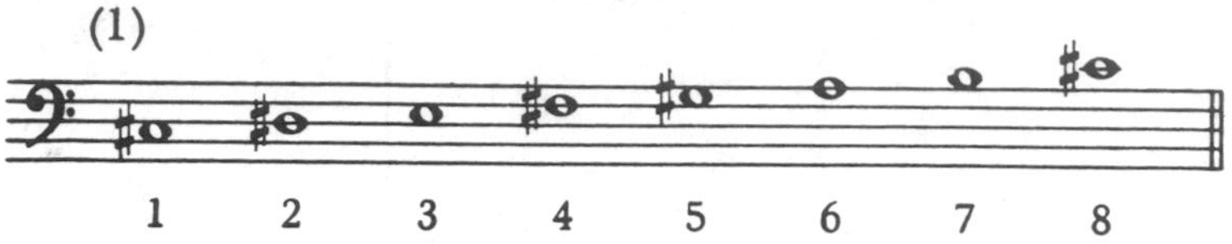

(2)

(2)

9.61 Which of the scales below is the *ascending* form of the G melodic minor scale? _____

(1)

(2)

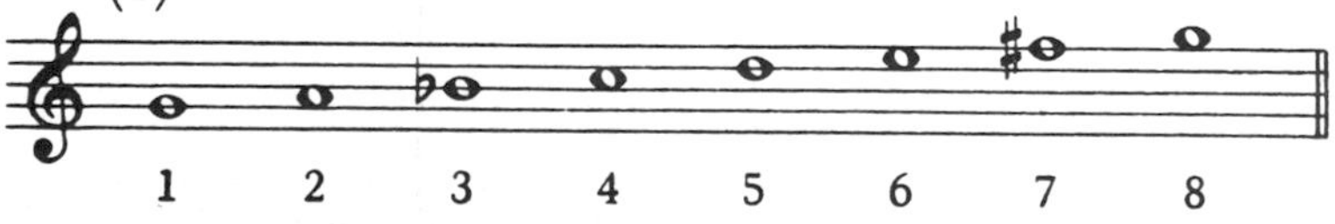

major

9.62 Scale (1) in the preceding frame is what type of scale? _____

the 3rd

9.63   Compare Scale (1) with Scale (2) in Frame 9.61.

What scale degree is different? _____

---

half

9.64   The ascending form of the melodic minor scale is the same as a major scale, except that the

3rd degree is a _____ step lower.

---

true

9.65   The lower tetrachord of all three types of minor scales consists of a whole step followed by a half step followed by a whole step. In the melodic minor scale, the *ascending* upper tetrachord is the same as in the major scale (whole step, whole step, half step); the *descending* upper tetrachord is the same as in the natural minor scale (whole step, half step, whole step).

The tetrachord below is the upper tetrachord of the B melodic minor scale, *ascending* form. (True/False)

_____

9.66   Write the upper tetrachord of the *D melodic minor scale, descending* form.

9.67 Write the upper tetrachord of the *E melodic minor scale*, *ascending* form.

9.68 Use accidentals to form the *C melodic minor scale*.

(ASCENDING FORM)

(DESCENDING FORM)

9.69 Use accidentals to form the *F melodic minor scale*.

(ASCENDING FORM)

(DESCENDING FORM)

9.70   Use accidentals to form the *G melodic minor scale.*

(ASCENDING FORM)

(DESCENDING FORM)

9.71   Use accidentals to form the *B-flat melodic minor scale.*

(ASCENDING FORM)

(DESCENDING FORM)

9.72   Use accidentals to form the *D melodic minor scale.*

(ASCENDING FORM)

(DESCENDING FORM)

9.73 Use accidentals to form the *E-flat melodic minor scale.*

(ASCENDING FORM)

(DESCENDING FORM)

9.74 Use accidentals to form the *A melodic minor scale.*

(ASCENDING FORM)

(DESCENDING FORM)

9.75 Write the *A-flat melodic minor scale.*

(ASCENDING FORM)

(DESCENDING FORM)

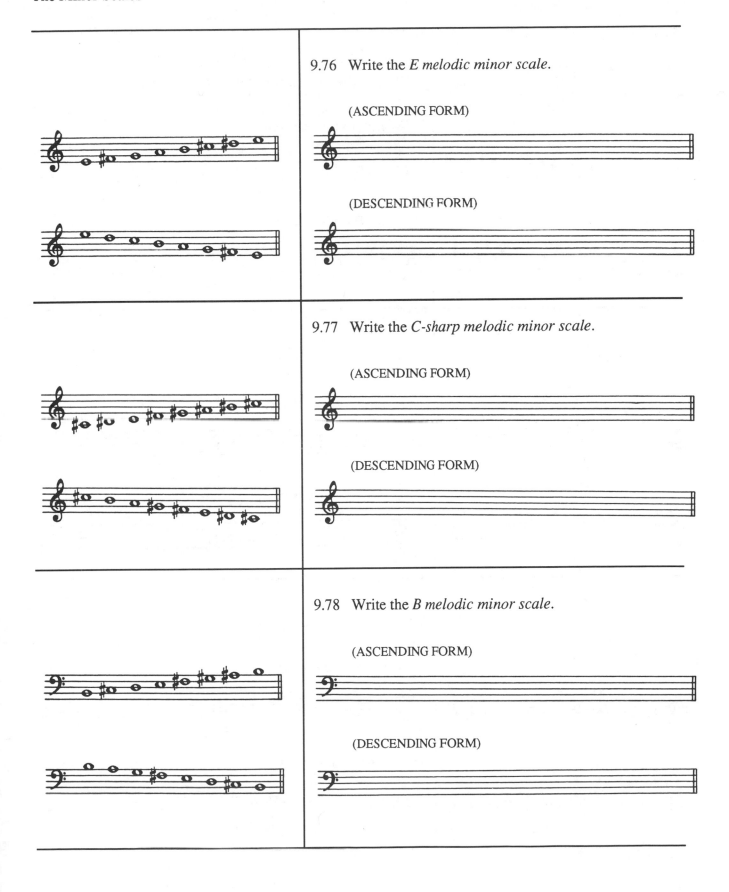

9.76   Write the *E melodic minor scale*.

(ASCENDING FORM)

(DESCENDING FORM)

9.77   Write the *C-sharp melodic minor scale*.

(ASCENDING FORM)

(DESCENDING FORM)

9.78   Write the *B melodic minor scale*.

(ASCENDING FORM)

(DESCENDING FORM)

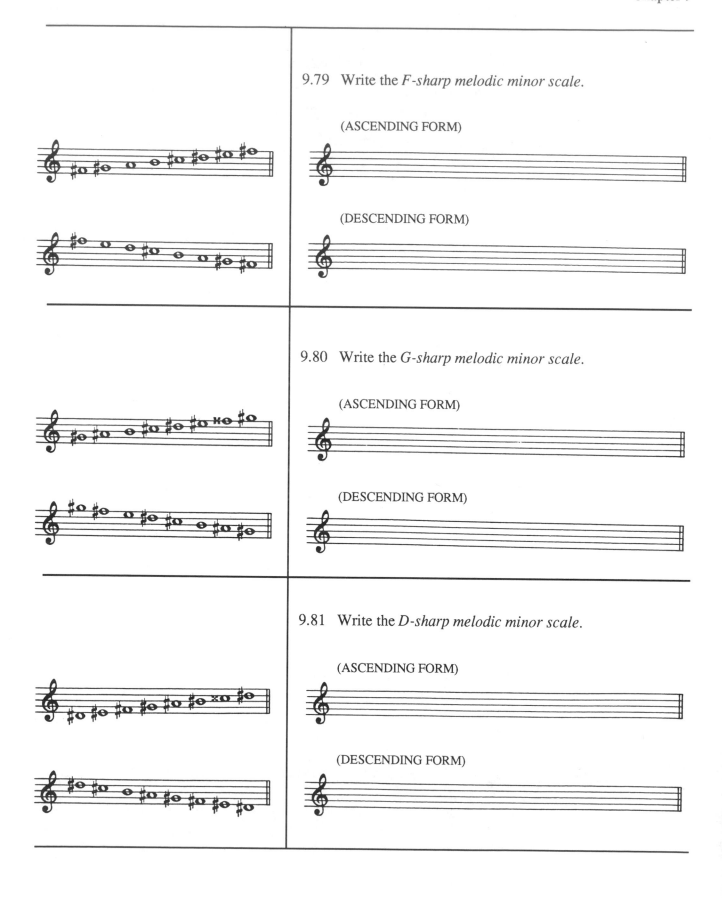

9.79   Write the *F-sharp melodic minor scale.*

(ASCENDING FORM)

(DESCENDING FORM)

9.80   Write the *G-sharp melodic minor scale.*

(ASCENDING FORM)

(DESCENDING FORM)

9.81   Write the *D-sharp melodic minor scale.*

(ASCENDING FORM)

(DESCENDING FORM)

9.82 Write the *A-sharp melodic minor scale.*

(ASCENDING FORM)

(DESCENDING FORM)

(2)

9.83 Which of the scales below is a *pure* minor scale?

_____

(1)

(2)

(2)

9.84 Which of the scales below is a *harmonic* minor scale?

_____

(1)

(2)

(1)

9.85 Which of the scales below is the *ascending* form of a *melodic* minor scale?

_____

(1)

(2)

(1)

9.86 Which of the scales below is the *descending* form of a *melodic* minor scale?

_____

(1)

(2)

no

9.87 All *major* and *minor* scales are *diatonic* scales. A diatonic scale consists of eight notes (including the octave duplication of the keynote) arranged stepwise. Does the chromatic half step occur in any

of the diatonic scales? _____

Summary

In all three forms of the *minor scale* the *lower tetrachord* is the same. The *intervals* are a *whole step*, followed by a *half step*, followed by a *whole step*. The *upper tetrachord*, however, is different in each case. This is shown in the schematic below. Notice that, in each pattern, the two *tetrachords* are separated by a *whole step*.

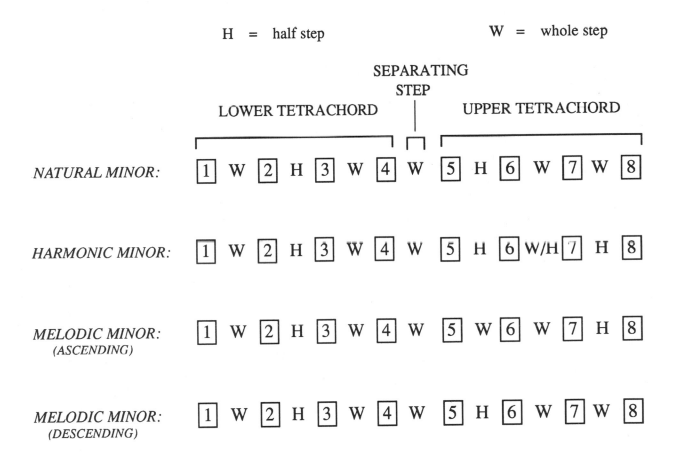

Mastery Frames

9–1   Name the type of minor scale that has the same pattern of half and whole steps as the Aeolian mode.

natural   (Frame 9.3)   _____

9–2   Add accidentals to produce natural minor scales.

(9.12–9.15)

9–3   Which type of minor scale contains three half steps?

harmonic   (9.20)   _____

9–4   Add accidentals to produce harmonic minor scales.

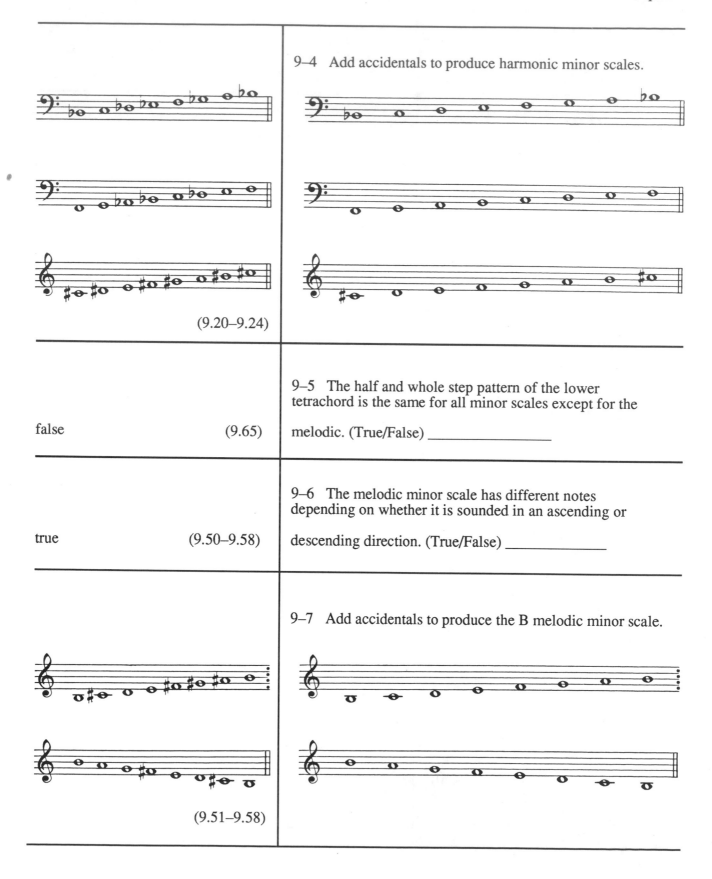

(9.20–9.24)

9–5   The half and whole step pattern of the lower tetrachord is the same for all minor scales except for the melodic. (True/False) _____

false   (9.65)

9–6   The melodic minor scale has different notes depending on whether it is sounded in an ascending or descending direction. (True/False) _____

true   (9.50–9.58)

9–7   Add accidentals to produce the B melodic minor scale.

(9.51–9.58)

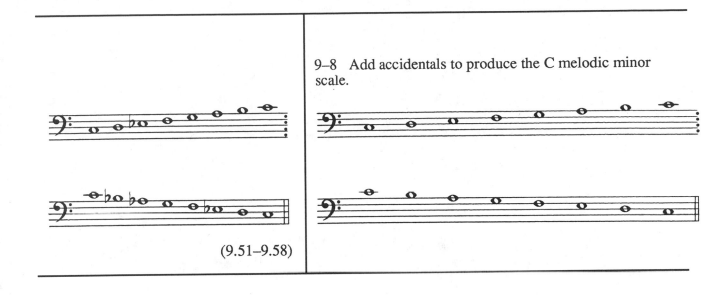

(9.51–9.58)

9–8   Add accidentals to produce the C melodic minor scale.

Supplementary Assignments

Assignment 9–1   Name: _____

1. What type of minor scale contains the interval of an augmented second? _____

2. Between which scale degrees do half steps occur in the natural minor scale? _____

3. Add one accidental to change the natural minor scale below to a harmonic minor scale.

4. Which of the scales is a natural minor scale? _____

5. Which of the scales is a harmonic minor scale? _____

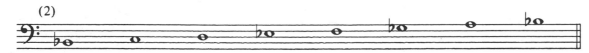

6. Add accidentals to produce natural minor scales.

7. Add accidentals to produce harmonic minor scales.

8. What interval occurs between the 6th and 7th degrees of the harmonic minor scale?

   _____

9. Which scale degrees have alternate forms in the melodic minor scale, depending on whether the scale is ascending or descending? _____

10. Add accidentals to produce melodic minor scales.

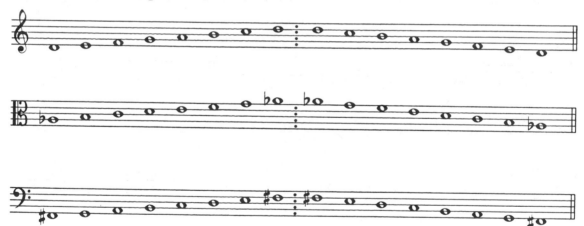

11. Between which scale degrees do half steps occur in the ascending form of the melodic minor scale? _____

12. Between which scale degrees do half steps occur in the descending form of the melodic minor scale? _____

Eartraining Activities

1. The *lower* tetrachord (scale degrees 1–4) of all three forms of the minor scale is the same. The interval pattern is whole-step/half step/whole step. Sing the following tetrachords:

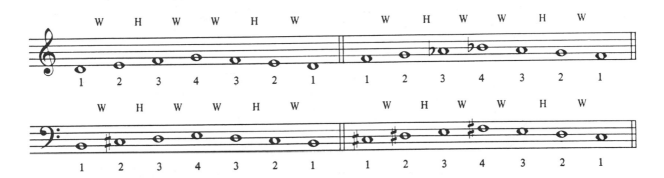

2. Focus your attention on the *upper* tetrachord as you sing the following three minor scales:

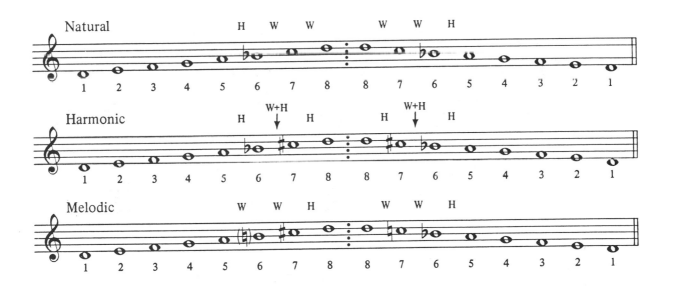

3. Practice singing the three forms of the minor scale beginning on various notes to achieve accuracy and fluency. Always be conscious of the half and whole step pattern. Check yourself at a keyboard, if necessary.

4. Use the notes given in the following to sing the various minor scales as directed. Rely on your ear and your knowledge of the intervallic pattern of each scale. Resort to a keyboard for aid, if necessary. End by writing out the notes of the scale.

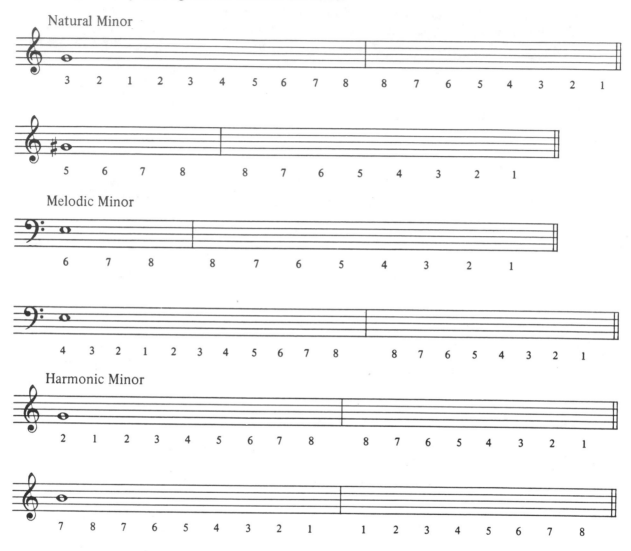

Natural Minor

Melodic Minor

Harmonic Minor

5. On your own, again search out compositions, select from those you may be performing, or seek suggestions from your instructor for examples to continue visually and aurally practicing (hearing in your head or singing) minor scale and mode identification.

10.0
Key Signatures

You have learned to write *major* and *minor* scales by applying *accidentals* to produce the desired *half* and *whole step* patterns. The *sharps* and *flats* used in a particular *scale* may be grouped together and placed on the *staff* immediately after the *clef sign*. This is called a *key signature*. With a key signature in place it is unnecessary to apply accidentals to each note; a sharp or flat in the key signature affects all such notes in any octave, unless superceded by an accidental. Also with a key signature in use, the music notation is thus less cluttered and easier to read. In this "gathering" of the recurring accidentals at the beginning of each staff, a system of key signatures has developed over the centuries, which will be explained in this chapter.

A	10.1 A scale organizes into a stepwise series of notes the tonal material of a particular KEY. The first and last note of a scale is called the KEYNOTE (or TONIC). The *keynote* of the A major scale is _____.
E-flat	10.2 The *key* of a composition is the same as the *keynote* of its principal scale. If a composition is based primarily upon the E-flat major scale, it is said to be in the key of _____ major.
scale	10.3 The term *key* is practically synonymous with TONALITY. Regardless of the term used, the *keynote* is the center to which the other tones of the scale relate. *Tonality* is the result of a *keynote* (or *tonic*) predominating over the remaining tones of the _____.

	10.4 Reiteration of the keynote is one possible way of causing it to predominate over the remaining tones of the scale, for any note which occurs more frequently than others automatically has special status. Another way is to use the keynote in strategic positions such as on metrical stresses, or at structural points such as beginnings and endings of phrases. *Harmonic relationships* also help establish *tonality*, but the study of the melody and harmony lies outside the scope of this work.
tonality	What is another word for key? _____
	10.5 Much of the music we hear today is based upon major and minor scales. Either of these can be written beginning on any note, provided the appropriate basic notes are adjusted by the use of accidentals.
	Accidentals are used to produce the desired pattern
half (and) whole	of _____ and _____ steps.
	10.6 The groupings of *sharps* or *flats* at the beginning of each *staff* line are necessary to produce the desired *half* and *whole step* pattern in a given *scale* are grouped together to form the KEY SIGNATURE. The *key signature* is placed on the *staff* immediately after the *clef* sign, as shown below:
	The *key signature* consists of a group of either
sharps or flats	_____ or _____.
	10.7 The sharps or flats of a key signature apply to *all* notes of that name in the composition, unless indicated otherwise by additional accidentals.
	A B-flat in the key signature means that each B appearing
B-flat	in the composition will be played as a_____.

key signature	10.8 The group of sharps or flats which appear just to the right of the clef sign is called the _____.
yes	10.9 Does a sharp or flat in the key signature affect all notes of that name regardless of where they may appear? _____
F-C-G-D-A-E-B	10.10 The sharps or flats which comprise a key signature always occur in a specific order. The order of the sharps is F-C-G-D-A-E-B. Key signatures consist of either sharps or flats.* The sharps are placed on the staff in the following order: _____-_____-_____-_____-_____-_____-_____ **_Learn the order of the sharps before proceeding with the next frame._** _____ *Two keys (C major and A minor) have a key signature of no sharps or flats.
the fourth	10.11 The sharps are placed on the staff in a particular order, creating this pattern: On which line of the treble staff does the fourth sharp appear? _____

the third	10.12 In which space does the sixth sharp appear on the bass staff? _____
	10.13 Write the seven sharps on the *grand* staff. ***Observe correct order and placement.***
no *(The third sharp on the bass staff should be an octave higher.)*	10.14 Are the sharps placed correctly in the example below? _____
yes *(see the next frame)*	10.15 When the C-clefs are used, the sharps are placed on the staff as below: Alto Clef Tenor Clef Do the sharps occur in the same order in each case above? _____

10.16   Even though they appear in a different pattern, the sharps occur in the *same* order on both the *alto* and *tenor* clefs. Write the order of the seven sharps as they occur in a key signature.

F-C-G-D-A-E-B

_____-_____-_____-_____-_____-_____-_____

10.17   Write the seven sharps on the alto clef.

10.18   Write the seven sharps on the tenor clef.

10.19   The flats are placed on the staff in the following order: B-E-A-D-G-C-F. Observe that the order of the flats is the reverse of the order of the sharps. Write the order of the flats:

B-E-A-D-G-C-F

_____-_____-_____-_____-_____-_____-_____

Learn the order of the flats before proceeding with the next frame.

10.20   The flats are placed on the staff in a particular order, creating this pattern:

On which line of the treble staff does the fifth

the second

flat appear? _____

10.21   Where on the bass staff is the seventh flat placed?

In the first space
below the staff.

_____

_____

10.22   Write the seven flats on the *grand* staff. ***Observe correct order and placement.***

10.23   Are the flats placed correctly in the example below?

no
*(The last flat on
both the treble
and bass staff
should be an
octave lower.)*

_____

10.24 Write once again on the grand staff the seven sharps.

10.25 Write once again on the grand staff the seven flats.

10.26 When the C-clefs are used, the flats are placed on the staff as below:

Alto Clef

Tenor Clef

Flats, when used in a key signature, are written in the *same* up and down pattern on both of the *C-clefs* as well as the *treble* and *bass* clefs.

Write the order of the seven flats as they occur in a key signature.

B-E-A-D-G-C-F

_____-_____-_____-_____-_____-_____-_____

10.27   Write the seven flats on the tenor clef.

10.28   Write the seven flats on the alto clef.

10.29   Each given *key signature* may indicate either a MAJOR or a MINOR KEY. We shall learn first how to determine the *major key*.

The C major scale uses only the basic (unaltered) notes. The key signature for the key of C major is

no   therefore _____ sharps or flats.

10.30   The *major key* with no sharps or flats in the

C major   signature is _____.

E	10.31 If the *key signature* consists of *sharps*, the *major key* can be determined by referring to the *last* sharp in the signature. This sharp indicates the *7th* scale degree. The *keynote*, therefore, is a half step higher. (The interval of a half step separates the 7th and 8th degrees of the major scale.) If the last sharp in the key signature is D-sharp, the key is _____ major.
the 7th	10.32 Which degree of the major scale is indicated by the last sharp of the key signature? _____
A	10.33 If the last sharp in the key signature is G-sharp, the key is _____ major.
D	10.34 If the last sharp in the key signature is C-sharp, the key is _____ major.
B	10.35 What *major key* is indicated by the signature below? _____ major.
G	10.36 What *major key* is indicated by the signature below? _____ major.

F-sharp

10.37 What *major key* is indicated by the signature below?

_____ major.

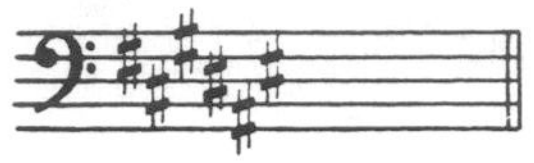

E

10.38 What *major key* is indicated by the signature below?

_____ major.

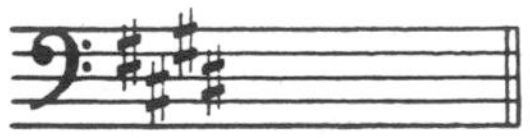

D

10.39 What *major key* is indicated by the signature below?

_____ major.

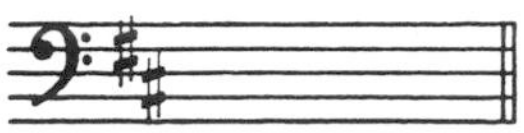

A

10.40 What *major key* is indicated by the signature below?

_____ major.

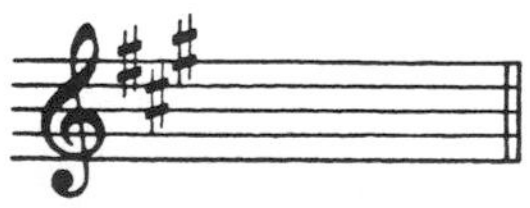

C-sharp

10.41 What *major key* is indicated by the signature below?

_____ major.

10.42   To write a key signature consisting of sharps for a given key, the process described in Frame 10.31 is reversed. For example, the signature for the key of E major can be determined as follows:

(1)   The 7th degree of the E major scale is D-sharp.
(2)   D-sharp will be the last sharp in the key signature.
(3)   The order of sharps up to and including D-sharp is F-C-G-D.
(4)   Therefore, the signature for the key of E major is four sharps.

The *last* sharp of the key signature is on which degree

the 7th

of the major scale? _____

10.43   Write on the *grand* staff the *key signature* for A major.

10.44   Write on the *grand* staff the *key signature* for D major.

10.45   Write on the *grand* staff the *key signature* for
E major.

10.46   Write on the *grand* staff the *key signature* for
G major.

10.47   Write on the *grand* staff the *key signature* for
B major.

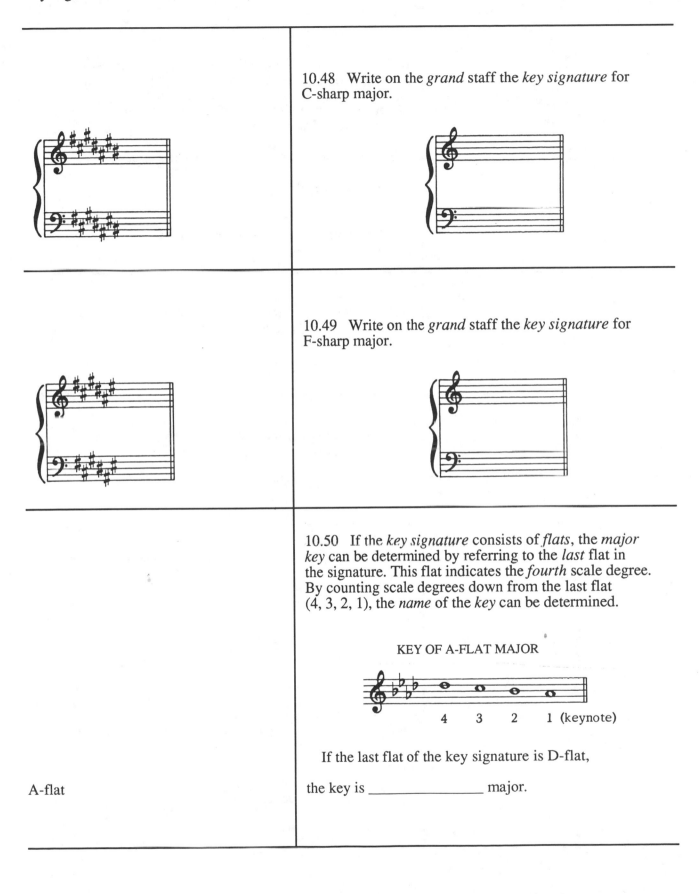

10.48   Write on the *grand* staff the *key signature* for C-sharp major.

10.49   Write on the *grand* staff the *key signature* for F-sharp major.

10.50   If the *key signature* consists of *flats*, the *major key* can be determined by referring to the *last* flat in the signature. This flat indicates the *fourth* scale degree. By counting scale degrees down from the last flat (4, 3, 2, 1), the *name* of the *key* can be determined.

KEY OF A-FLAT MAJOR

4   3   2   1   (keynote)

If the last flat of the key signature is D-flat,

the key is _____ major.

A-flat

the 1st

10.51 Notice in the preceding frame that the *name* of the *key* (A-flat) is the *same* as the *next-to-the-last* flat. *This will always be the case.* You may wish to make use of this method when identifying *key signatures* which contain *flats.**

The next-to-the-last flat indicates which degree

of the major scale? _____

---

*The key with one flat (F major) is the only key which cannot be identified in this way.

D-flat

10.52 If the next-to-the-last flat in the key signature is D-flat, what is the name of the key?

_____ major.

E-flat

10.53 If the next-to-the-last flat in the key signature is E-flat, what is the name of the key?

_____ major.

D-flat

10.54 What *major key* is indicated by the signature below?

_____ major.

F

10.55 What *major key* is indicated by the signature below?

_____ major.

G-flat	10.56 What *major key* is indicated by the signature below? _____ major.
A-flat	10.57 What *major key* is indicated by the signature below? _____ major.
B-flat	10.58 What *major key* is indicated by the signature below? _____ major.
E-flat	10.59 What *major key* is indicated by the signature below? _____ major.
C-flat	10.60 What *major key* is indicated by the signature below? _____ major.

10.61   The signature of a key containing flats can be determined as follows:

> (1)   Go through the order of the flats until you reach the flat which is identical with the name of the key.
>
> (2)   Add the next flat in the series of flats.

The *next-to-the-last* flat is on which degree of

the 1st   the major scale? _____

10.62   The *last* flat is on which degree of the major scale?

the 4th   _____

10.63   Write on the *grand* staff the *key signature* for E-flat major.

10.64   Write on the *grand* staff the *key signature* for B-flat major.

10.65 Write on the *grand* staff the *key signature* for A-flat major.

10.66 Write on the *grand* staff the *key signature* for F major.

10.67 Write on the *grand* staff the *key signature* for D-flat major.

10.68 Write on the *grand* staff the *key signature* for C-flat major.

10.69 Write on the *grand* staff the *key signature* for G-flat major.

10.70 Keys with two or more flats in their signatures have the word *flat* in their name. There are, for example, the keys of B-*flat*, E-*flat*, A-*flat*, and so forth. The key of F major (one flat) is the only *flat* key which does not have the word *flat* in its name.

The word *flat* is part of the name of all the *major* keys which contain flats in their signatures

except the key of _____ major.

F

sharps

10.71 Would the signature for the key of E major consist of sharps or flats?

_____

flats

10.72 Would the signature for the key of A-flat major consist of sharps or flats?

_____

flats

10.73 Would the signature for the key of G-flat major consist of sharps or flats?

_____

sharps

10.74 Would the signature for the key of B major consist of sharps or flats?

_____

10.75 Write on the *grand* staff the *key signature* for D major.

10.76 Write on the *grand* staff the *key signature* for D-flat major.

10.77 Write on the *grand* staff the *key signature* for G major.

10.78 Write on the *grand* staff the *key signature* for C major.

10.79 Write on the *grand* staff the *key signature* for F major.

10.80 Write on the *grand* staff the *key signature* for B major.

10.81 Write on the *grand* staff the *key signature* for B-flat major.

10.82   The *system* of *major keys* may be arranged in a *pattern* called the CIRCLE OF FIFTHS.

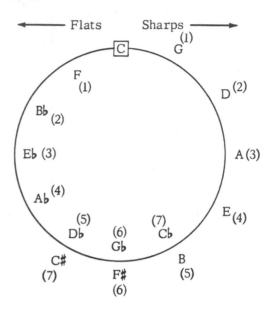

You may find the *circle of fifths* to be an aid in remembering the various *major key signatures*. Examine the order in which the sharp keys occur (reading clockwise from C major).

Each additional sharp added to the signature produces a

perfect 5th

key the interval of a _____ higher than the preceding key.

10.83   Refer again to the *circle of fifths* in the preceding frame. Examine the order in which the flat keys occur (reading counterclockwise from C major).

Each additional flat added to the signature produces

lower

a key the interval of a perfect 5th _____ than the preceding key.

10.84 The *circle of fifths* makes it clear that some of the flat keys sound the same as some of the sharp keys. The key of five flats (D-flat), for example, sounds the same as the key of seven sharps (C-sharp). Keys which contain the same pitches, but are notated differently are ENHARMONIC KEYS.

Which key is *enharmonic* with B major?

C-flat major

_____

10.85 What is the signature of the key which is *enharmonic* with G-flat major? _____

six sharps
(F-sharp major)

10.86 Each *key signature* may indicate either a *major* key or a *minor* key. The *major* and *minor* keys which share the *same* signature are called RELATIVE KEYS.

Each *major* key has a *relative* minor key, and

each *minor* key has a *relative* _____ key.

major

10.87 The relation between a *major* key and its *relative minor* is shown in the example below:

White note = major keynote.
Black note = minor keynote.

The *keynote* of the *relative minor* key is located on the *6th* degree of the *major* scale. The *keynote* of

the *relative major* key is located on the _____ degree of the *minor* scale.

3rd

below	10.88 The *keynotes* of *relative major* and *minor* keys are a *minor 3rd* apart. The *keynote* of a *minor* key is a *minor 3rd* (above/below) _____ the *keynote* of its *relative major*.
relative	10.89 The two keys (one major and one minor) which utilize the same key signature are called _____ keys.
the 6th	10.90 *There is a relative minor key for each major key.* Upon which degree of the major scale is the keynote of its relative minor located? _____
the 3rd	10.91 *There is a relative major key for each minor key.* Upon which degree of the minor scale is the keynote of its relative major located? _____
the minor 3rd	10.92 You must not think that because the keynote of the relative minor is located below the keynote of the major, or because major key signatures have been presented first, that minor keys are inferior to major keys. On the contrary, composers have long treated minor keys as in every way equal to major keys. A minor key does not *borrow* its signature from the relative major; a *single* signature is *shared* by the two keys. What is the interval which separates the keynotes of relative major and minor keys? _____

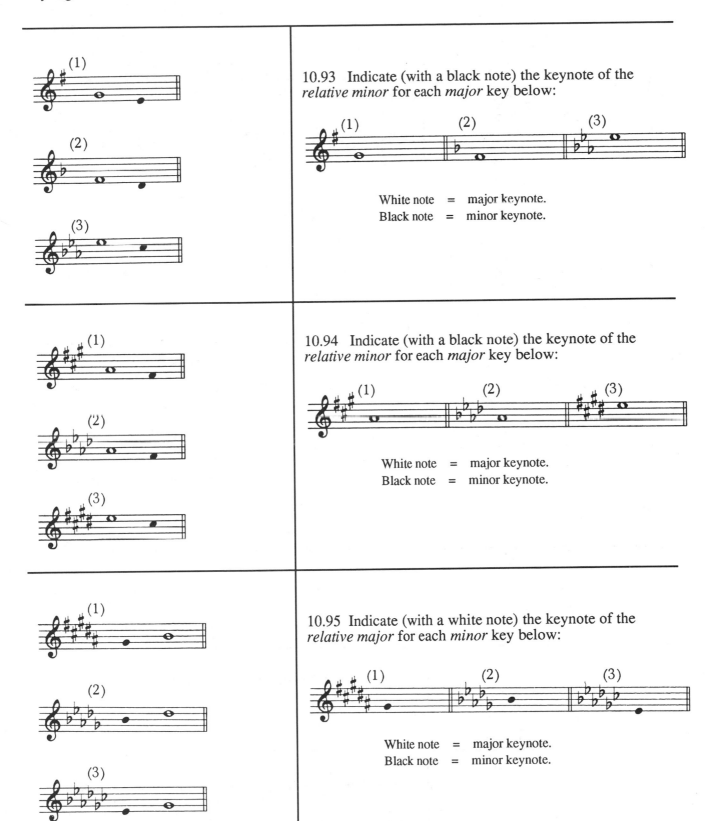

10.93 Indicate (with a black note) the keynote of the *relative minor* for each *major* key below:

White note = major keynote.
Black note = minor keynote.

10.94 Indicate (with a black note) the keynote of the *relative minor* for each *major* key below:

White note = major keynote.
Black note = minor keynote.

10.95 Indicate (with a white note) the keynote of the *relative major* for each *minor* key below:

White note = major keynote.
Black note = minor keynote.

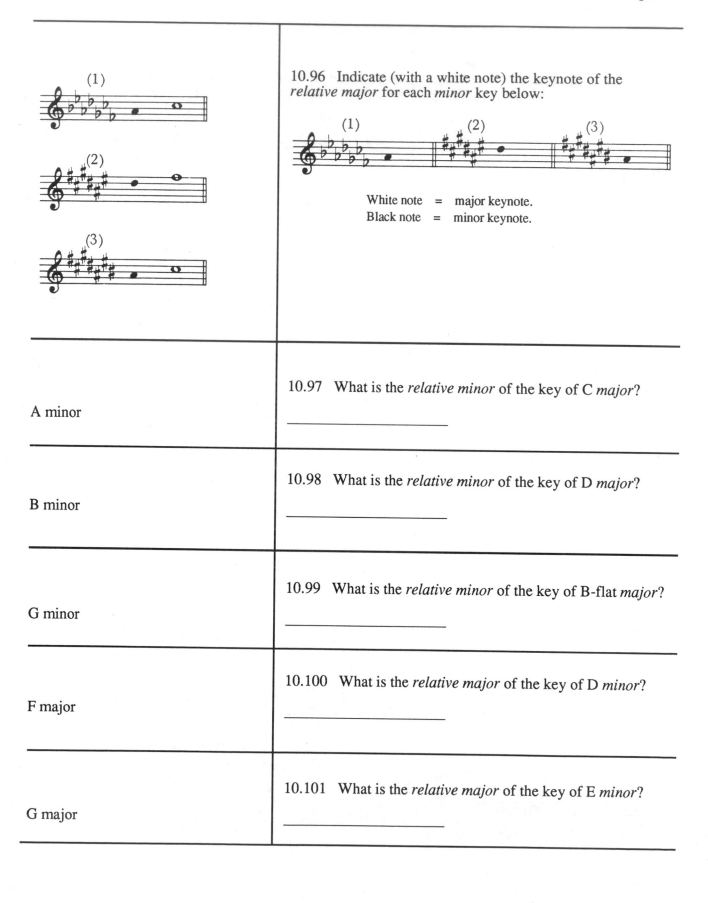

(1)

(2)

(3)

10.96 Indicate (with a white note) the keynote of the *relative major* for each *minor* key below:

(1)   (2)   (3)

White note = major keynote.
Black note = minor keynote.

A minor

10.97 What is the *relative minor* of the key of C *major*?

_____

B minor

10.98 What is the *relative minor* of the key of D *major*?

_____

G minor

10.99 What is the *relative minor* of the key of B-flat *major*?

_____

F major

10.100 What is the *relative major* of the key of D *minor*?

_____

G major

10.101 What is the *relative major* of the key of E *minor*?

_____

A major

10.102 What is the *relative major* of the key of F-sharp *minor*?

_____

C minor

10.103 What is the *relative minor* of the key of E-flat *major*?

_____

10.104 A *circle of fifths* can be written for *minor* keys as well as *major* keys.

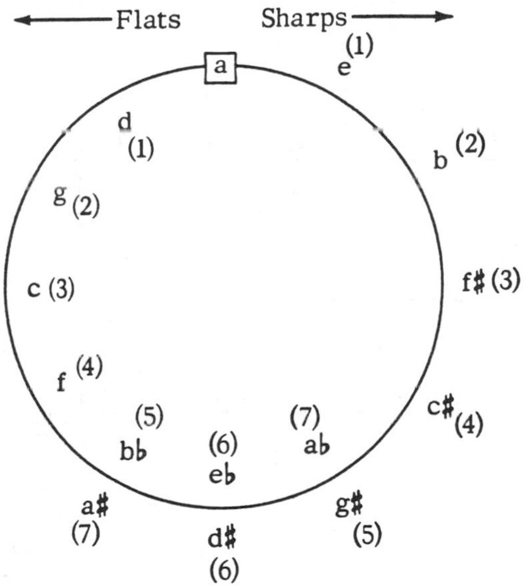

You may use the *circle of fifths* above as an aid in remembering *minor key signatures*. As in the case of major keys, each additional sharp in the signature produces a key a perfect 5th higher than the preceding key.

The keys of E-flat minor and D-sharp minor are

enharmonic   _____ keys.

10.105 Write on the *grand* staff the *key signature* for C-sharp minor.

10.106 Write on the *grand* staff the *key signature* for F minor.

10.107 Write on the *grand* staff the *key signature* for B-flat minor.

10.108 Write on the *grand* staff the *key signature* for G-sharp minor.

10.109 Write on the *grand* staff the *key signature* for E-flat minor.

10.110 Write on the *grand* staff the *key signature* for D-sharp minor.

10.111 Write on the *grand* staff the *key signature* for A-flat minor.

10.112 Write on the *grand* staff the *key signature* for A-sharp minor.

10.113 The sharps or flats of the key signature produce the half and whole step pattern of the NATURAL MINOR SCALE.

THE C NATURAL MINOR SCALE

1   2   3   4   5   6   7   8

What *type* of minor scale results when the notes are limited to the sharps or flats of the key signature?

natural

The _____ minor.

10.114 *Accidentals in addition* to the sharps or flats of the key signature are necessary to transform the *natural* minor scale into the *harmonic* and *melodic* types. These accidentals are applied to the individual notes as needed.

THE C HARMONIC MINOR SCALE

1   2   3   4   5   6   7   8

If the 7th degree of a natural minor scale is

raised a half step, the result is the _____ minor scale.

harmonic

10.115 Transform the *natural* minor scale below into a *harmonic* minor scale.

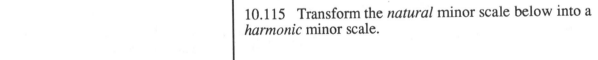

10.116 Transform the *natural* minor scale below into a *harmonic* minor scale.

10.117 Transform the *natural* minor scale below into a *harmonic* minor scale.

10.118 Transform the *natural* minor scale below into a *harmonic* minor scale.

10.119 The *melodic* minor scale (*ascending* form) is formed by *raising* the 6th and 7th degrees of the *natural* minor scale each by a *half step*.

THE C MELODIC MINOR SCALE, ASCENDING FORM

If the 6th and 7th degrees of the natural minor scale are raised each by a half step, the result is the

_____ form of the melodic minor scale.

ascending

10.120 Since the *descending* form of the *melodic* minor scale is identical with the *natural* minor scale, the 6th and 7th degrees *must be returned to their previous state* by the use of accidentals.

THE C MELODIC MINOR SCALE

The descending form of the melodic minor scale

is the same as the _____ minor scale.

natural

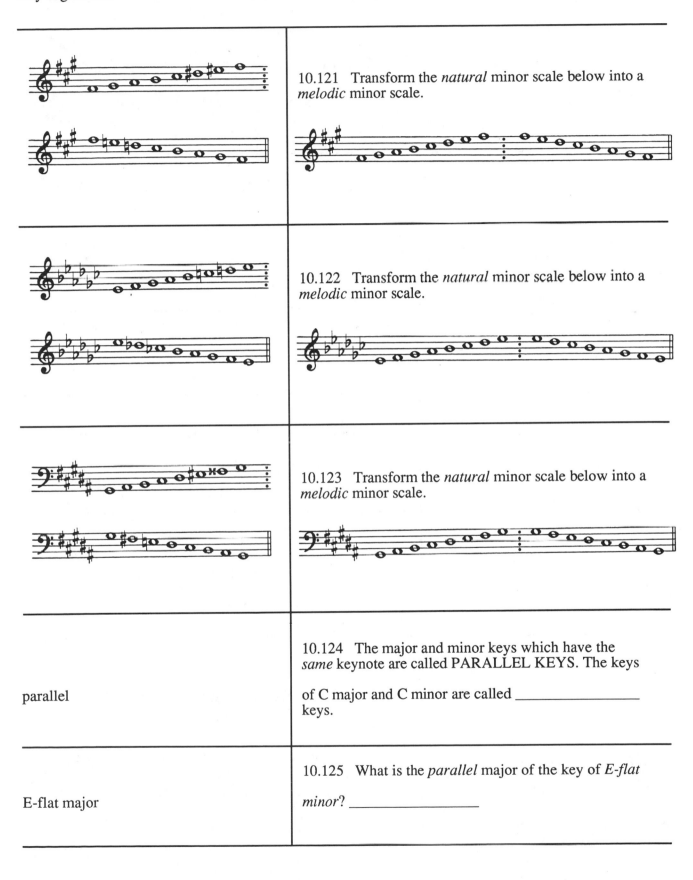

10.121 Transform the *natural* minor scale below into a *melodic* minor scale.

10.122 Transform the *natural* minor scale below into a *melodic* minor scale.

10.123 Transform the *natural* minor scale below into a *melodic* minor scale.

parallel

10.124 The major and minor keys which have the *same* keynote are called PARALLEL KEYS. The keys of C major and C minor are called _____ keys.

E-flat major

10.125 What is the *parallel* major of the key of *E-flat minor*? _____

B major	10.126 What is the *parallel* major of the key of *B minor*? _____
E minor	10.127 What is the *parallel* minor of the key of *E major*? _____
F-sharp minor	10.128 What is the *parallel* minor of the key of *F-sharp major*? _____
no	10.129 Parallel keys have the same keynote. Do they have the same key signature? _____
no	10.130 Relative keys have the same key signature. Do they have the same keynote? _____
(1) (2)	10.131 Use black notes to show the *keynotes* of the *relative* and *parallel keys* of E major. E Major (1) Relative Key (2) Parallel Key

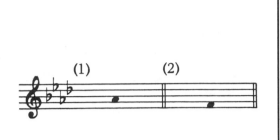

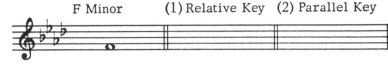

10.132   Use black notes to show the *keynotes* of the *relative* and *parallel* keys of F minor.

Summary

The signature of no sharps or flats denotes the keys of C major and A minor. All other keys have signatures of one or more sharps or flats. If there are *sharps* in the signature, the *last* sharp falls on the *seventh* degree of the major scale; if there are *flats*, the *last* flat falls on the *fourth* degree of the major scale, or the key may be derived from the *next-to-last flat*, except for the key of F major.

Any *key signature* serves for both a *major* and a *minor key*. The two *keys* that use the *same signature* are called *relative keys*. The *keynote* of the *relative minor* is located a *minor* 3rd **below** the *keynote* of the *major* (on the sixth scale degree); the *keynote* of the *relative major* is located a *minor* 3rd **above** the *keynote* of the *minor* (on the third scale degree). *Parallel keys* must not be confused with *relative keys*. *Parallel keys* have the *same keynotes* but **not** the *same signatures*.

Mastery Frames

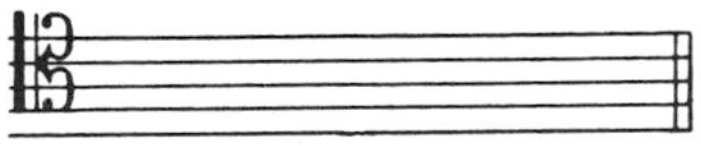

Treble

Tenor

(Frames 10.11, 10.15)

10–1   Write the seven sharps on the treble and tenor clefs as they would appear in a key signature.

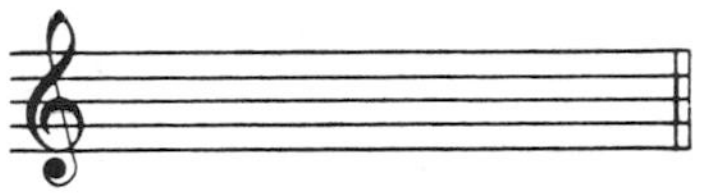

Treble

Tenor

Bass

Alto

(10.20, 10.26)

10–2   Write the seven flats on the bass and alto clefs as they would appear in a key signature.

Bass

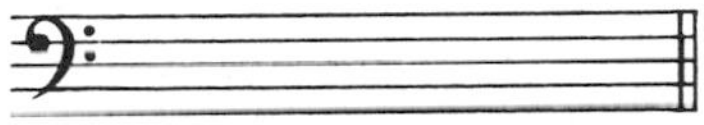

Alto

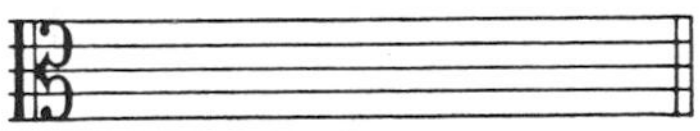

---

false   (10.31)

10–3   If sharps appear in the key signature, the major keynote is located a half step above the next-to-the-last sharp. (True/False) _____

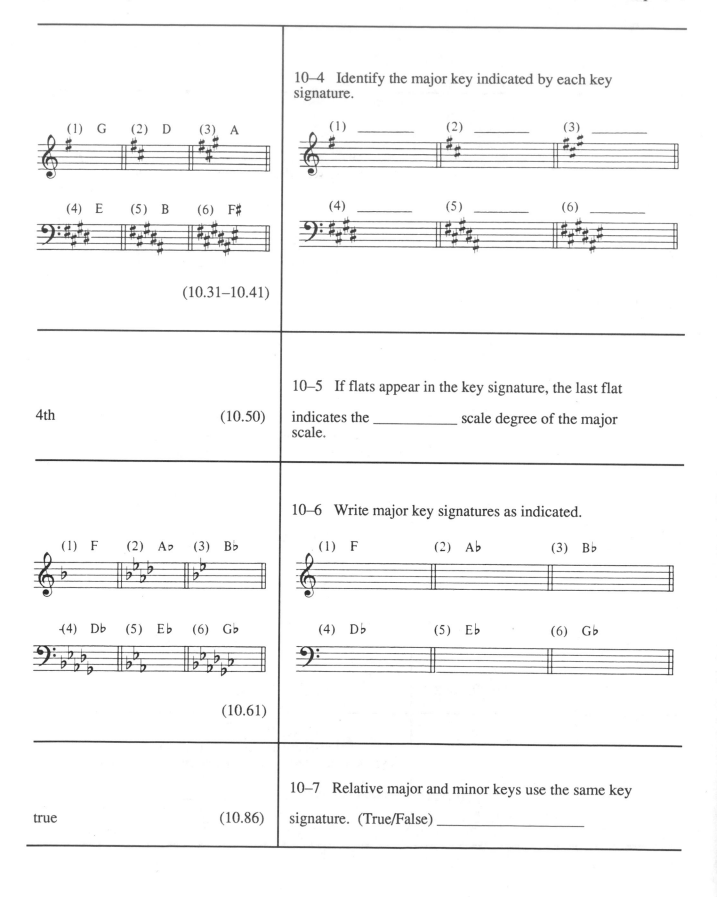

10–4 Identify the major key indicated by each key signature.

(1) G   (2) D   (3) A

(4) E   (5) B   (6) F♯

(10.31–10.41)

(1) _____   (2) _____   (3) _____

(4) _____   (5) _____   (6) _____

4th   (10.50)

10–5 If flats appear in the key signature, the last flat indicates the _____ scale degree of the major scale.

(1) F   (2) A♭   (3) B♭

(4) D♭   (5) E♭   (6) G♭

(10.61)

10–6 Write major key signatures as indicated.

(1) F   (2) A♭   (3) B♭

(4) D♭   (5) E♭   (6) G♭

true   (10.86)

10–7 Relative major and minor keys use the same key signature. (True/False) _____

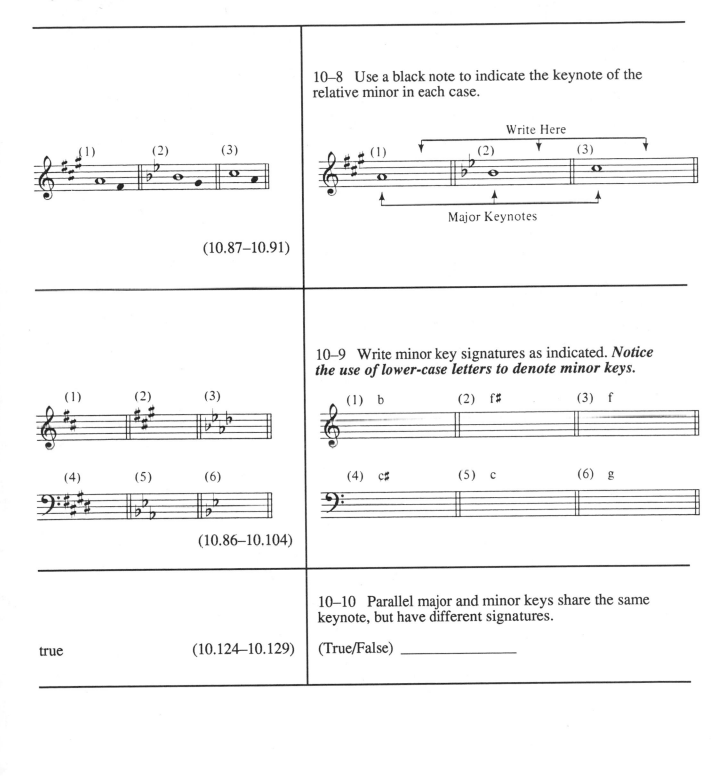

10-8 Use a black note to indicate the keynote of the relative minor in each case.

Write Here

Major Keynotes

(10.87-10.91)

10-9 Write minor key signatures as indicated. *Notice the use of lower-case letters to denote minor keys.*

(1) b   (2) f♯   (3) f

(4) c♯   (5) c   (6) g

(10.86-10.104)

10-10 Parallel major and minor keys share the same keynote, but have different signatures.

true   (10.124-10.129)   (True/False) _____

Supplementary Assignments

Assignment 10–1   Name: _____

1. Write the seven sharps and flats on the staffs below as they would appear in a key signature. *(Use correct order and placement.)*

SHARPS   FLATS

2. What is the key signature for the key of C major? _____

3. Explain how the major key is determined if the signature contains flats.

    _____

    _____

4. Explain how the major key is determined if the signature contains sharps.

    _____

    _____

5. Each major key has a relative minor key which uses the same signature. The minor key is located a minor 3rd (above/below) _____ the major key.

6. Which key signature indicates the relative major of F-sharp minor? _____

7. Name the major and minor keys indicated by each of the key signatures below:

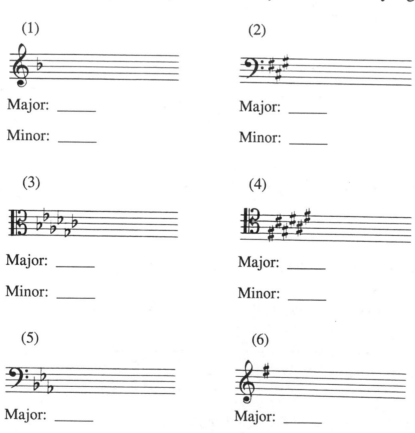

(1)

Major: _____

Minor: _____

(2)

Major: _____

Minor: _____

(3)

Major: _____

Minor: _____

(4)

Major: _____

Minor: _____

(5)

Major: _____

Minor: _____

(6)

Major: _____

Minor: _____

Assignment 10–2   Name: _____

1. Which key signature indicates the parallel major of B-flat minor? _____

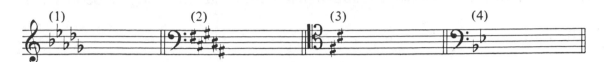

2. Which key signature indicates the relative minor of D major? _____

3. Write key signatures on the grand staff as directed. *(Capital letters indicate major keys; lower-case letters indicate minor keys.)*

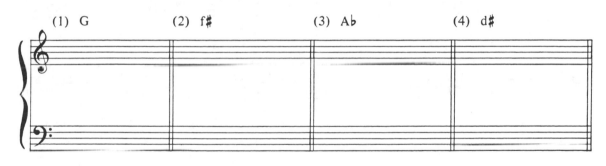

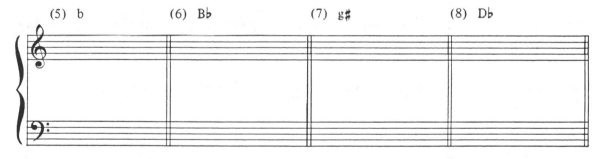

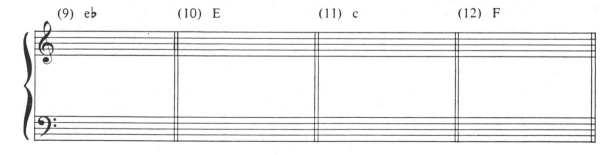

4. What form of the minor scale uses only the notes provided by the key signature?

_____

5. What form of the minor scale requires that the seventh scale degree be raised a

half step? _____

6. Transform the scales below into harmonic minor scales by applying the necessary accidentals.

f:

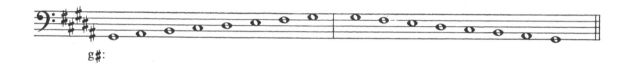

g♯:

g:

7. Transform the scales below into melodic minor scales by applying the necessary accidentals.

a:

b♭:

f♯:

Eartraining Activities

1. The circle of fifths (Frames 10.82 and 10.104 in the text) is helpful in remembering the various key signatures. It is also helpful for understanding harmonic relations such as chord progressions and modulations, topics of more advanced theory study (covered in the authors' *Harmonic Materials of Tonal Music, Parts I & II*). If you begin on the lowest C of the piano or a full-size keyboard, you may play the entire series of fifths in ascending motion.

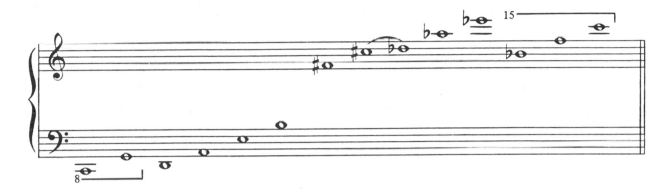

2. As a more advanced exercise for those wishing the challenge, the series can be sung within your vocal range by bringing all the notes within a limited range. Sing the circle of fifths as notated in the following (or transpose to a more convenient level):

The three basic elements of traditional music are *melody, rhythm, and harmony*. The harmonic element is based on three-note chords called *triads*. The major-minor scale system generates four types of triads: *major, minor, diminished, and augmented*. These names reflect the *intervals* contained in the triads. Triads may be built on any note of a scale. They vary not only in quality, but also in the way they function within a tonality. Because of the important role harmony plays in music, you must have a thorough knowledge of triads. It is also essential that you cultivate sensitivity to their sounds.

three	11.1 Three or more tones sounding together form a CHORD. An *interval* consists of *two* tones, but a *chord* consists of _____ or more tones.
chord	11.2 Three or more tones sounding together form a _____
triad	11.3 For our purposes, the term TRIAD refers specifically to a chord with *three* different tones. A *chord* of three tones is called a _____
triad	11.4 *Triads* are usually based on the TERTIAN system of harmony. In this system the tones of the *triad* are related to one another by the interval of the 3rd. A *chord* consisting of two superimposed 3rds is called a _____.

11.5 A triad may be constructed on any note of the basic scale.

seven

These triads are called BASIC TRIADS. What is the total number of *basic triads*? _____

C E G

11.6 Spell the *basic triad* based on C. _____

D F A

11.7 Spell the *basic triad* based on D. _____

E G B

11.8 Spell the *basic triad* based on E. _____

F A C

11.9 Spell the *basic triad* based on F. _____

G B D

11.10 Spell the *basic triad* based on G. _____

A C E

11.11 Spell the *basic triad* based on A. _____

B D F

11.12 Spell the *basic triad* based on B. _____

11.13 Play the seven basic triads at a keyboard and compare the sound of each. It is apparent they do not all sound alike. This is because the intervallic structure is not the same for all basic triads, due to the *half steps* which occur between E and F, and between B and C in the *basic scale*.

Do the seven basic triads sound alike? _____

no

11.14 There are four types of triads which originate in the major-minor scale system: MAJOR, MINOR, DIMINISHED, and AUGMENTED. We shall examine each type separately.

Name the four types of triads.

(1) _____

(2) _____

(3) _____

(4) _____

(1) major

(2) minor

(3) diminished

(4) augmented
(any order)

11.15 The three tones of the MAJOR TRIAD correspond to the 1st, 3rd, and 5th degrees of the *major scale*.

When sounding together, the 1st, 3rd, and 5th degree

of the major scale produce a _____ triad.

major

11.16 The *lowest* tone of a triad, when the tones are arranged in 3rds, is called the ROOT. It is the generating tone of the triad and exerts a strong influence over the other two members (the 3rd and 5th).

The lowest tone of a triad (when arranged in 3rds)

is called the _____.

root

5th	11.17 The *uppermost* tone of a triad (when the tones are arranged in 3rds) is called the _____.
3rd	11.18 The tone between the *root* and the 5th of a triad is called the _____.
1st, 3rd, (and) 5th	11.19 The major triad consists of the _____, _____, and _____ degrees of the major scale.
perfect 5th	11.20 Observe in the example below the *intervals* which constitute the *major triad*. In the major triad the interval from 1 up to 3 is a major 3rd, the interval from 3 up to 5 is a minor 3rd, and the interval from 1 up to 5 is a _____.
minor 3rd	11.21 What is the *interval* from 3 up to 5 of a *major triad*? _____
major 3rd	11.22 What is the *interval* from 1 up to 3 of a *major triad*? _____

perfect 5th

11.23   What is the *interval* from 1 up to 5 of a *major triad*?

_____

11.24   Three of the *basic triads* are *major triads*.
These are C E G, F A C, and G B D.

Observe that the tones of each triad fall into
the *major scale* of the *root*.

When sounding together, the 1st, 3rd, and 5th degrees

major

of the major scale produce a _____ triad.

11.25   A *major triad* may be written on any note by
either relating the three tones of the triad to the
major scale of the root, or by observing the correct
intervallic relationship between the triad tones. Try
both methods; check one against the other.

Write *major triads* (the given note is the *root*).

11.26   Write *major triads* (the given note is the *root*).

11.27 Write *major triads* (the given note is the *root*).

11.28 Write *major triads* (the given note is the *root*).

11.29 Write *major triads* (the given note is the *root*).

11.30 Write *major triads* (the given note is the *3rd*).

11.31 Write *major triads* (the given note is the *3rd*).

11.32 Write *major triads* (the given note is the *3rd*).

11.33 Write *major triads* (the given note is the *3rd*).

11.34 Write *major triads* (the given note is the *5th*).

11.35 Write *major triads* (the given note is the *5th*).

11.36 Write *major triads* (the given note is the *5th*).

11.37 Write *major triads* (the given note is the *5th*).

(1)   (2)   (3)

C E G; F A C; G B D

11.38 List the three *basic triads* which are *major*.

_____   _____   _____

11.39 A MINOR TRIAD consists of the 1st, 3rd, and 5th degrees of the *minor scale*.

1 2 3 4 5 6 7 8   5
                              3
                              1

When sounding together, the 1st, 3rd, and 5th degrees

minor

of the minor scale produce a _____ triad.

11.40 A minor triad consists of the 1st, 3rd, and 5th

minor

degrees of a _____ scale.

11.41 The *intervals* which constitute the *minor triad* are shown below:

M3

P5   m3

What is the *interval* from 1 up to 3 of a *minor triad*?

minor 3rd

_____

major 3rd	**11.42** What is the *interval* from 3 up to 5 of a *minor triad*? _____
perfect 5th	**11.43** What is the *interval* from 1 up to 5 of a *minor triad*? _____
major	**11.44** As compared with the major triad, the *order* of major and minor 3rds is *reversed* in the minor triad. MAJOR TRIAD MINOR TRIAD 1 up to 3 major 3rd minor 3rd 3 up to 5 minor 3rd major 3rd 1 up to 5 perfect 5th perfect 5th The interval from 1 up to 5 is a perfect 5th in both the major and minor triad. The interval from 3 up to 5 in the major triad is a minor 3rd; but in the minor triad the interval from 3 up to 5 is a_____ 3rd.
1st, 3rd, (and) 5th	**11.45** Three of the *basic triads* are *minor triads*. These are D F A, E G B, and A C E. The minor triad consists of the _____, _____, and _____ degrees of the minor scale.
(1) (2) (3)	**11.46** Write *minor triads* (the given note is the *root*). (1) (2) (3)

11.47 Write *minor triads* (the given note is the *root*).

11.48 Write *minor triads* (the given note is the *root*).

11.49 Write *minor triads* (the given note is the *root*).

11.50 Write *minor triads* (the given note is the *root*).

11.51 Write *minor triads* (the given note is the *3rd*).

11.52 Write *minor triads* (the given note is the *3rd*).

11.53 Write *minor triads* (the given note is the *3rd*).

11.54 Write *minor triads* (the given note is the *3rd*).

11.55 Write *minor triads* (the given note is the *5th*).

11.56 Write *minor triads* (the given note is the *5th*).

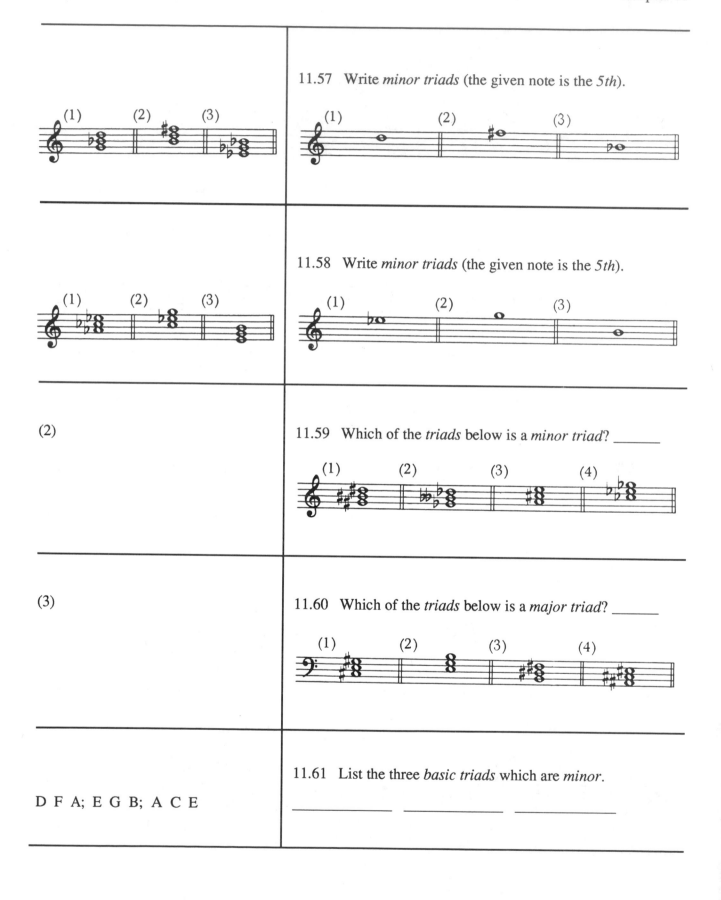

11.57 Write *minor triads* (the given note is the *5th*).

11.58 Write *minor triads* (the given note is the *5th*).

(2)

11.59 Which of the *triads* below is a *minor triad*? _____

(3)

11.60 Which of the *triads* below is a *major triad*? _____

D F A; E G B; A C E

11.61 List the three *basic triads* which are *minor*.

_____ _____ _____

11.62 The DIMINISHED TRIAD can be produced by *lowering* the *5th* of a *minor* triad a *half step*.

MINOR   DIMINISHED

If the 5th of a minor triad is lowered a half step,

the result is a _____ triad.

diminished

11.63 Transform the *minor* triads below into *diminished* triads by *lowering* the *5th* a *half step*.

Apply the proper accidentals to the second triad in each case.

(1)   (2)   (3)
MINOR   DIM.   MINOR   DIM.   MINOR   DIM.

(1)   (2)   (3)

11.64 The *diminished* triad can be produced by *raising* the *root* and *3rd* of a *minor* triad a *half step*.

MINOR   DIMINISHED

If the root and 3rd of a minor triad are raised a

half step, the result is a _____ triad.

diminished

11.65 Transform the *minor* triads below into *diminished* triads by *raising* the *root* and *3rd* a *half step*.

Apply the proper accidentals to the second triad in each case.

(1)   (2)   (3)
MINOR DIM.   MINOR DIM.   MINOR DIM.

(1)   (2)   (3)

raised

11.66 The diminished triad is the same as a minor triad whose 5th has been lowered a half step, or whose root

and 3rd have been _____ a half step.

11.67 Observe the *intervals* which constitute the *diminished triad*.

The diminished triad is named for the diminished 5th between the root and the 5th of the triad. What is

minor 3rd

the *interval* from 3 up to 5? _____

11.68 What is the *interval* from 1 up to 3 of a *diminished*

minor 3rd

triad? _____

minor	11.69 The diminished triad consists of two superimposed _____ 3rds.
B D F	11.70 One of the *basic triads* is a *diminished triad.* Spell this triad. _____
	11.71 Write *diminished triads* (the given note is the *root*).
	11.72 Write *diminished triads* (the given note is the *root*).
	11.73 Write *diminished triads* (the given note is the *root*).
	11.74 Write *diminished triads* (the given note is the *root*).
	11.75 Write *diminished triads* (the given note is the *3rd*).

(1)   (2)   (3)

11.76 Write *diminished triads* (the given note is the *3rd*).

(1)   (2)   (3)

(1)   (2)   (3)

11.77 Write *diminished triads* (the given note is the *3rd*).

(1)   (2)   (3)

(1)   (2)   (3)

11.78 Write *diminished triads* (the given note is the *3rd*).

(1)   (2)   (3)

(1)   (2)   (3)

11.79 Write *diminished triads* (the given note is the *5th*).

(1)   (2)   (3)

(1)   (2)   (3)

11.80 Write *diminished triads* (the given note is the *5th*).

(1)   (2)   (3)

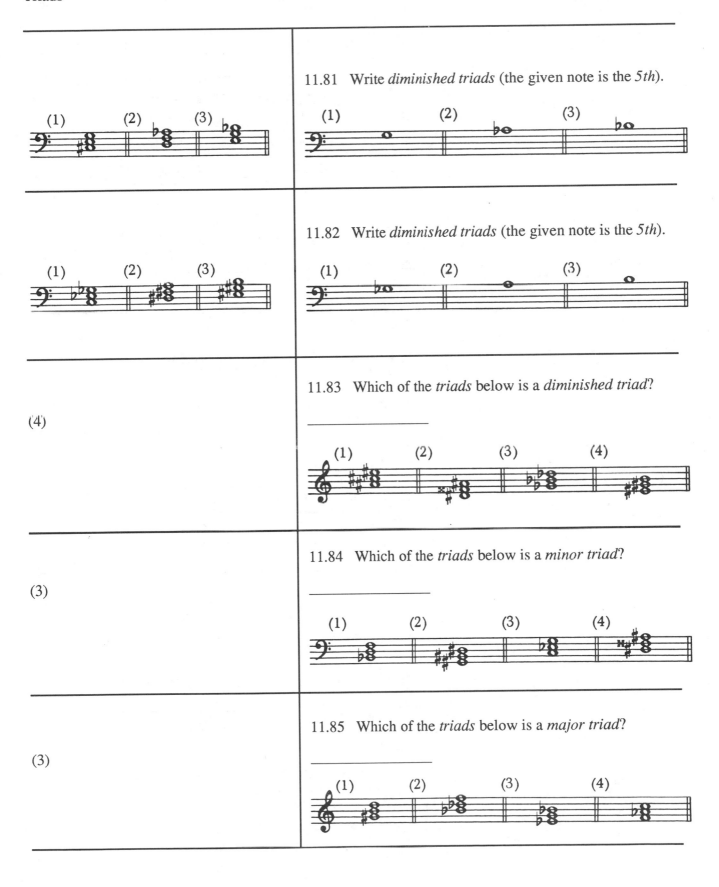

11.81 Write *diminished triads* (the given note is the *5th*).

(1)   (2)   (3)

11.82 Write *diminished triads* (the given note is the *5th*).

(1)   (2)   (3)

(4)

11.83 Which of the *triads* below is a *diminished triad*?

_____

(1)   (2)   (3)   (4)

(3)

11.84 Which of the *triads* below is a *minor triad*?

_____

(1)   (2)   (3)   (4)

(3)

11.85 Which of the *triads* below is a *major triad*?

_____

(1)   (2)   (3)   (4)

11.86 The AUGMENTED TRIAD can be produced by *raising* the *5th* of a *major* triad by a *half step*.

MAJOR   AUGMENTED

If the 5th of a major triad is raised a half-step,

augmented

the result is a(n) _____ triad.

11.87 Transform the *major* triads below into *augmented* triads by *raising* the *5th* a *half step*.

Apply the proper accidentals to the second triad in each case.

(1)   (2)   (3)
MAJOR   AUG.   MAJOR   AUG.   MAJOR   AUG.

(1)   (2)   (3)

11.88 The *augmented* triad can be produced by *lowering* the *root* and *3rd* of a *major* triad a *half step*.

MAJOR   AUGMENTED

If the root and 3rd of a major triad are lowered a

augmented

half step, the result is a(n) _____ triad.

11.89   Transform the *major* triads below into *augmented* triads by *lowering* the *root* and *3rd* a *half step*.

Apply the proper accidentals to the second triad in each case.

11.90   The augmented triad is the same as a major triad whose 5th has been raised a half step, or whose root

lowered

and 3rd have been _____ a half step.

11.91   Observe the *intervals* which constitute the *augmented triad*.

In the augmented triad the *intervals* from 1 up to 3, and from 3 up to 5 are both major 3rds.

What is the *interval* from 1 up to 5?

an augmented 5th

_____

11.92   The augmented triad consists of two super-

major

imposed _____ 3rds.

major; minor;

diminished

11.93 The *augmented triad* **does not exist** as a *basic triad*. List the three types of triads which do occur as *basic triads.* _____

_____

(1)   (2)   (3)

11.94 Write *augmented triads* (the given note is the *root*).

(1)   (2)   (3)

(1)   (2)   (3)

11.95 Write *augmented triads* (the given note is the *root*).

(1)   (2)   (3)

(1)   (2)   (3)

11.96 Write *augmented triads* (the given note is the *root*).

(1)   (2)   (3)

(1)   (2)   (3)

11.97 Write *augmented triads* (the given note is the *root*).

(1)   (2)   (3)

11.98 Write *augmented triads* (the given note is the *3rd*).

11.99 Write *augmented triads* (the given note is the *3rd*).

11.100 Write *augmented triads* (the given note is the *3rd*).

11.101 Write *augmented triads* (the given note is the *3rd*).

11.102 Write *augmented triads* (the given note is the *5th*).

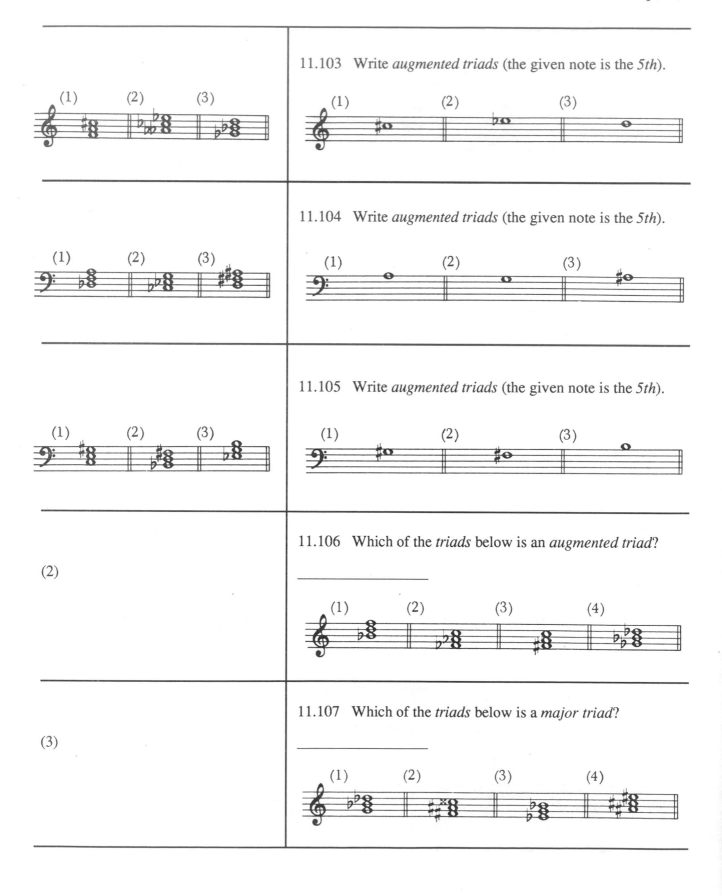

11.103   Write *augmented triads* (the given note is the *5th*).

(1)   (2)   (3)

11.104   Write *augmented triads* (the given note is the *5th*).

(1)   (2)   (3)

11.105   Write *augmented triads* (the given note is the *5th*).

(1)   (2)   (3)

(2)

11.106   Which of the *triads* below is an *augmented triad*?

_____

(1)   (2)   (3)   (4)

(3)

11.107   Which of the *triads* below is a *major triad*?

_____

(1)   (2)   (3)   (4)

(4)

11.108   Which of the *triads* below is an *diminished triad*?

_____

(1)   (2)   (3)   (4)

(3)

11.109 Which of the *triads* below is an *minor triad*?

_____

(1)   (2)   (3)   (4)

major

11.110   The *major triad* consists of a major 3rd (1 up to 3) and a minor 3rd (3 up to 5). The *minor triad* consists of a minor 3rd (1 up to 3) and a _____ 3rd (3 up to 5).

minor

11.111   The two 3rds which constitute the major and minor triads are "unequal." One is major and one is _____.

major

11.112   The *diminished triad* consists of two minor 3rds (1 up to 3, and 3 up to 5). The *augmented triad* consists of two _____ 3rds (1 up to 3, and 3 up to 5).

minor

11.113   The diminished and augmented triads are composed of "equal" intervals. Both of the 3rds in the diminished triad are _____ 3rds.

augmented

11.114 The triad which consists of two superimposed major 3rds is the _____ triad.

(As follows or with accidental signs.)
(1) D F-sharp A

(2) D F A

(3) D F A-flat

(4) D F-sharp A-sharp

11.115   Spell triads as directed.

(1) D is 1 of the *major* triad _____

(2) D is 1 of the *minor* triad _____

(3) D is 1 of the *diminished* triad _____

(4) D is 1 of the *augmented* triad _____

---

(1) E-flat G B-flat

(2) E G B

(3) E G B-flat

(4) E-flat G B

11.116   Spell triads as directed.

(1) G is 3 of the *major* triad _____

(2) G is 3 of the *minor* triad _____

(3) G is 3 of the *diminished* triad _____

(4) G is 3 of the *augmented* triad _____

---

(1) F A C

(2) F A-flat C

(3) F-sharp A C

(4) F-flat A-flat C

11.117   Spell triads as directed.

(1) C is 5 of the *major* triad _____

(2) C is 5 of the *minor* triad _____

(3) C is 5 of the *diminished* triad _____

(4) C is 5 of the *augmented* triad _____

---

(1) B-flat D-flat F

(2) A-flat C E-flat

(3) F A-flat C-flat

(4) C E G-sharp

11.118   Spell triads as directed.

(1) B-flat is 1 of the *minor* triad _____

(2) E-flat is 5 of the *major* triad _____

(3) A-flat is 3 of the *diminished* triad _____

(4) G-sharp is 5 of the *augmented* triad _____

(1) C-sharp E G

(2) B-flat D F-sharp

(3) D-flat F-flat A-flat

(4) C-sharp E-sharp G-sharp

11.119 Spell triads as directed.

(1) G is 5 of the *diminished* triad _____

(2) D is 3 of the *augmented* triad _____

(3) A-flat is 5 of the *minor* triad _____

(4) C-sharp is 1 of the *major* triad _____

11.120 The example below shows triads built on each degree of the D major scale. Indicate the quality of each triad.

Use the following abbreviations: M = major; m = minor; d = diminished; A = augmented.

11.121 The previous frame shows that the major scale produces three major triads, three minor triads, and one diminished triad.

List the scale degrees on which the various triad types occur.

Triad Types	Scale Degrees
Major:	1, 4, 5
Minor:	2, 3, 6
Diminished:	7

Triad Types	Scale Degrees
Major	_____
Minor	_____
Diminished	_____

11.122   ROMAN NUMERALS are used to *identify* the *scale degree* on which triads are built. This is shown in the example below:

KEY OF D MAJOR

Notice that major triads are represented by *capital Roman numerals*, minor triads are represented by *lower-case Roman numerals*, and the diminished triad is represented by a *small circle added to a lower-case Roman numeral.*

(no response required)

11.123   Write *Roman numerals* to identify the triads built on the tones of the E-flat major scale.

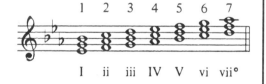

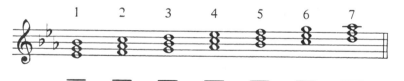

11.124   The example below shows triads built on each degree of the E harmonic minor scale. Indicate the *quality* of each triad.

Use the abbreviations M, m, d, and A, as needed.

11.125 The harmonic minor scale produces *a different array of triad* types than the major scale. There are *two* major triads, *two* minor triads, *two* diminished triads, and *one* augmented triad.

List the scale degrees on which the various triad types occur.

Triad Types	Scale Degrees
Major	_____
Minor	_____
Diminished	_____
Augmented	_____

Triad Types	Scale Degrees
Major:	5, 6
Minor:	1, 4
Diminished:	2, 7
Augmented:	3

11.126 *Roman numerals* are used to *identify* the *scale degree* on which triads are built. This is shown below:

KEY OF E MINOR

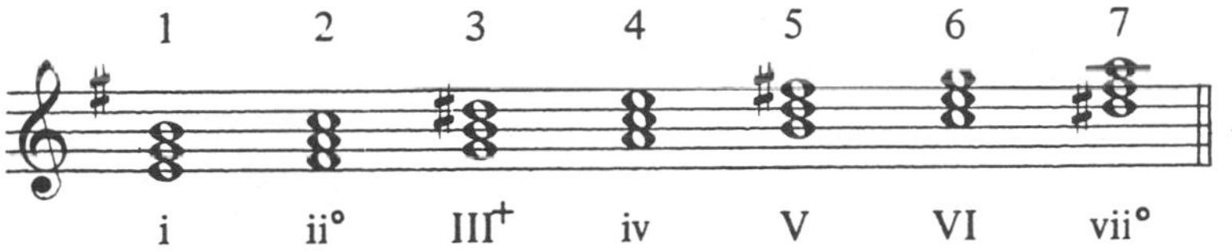

i   ii°   III⁺   iv   V   VI   vii°

As in the case of the major scale (see Frame 11.122), various *Roman numerals* are used to represent the *quality* of each triad produced by the minor scale. Notice that the augmented triad is represented by a *small cross added to a capital Roman numeral.*

(no response required)

---

i   ii°   III⁺   iv   V   VI   vii°

11.127 Write Roman numerals to identify the triads built on the tones of the C harmonic minor scale.

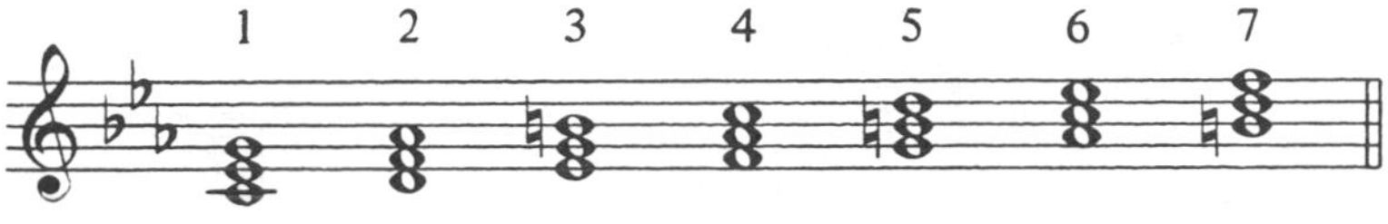

___   ___   ___   ___   ___   ___   ___

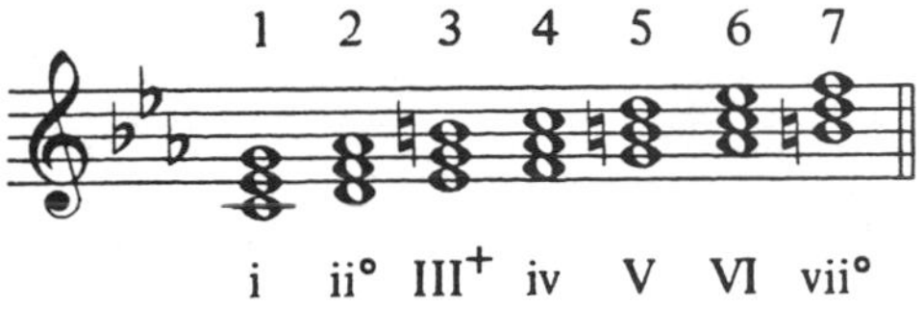

11.128 By using various Roman numerals, you are made aware of the *specific quality of each triad.* Your sensitivity to the actual sounds represented by the notes is thereby enhanced.

As an adjunct to Roman numerals, the *key* is identified *by an abbreviation of its name followed by a colon (:).*

Compare the designations below:

A-flat major = A♭
A-flat minor = a♭

Notice that a *capital letter* signifies a *major key,* whereas a *lower-case letter* signifies a *minor key.*

Write the proper designation for each key.

(1) F-sharp minor   _____

(2) G major   _____

(3) E-flat major   _____

(1) f♯:

(2) G:

(3) E♭:

11.129 What key is indicated by each symbol.

(1) B♭ : _____

(2) g♯ : _____

(3) c : _____

(1) B-flat major

(2) G-sharp minor

(3) C minor

11.130 Write the proper Roman numeral for each triad.

d: ___   A: ___   B♭: ___

d: V   A: vii°   B♭: ii

Eb: IV   b: III⁺   a: ii°

11.131 Continue as in the preceding frame.

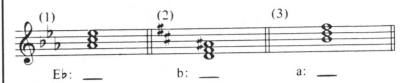

Eb: ___   b: ___   a: ___

f#: vii°   Ab: iii   d: V

11.132 Write the triads indicated by the Roman numerals.

f#: vii°   Ab: iii   d: V

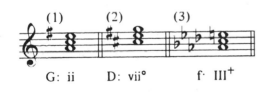

G: ii   D: vii°   f: III⁺

11.133 Continue as in the preceding frame.

G: ii   D: vii°   f: III⁺

Summary

Triads are chords consisting of three tones. In traditional music there are four types of triads: *major, minor, diminished,* and *augmented.* A *major triad* consists of the 1st, 3rd, and 5th tones of a *major scale*; a *minor triad* consists of the 1st, 3rd, and 5th tones of a *minor scale.* A *major triad* can be converted to an *augmented triad* by either *raising* the 5th a half step, or by *lowering* the root and 3rd a half step. A *minor triad* can be converted to a *diminished triad* by either *lowering* the 5th a half step, or by *raising* the root and 3rd a half step.

Triads can be built on *each degree* of a *major* or *minor scale.* The *quality* of the various triads is summarized below:

TRIAD QUALITY

Scale Degree	Major	Harmonic Minor
1	Major	Minor
2	Minor	Diminished
3	Minor	Augmented
4	Major	Minor
5	Major	Major
6	Minor	Major
7	Diminished	Diminished

Roman numerals are used to *identify* the *scale degrees* on which triads are built. *Various forms* of *Roman numerals* are used to *indicate* triad *quality,* as shown below:

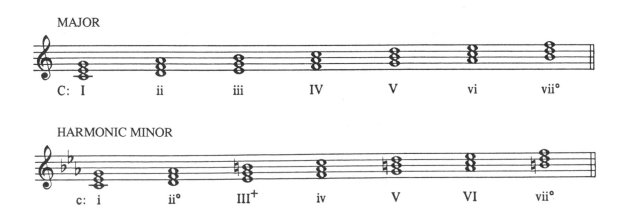

Mastery Frames

11–1 Indicate the quality of each basic triad.

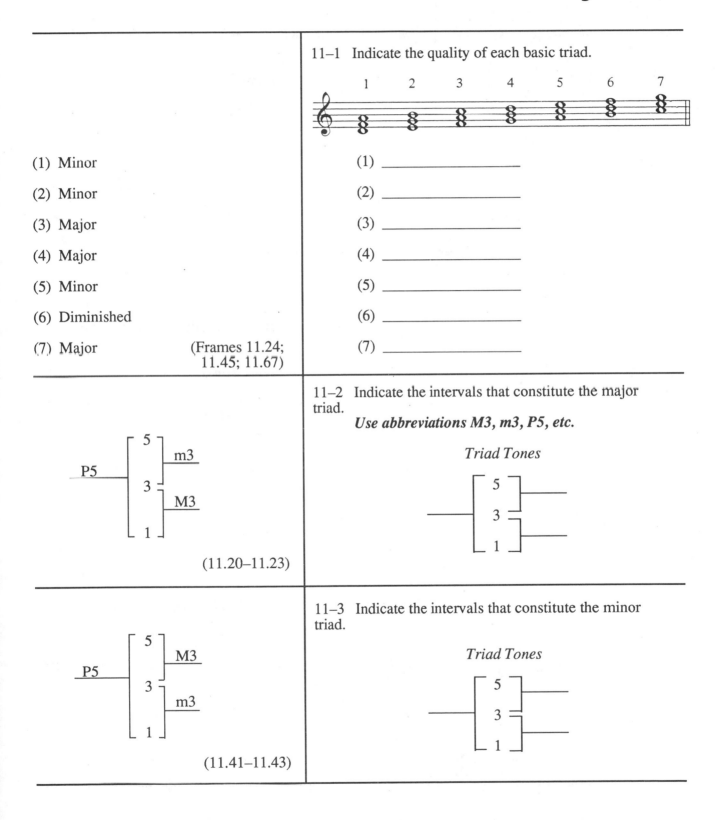

(1) Minor	(1) _____
(2) Minor	(2) _____
(3) Major	(3) _____
(4) Major	(4) _____
(5) Minor	(5) _____
(6) Diminished	(6) _____
(7) Major (Frames 11.24; 11.45; 11.67)	(7) _____

11–2 Indicate the intervals that constitute the major triad.

Use abbreviations M3, m3, P5, etc.

Triad Tones

(11.20–11.23)

11–3 Indicate the intervals that constitute the minor triad.

Triad Tones

(11.41–11.43)

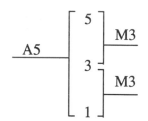

(11.67–11.69)

11–4   Indicate the intervals that constitute the diminished triad.

Triad Tones

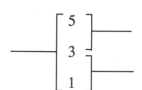

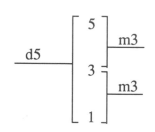

(11.91–11.92)

11–5   Indicate the intervals that constitute the augmented triad.

Triad Tones

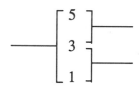

(11.15–11.25;
11.39–11.43;
11.62–11.70)

11–6   Write triads as indicated. *(The given note is the root.)*

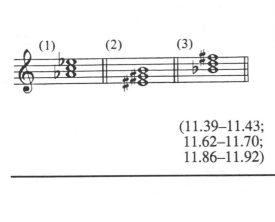

(11.39–11.43;
11.62–11.70;
11.86–11.92)

11–7 Write triads as indicated. *(The given note is the 3rd.)*

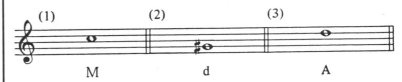

M   d   A

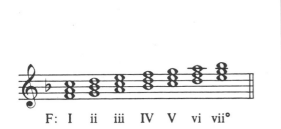

(11.86–11.92;
11.15–11.25;
11.39–11.43)

11–8 Write triads as indicated. *(The given note is the 5th.)*

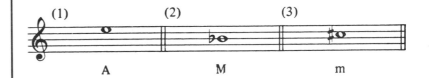

A   M   m

11–9 Write Roman numerals to identify the triads built on the tones of the F major scale.

F: __   __   __   __   __   __   __

F: I ii iii IV V vi vii°

(11.122–11.123)

11–10 Write Roman numerals to identify the triads built on the tones of the D harmonic minor scale.

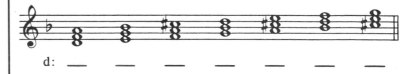

d: __   __   __   __   __   __   __

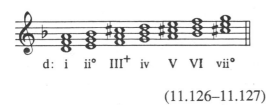

d: i ii° III⁺ iv V VI vii°

(11.126–11.127)

Supplementary Assignments

Assignment 11–1   Name: _____

1.   On the staff below, write the seven basic triads. Identify the quality of each triad.
     (Use the abbreviations M, m, d, and A, as needed.)

2.   Name the triad that consists of two minor thirds. _____

3.   Name the triad that consists of a major third over a minor third. _____

4.   Name the triad that consists of a minor third over a major third. _____

5.   Name the triad that consists of two major thirds. _____

6.   Write major triads as indicated.

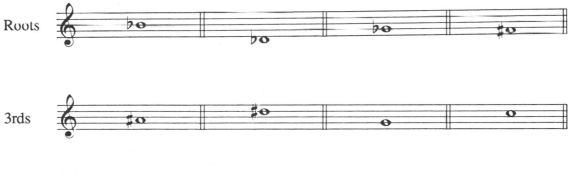

7. Write minor triads as indicated.

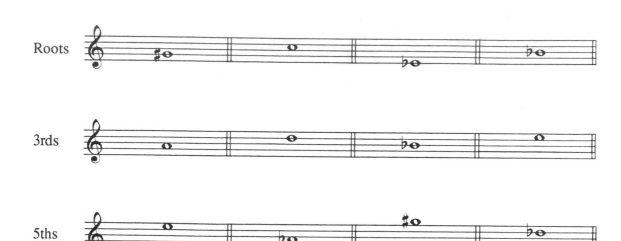

Assignment 11–2

1. Write diminished triads as indicated.

2. Write augmented triads as indicated.

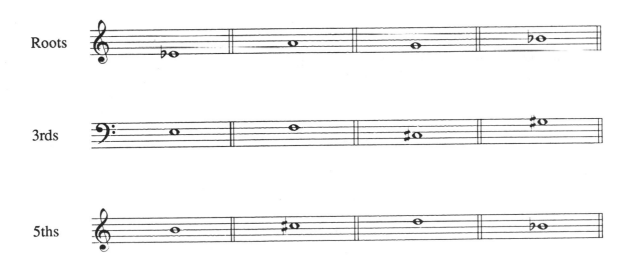

3. Write the proper Roman numeral for each of the triads in the key of G-flat major.

Gb: ___ ___ ___ ___ ___ ___ ___

4. Write the proper Roman numeral for each of the triads in the key of F-sharp minor.

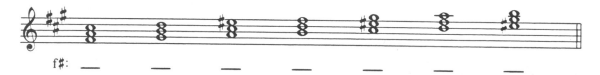

f#: ___ ___ ___ ___ ___ ___ ___

5. Write the triad indicated by each chord symbol. *(Provide the necessary accidentals.)*

(1)

Db: V   iii   vi   IV   vii°

(2)

c: i   III⁺   VI   vii°   ii°

6. Provide the correct Roman numeral for each chord.

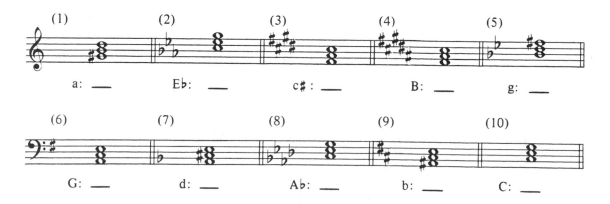

(1)   (2)   (3)   (4)   (5)

a: ___   Eb: ___   c#: ___   B: ___   g: ___

(6)   (7)   (8)   (9)   (10)

G: ___   d: ___   Ab: ___   b: ___   C: ___

Eartraining Activities

1. Play the seven *basic* triads at a keyboard, taking note of the effect of each type.

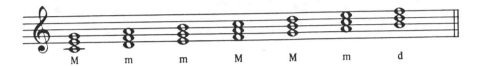

2. Sing the *basic* triads according to the following model:

3. Sing *major* triads as indicated by the following:

4. Sing *minor* triads as indicated by the following:

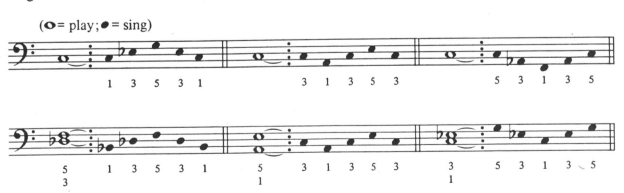

5. Sing *diminished* triads as indicated by the following:

6. Sing *augmented* triads as indicated by the following:

A (It., Fr.) - At, to, by, in, with.
A battuta (It.) - In strict time.
A piacere (It.) - At pleasure, in free time.
A tempo (It.) - Return to original tempo.
A volonta (It.) - At pleasure.
A volonté (Fr.) - At pleasure.
Aber (Ger.) - But.
Accelerando (It.) - Gradually growing faster.
Ad libitum (Lat.) - At pleasure, freely.
Adagio (It.) - Slowly, smoothly, gently.
Affettuosamente (It.) - Affectionately, tenderly.
Affrettando (It.) - Becoming faster, excited.
Affrettoso (It.) - Hurried.
Agevole (It.) - Light, easy, smooth, facile.
Agitato (It.) - Agitated, excited.
Aimable (Fr.) - Pleasant, agreeable.
Aisément (Fr.) - Easily, comfortably.
Al (It.) - At the, to the, on the.
Al fine (It.) - To the end.
Al segno (It.) - To the sign.
Alla (It.) - In the style of.
Alla breve (It.) - Rapid duple-simple meter in
   which the half note is the unit.
Alla marcia (It.) - In march style.
Alla turca (It.) - In Turkish style.
Allargando (It.) - Growing gradually slower.
Allegretto (It.) - Fast, but slower than *allegro*
Allegro (It.) - Fast
Am (Ger.) - On, by, near.
Amabile (It.) - Agreeable, tender, lovely.
Amoroso (It.) - Amorous.
Ancora (It.) - Again, yet, still, more.
Ancora una volta (It.) -Once more.
Andante (It.) - Moderately slow.
Andantino (It.) - Diminutive of *andante*.
   Usually interpreted as slightly quicker
   than *andante,* but may also have the opposite
   meaning.
Animato (It.) - Animated, spirited, brisk, buoyant.
Animé (Fr.) - Animated.
Anmutig (Ger.) - Graceful, charming, pleasant.
Appassionata (It.) - With passion.
Aria (It.) - Air, song.
Arioso (It.) - Melodious.
Assai (It.) - Much, very much.
Assez (Fr.) - Enough, quite.
Attacca (It.) - Join, attach, bind.
Au (Fr.) - To the, in the, at, for.

Au mouvement (Fr.) - Return to the original tempo.
Aufhalten (Ger.) - To retard.
Ausdruck (Ger.) - Expression.
Avec (Fr.) - With.

Battuta (It.) - Beat (see *A battuta*).
Beaucoup (Fr.) - Very, considerably.
Behaglich (Ger.) - Without haste, placid, comfortable.
Bei (Ger.) - With, at, for.
Belebt (Ger.) - Lively, animated.
Ben (It.) - Well, very.
Beruhigend (Ger.) - Calming.
Bewegter (Ger.) - Faster, more animated.
Bien (Fr.) - Well, very.
Bis (Ger.) - Until, up to.
Bis zu Ende (Ger.) - Until the end.
Bravura (It.) - Spirit, dash, skill.
Breit (Ger.) - Broad, stately.
Brillante (It.) - Sparkling, brilliant, glittering.
Brio (It.) - Vigor, spirit, animation.
Brioso (It.) - Vivacious, sprightly, animated.
Buffa (It.) - Comic, burlesque.

Cadenza (It.) - An ornamental unaccompanied
   passage, cadence.
Calando (It.) - Growing softer.
Calore (It.) - Warmth, ardour.
Cantabile (It.) - In a singing style.
Capo (It.) - Head, beginning.
Capriccioso (It.) - Whimsical, capricious.
Cedendo (It.) - Growing gradually slower.
Cédez (Fr.) - Growing gradually slower.
Clair (Fr.) - Light, clear, bright.
Coda (It.) - Literally "tail," the closing section of
   a composition or movement.
Codetta (It.) - A short *coda*.
Col, coll, colla (It.) - With the.
Colla parte (It.) - With the principal part.
Collera (It.) - Anger, rage.
Come (It.) - As, like.
Come prima (It.) - As before.
Come sopra (It.) - As above.
Commodo (It.) - Easy, without haste.
Con (It.) - With.
Con animo (It.) - With animation.
Con moto (It.) - With motion.
Con spirito (It.) - With spirit.
Corto (It.) - Short, brief.

Coulé (Fr.) - Smoothly.
Crescendo (Cresc.) (It.) - Gradually growing louder
  (often notated: ◁———————▷).
Cuivré (Fr.) - Play in a "brassy" way.

Da, dal, dallo, dalla (It.) - From, at, by, to, for, like.
Da capo (D.C.) (It.) - From the beginning.
Dal segno (D.S.) (It.) -From the sign.
Dans (Fr.) - In, within.
Décidé (Fr.) - Decided, resolute.
Deciso (It.) - Decided, bold.
Decrescendo (Decresc.) (It.) - Gradually growing
  softer (often notated: ———————▷).
Del, dell', della, delle, dello (It.) - Of the, than the.
Demi (Fr.) - Half.
Desto (It.) - Sprightly, lively.
Détaché (Fr.) - Detached, short.
Deutlich (Ger.) - Clear, distinct.
Di (It.) - To, by, of, for, with.
Di molto (It.) - Extremely.
Diminuendo (Dim.) (It.) - Gradually growing softer
  (often notated: ———————▷).
Dolce (It.) - Sweet, soft, pleasant, mild, charming.
Dolente (It.) - Sad, painful, sorrowful.
Dolore (It.) - Sorrow, pain, grief, regret.
Doppio (It.) - Double, twice as much.
Doppio movimento (It.) - Twice as fast.
Doppio più lento (It.) - Twice as slow.
Douce (Fr.) - Sweet, soft, mild, calm, charming.
Drängend (Ger.) - Hastening, pressing ahead.
Drückend (Ger.) - Heavy, stressed.

E, ed (It.) - And.
Edelmütig (Ger.) - Noble, lofty.
Eifrig (Ger.) - Ardently.
Eilig (Ger.) - Hurried.
Einfach (Ger.) - Simple.
En (Fr.) - In, into, as, like, in the form of.
En cédant (Fr.) - Growing gradually slower.
En dehors (Fr.) -Outside of, to be brought out.
En mouvement (Fr.) - Return to original tempo.
Espressione (It.) - Expression, feeling.
Espressivo (It,) - Expressive, vivid.
Et (Fr.) - And.
Etwas (Ger.) - Somewhat.

Facile (It., Fr.) - Easy, simple.
Feirlich (Ger.) - Festive.
Fermamente (It.) - Firmly, resolutely.
Fermata (⌢) (It.) - Pause.
Feroce (It.) - Wild, fierce, savage.
Festevole (It.) - Festive, joyful, gay.
Feu (Fr.) - Fire, ardour, passion, spirit.

Feuer (Ger.) - Fire, ardour, spirit.
Fière (Fr.) - Proud, lofty.
Fin (Fr.) - End, close.
Fine (It.) - End, close.
Flautando (It.) - Flutelike, clear.
Flüchtig (Ger.) - Delicately, airily.
Forte (f) (It.) - Loud, strong.
Fortissimo (ff) (It.) - Very loud.
Forzando (It.) - With force.
Forzato (It.) - Forced.
Frei (Ger.) - Free.
Freimütig (Ger.) - Frankly, broad.
Frisch (Ger.) - Brisk, lively.
Fröhlich (Ger.) - Joyful, gay.
Früheres Zeitmass (Ger.) - The original tempo.
Funebre (It., Fr.) - Funereal, gloomy, dismal.
Fuoco (It.) - Fire.
Furente (It.) - Furious, frantic.
Furioso (It.) - Furious, violent, frantic.

Gai (Fr.) - Gay, cheerful, lively, pleasant.
Gefühl (Ger.) - Feeling, expression.
Gehend (Ger.) - Moderately slow (at a "walking"
  tempo).
Geist (Ger.) - Spirit.
Gemächlich (Ger.) - Comfortably, without haste.
Gewichtig (Ger.) - Ponderous, heavy.
Giocoso (It.) - Playful, gay, humorous.
Giusto (It.) - Strict, exact, precise.
Glänzend (Ger.) - Sparkling, brilliant.
Gracieux (Fr.) - Graceful, gracious.
Grave (It., Fr.) - Solemn, heavy, serious.
Grazioso (It.) - Graceful, charming, pretty.

Heftig (Ger.) - Impetuous, intense, furious.
Heimlich (Ger.) - Mysterious, stealthy.
Heiter (Ger.) - Serene, bright, cheerful.
Hübsch (Ger.) - Charming, pretty.
Hurtig (Ger.) - Rapid.

I, il (It.) - The.
Im ersten Zeitmass (Ger.) - In original tempo.
Immer (Ger.) - Always, ever.
Immer belebter (Ger.) - Growing more lively.
Immer langsamer werden (Ger.) - Growing
  gradually slower.
Innig (Ger.) - Intimate, heartfelt, ardent.
Istesso (It.) - Same, like.
Istesso tempo (It.) - The same tempo.

Kräftig (Ger.) - Strong, powerful.

Lacrimoso (It.) - Mournful, plaintive, tearful.

Lamentoso (It.) - Mournful, plaintive, doleful.
Ländlich (Ger.) Rustic, simple.
Langsam (Ger.) - Slow.
Largamente (It.) - Broadly.
Larghetto (It.) - Slow, but quicker than *largo*.
Largo (It.) - Extremely slow, broad.
Le même mouvement (Fr.) - The same tempo.
Lebhaft (Ger.) - Lively, animated, brilliant.
Legato (It.) - Smooth, connected.
Léger (Fr.) - Light, delicate, nimble.
Leggiero (It.) - Light, delicate, nimble, quick.
Leicht (Ger.) - Light, easy.
Leicht bewegt (Ger.) - Light, agitated.
Leise (Ger.) - Soft, gentle.
Lent (Fr.) - Slow.
Lento (It.) - Slow.
Lesto (It.) - Quick, nimble, lively.
Licenza (It.) - Freedom, license.
Lieblich (Ger.) - Charming, sweet.
L'istesso tempo (It.) - The same tempo.
Lontano (It.) - Distant, soft.
Lungo (It.) - Long.
Lustig (Ger.) - Playful, merry.

Ma (It.) - But, however.
Ma non troppo (It.) - But not too much.
Mächtig (Ger.) - Powerful.
Maestoso (It.) - Majestic, stately, grand.
Mais (Fr.) - But.
Mais pas trop (Fr.) - But not too much.
Mal (Ger.) - Time, occurrence.
Mancando (It.) - Decreasing, dying away.
Marcato (It.) - Marked, accentuated, pronounced.
Marcia (It.) - March.
Marcia funebre (It.) - Funeral march.
Marziale (It.) - Martial, warlike.
Mässig (Ger.) - Moderate, the equivalent of *andante*.
Mässig bewegt (Ger.) - With moderate animation.
Mehr (Ger.) - More.
Même (Fr.) - Same.
Même mouvement (Fr.) - The same tempo.
Meno (It.) - Less.
Mesto (It.) - Sad, mournful, gloomy.
Mezzo (It.) - Half, middle.
Mezzo forte (*mf*) (It.) - Moderately loud.
Mezzo piano (*mp*) (It.) - Moderately soft.
Misura (It.) - Measure.
Mit (Ger.) - With.
Moderato (It.) - At a moderate tempo.
Modéré (Fr.) - Moderate, reasonable.
Möglich (Ger.) - Possible.
Möglichst (Ger.) - As much as possible.
Moins (Fr.) - Less

Molto (It.) - Very, greatly, well.
Morendo (It.) - Dying away.
Mosso (It.) - Rapid, animated.
Moto (It.) - Motion, movement.
Munter (Ger.) - Lively, vigorous, the equivalent of *allegro*.

Nicht (Ger.) - Not.
Nicht zu schnell (Ger.) - Not too fast.
Nicht zu viel (Ger.) - Not too much.
Nieder (Ger.) - Low.
Niente (It.) - Nothing.
Noch (Ger.) - Yet, still.
Noch einmal (Ger.) - Once more.
Non (It.) - Not, no.
Non tanto; Non troppo (It.) - Not too much.
Nur (Ger.) - Only, merely.

Oder (Ger.) - Or, or else.
Ohne (Ger.) - Without.
Opus (Lat.) - Work.
Oscuro (It.) - Dark, dim, mysterious.
Ossia (It.) - Or, or rather.
Ou (Fr.) - Or.

Parlando (It.) - In a speaking manner.
Pas (1) (Fr.) - Step, pace, dance.
Pas (2) (Fr.) - Not, no.
Pas beaucoup (Fr.) - Not too much.
Pas du tout (Fr.) - Not at all.
Pausa (It.) - Pause, rest.
Perdendosi (It.) - Dying away.
Pesante (It.) - Heavy, ponderous.
Peu (Fr.) - Little, not much, not very.
Peu à peu (Fr.) - Little by little, gradually.
Piacere (It.) - Pleasure, delight (see *A piacere*).
Piacevole (It.) - Agreeable.
Pianissimo (*pp*) (It.) - Very soft.
Piano (*p*) (It.) - Soft, quiet.
Pietoso (It.) - Doleful, pitiful, plaintive.
Più (It.) - More.
Più mosso (It.) - Faster.
Più moto (It.) - More motion, faster.
Placabile (It.) - Placid, mild.
Plötzlich (Ger.) - Sudden, abrupt.
Plus (Fr.) - More.
Po (It.) - Little.
Pochissimo (It.) - Very little.
Poco (It.) - Little.
Poco a poco (It.) - Little by little.
Poi (It.) - Then, afterwards.
Portamento (It.) - Connected, very legato.
Portato (It.) - Sustained, lengthened.

Precipitato (It.) - Sudden, hurried.
Pressé (Fr.) - Hurried, in haste.
Pressez (Fr.) - Hurry, press ahead.
Prestissimo (It.) - Extremely fast.
Presto (It.) - Very fast.
Prima (It.) - First.
Prima volta (It.) - The first time.

Quasi (It.) - Almost, as if, nearly.

Rallentando (It.) - Gradually becoming slower.
Rasch (Ger.) - Rapid, lively.
Recitativo (It.) - A speechlike passage.
Retenir (Fr.) - To hold back, to moderate.
Risoluto (It.) - Resolute, energetic, determined.
Ritardando (rit., ritard.) (It.) - Gradually becoming slower.
Ritenendo (It.) - Becoming slower.
Ritenuto (It.) - Held back.
Rubato (It.) - Robbed, irregular time.
Ruhig (Ger.) - Quiet, tranquil.

Sans (Fr.) - Without, free form.
Scherzando (It.) - Joking, playful.
Scherzo (It.) - Joke, jest.
Schnell (Ger.) - Rapid, equivalent of *presto*.
Schwer (Ger.) - Heavy, ponderous.
Secco (It.) - Dry, hard, short.
Segno (It.) - The sign.
Segue (It.) - Follows.
Sehr (Ger.) - Very, much, greatly.
Semplice (It.) - Simple, easy, unpretentious.
Semplicemente (It.) - Simply, plainly.
Sempre (It.) - Always, ever.
Senza (It.) - Without, free from.
Sforzando (*sfz* or *sfz*) (It.) - A sudden, strong accent.
Sforzata (It.) - Forced.
Simile (It.) - Similar, in the same manner.
Sin' al fine (It.) - Until the end.
Sin' al segno (It.) - Until the sign.
Singend (Ger.) - In a singing style.
Slancio (It.) - With dash, boldly.
Smorzando (It.) - Extinguishing the sound, growing softer.
Sostenuto (It.) - Sustained.
Sotto (It.) - Under, below.
Sotto voce (It.) - In a low, soft voice.
Später (Ger.) - Later, after.
Spirito (It.) - Spirit.
Spiritoso (It.) - Spirited, vivacious, jocular.
Staccato (It.) - Detached, short.
Stark (Ger.) - Strong, heavy, loud.
Streng (Ger.) - Strict.

Stretto (It.) - Pressed, hurried.
Stringendo (It.) - Hastening, accelerating.
Stürmisch (Ger.) - Stormy, impetuous.
Subito (It.) - Sudden, quick, at once.

Tacet (It.) - To be silent.
Takt (Ger.) - Measure, beat, tempo.
Takthalten (Ger.) - In strict time.
Tanto (It.) - So much, as much (*Non tanto* - Not too much).
Tempo (It.) - Time, movement, rate of speed.
Tempo primo (It.) - The original tempo.
Tenir (Fr.) - To hold.
Tenuto (It.) - Sustained, held.
Toujours (Fr.) - Always, ever.
Tranquillo (It.) - Tranquil, quiet, peaceful, calm.
Traurig (Ger.) - Sad, pensive.
Très (Fr.) - Very, greatly.
Triste (It., Fr.) - Sorrowful, mournful, sad.
Trop (Fr.) - Too, too much.
Troppo (It.) - Too, too much (*Non troppo* - Not too much).
Tutti (It.) - All, whole.

Übermütig (Ger.) - Gay, playful.
Un, una, uno (It.) - One.
Un, une (Fr.) - One.
Un peu (Fr.) - A little.
Ungefähr (Ger.) - Approximate.
Unruhig (Ger.) - Restless, agitated.

Va (It.) - Continue.
Veloce (It.) - Rapid, quick, nimble.
Vif (Fr.) - Brisk, lively, animated.
Vigoroso (It.) - Vigorous, robust.
Vivace (It.) - Lively, vivacious.
Vivo (It.) - Lively, brisk, animated.
Voce (It.) - Voice.
Voix (Fr.) - Voice, tone, sound.
Volante (It.) - With delicate, rapid execution.
Volta (It.) - Time occurrence.

Wehmütig (Ger.) - Doleful.
Wenig (Ger.) - Little.
Weniger (Ger.) - Less.
Wie (Ger,) - As, like.
Wütend (Ger.) - Furious.

Zart (Ger.) - Tender, soft, delicate.
Zeitmass (Ger.) - Tempo, time.
Ziemlich (Ger.) - Moderately.
Zögernd (Ger.) - Growing gradually slower.
Zurückhalten (Ger.) - Hold back.

Bibliography for Further Study

ACOUSTICS

Backus, John. *Acoustical Foundations of Music*, 2nd. ed. 1977. (ISBN 0-393-09029-9). New York: W.W. Norton.

Benade, A.H. *Fundamentals of Musical Acoustics*. 1976. (ISBN 0-19-502030-8). Fairlawn, N.J.: Oxford University Press, Inc.

_____. *Horns, Strings & Harmony*. 1979. Reprint of 1960 ed. (ISBN 0-313-20771-2, BEHO). Westport, Conn.: Greenwood Press.

Bienvenue, Gordon F. & Prout, James H. *Acoustics for You*. 1990. Malabar, Fla.: R. E. Krieger Pub. Co.

Campbell, D.W. & Greated, Clive A. *The Musicians Guide to Acoustics*. 1987. (ISBN 0-02-870161-5). New York: Schirmer Books.

Erickson, Robert. *Sound Structure in Music*. 1975. (ISBN 0-520-02376-5). Berkeley, Calif.: University of California Press.

Moravcsik, Michael J. *Musical Sound: An Introduction to the Physics of Music*. 1987. (ISBN 0-913729-39-6). New York: Paragon House.

Pierce, John R. *The Science of Musical Sound*. 1983. (ISBN 0-7167-1508-2). New York: W.H. Freeman.

Slawson, Wayne. *Sound Color*. 1985. (ISBN 0-520-05185-8). Berkeley, Calif.: University of California Press.

COMPOSITION

Austin, Larry & Clark, Thomas. *Learning to Compose - Modes, Materials and Models of Musical Invention*. 1989. (ISBN 3495). Madison, Wis.: WCB Brown & Benchmark.

Cope, David. *New Music Composition*. 1977. (ISBN 0-02-870630-7). New York: Schirmer Books.

Dallin, Leon. *Techniques of Twentieth Century Composition: A Guide to the Materials of Modern Music*. 3rd ed. 1974. (ISBN 0-697-03614-6). Madison, Wis.: WCB Brown & Benchmark.

Hanson, Howard. *Harmonic Materials of Modern Music: Resources of the Tempered Scale*. 1960. New York: Appleton-Century-Crofts.

Marquis, G. Welton. *Twentieth-Century Music Idioms*. Reprint of 1964 ed. 1981. (ISBN 0-313-22624-5, MATC). Westport, Conn.: Greenwood Press.

Persichetti, Vincent. *Twentieth-Century Harmony: Creative Aspects and Practice*. 1961. New York: W.W. Norton.

Russo, William & Ainis, Jeffrey. *Composing Music: A New Approach*. 1983. (ISBN 0-13-164756-3). Englewood Cliffs, N.J.:Prentice-Hall.

Wourinen, Charles. *Simple Composition*. 1979. (ISBN 0-582-28059-1). New York: Longman.

COUNTERPOINT

Benjamin, Thomas. *Counterpoint in the Style of J.S. Bach*. 1986. (ISBN 0-02-870280-8). New York: Schirmer Books.

_____. *The Craft of Modal Counterpoint: A Practical Approach*. 1979. (ISBN 0-02-870480-0). New York: Schirmer Books.

Gauldin, Robert. *A Practical Approach to Sixteenth Century Counterpoint*. 1985. (ISBN 0-13-689258-2). Englewood Cliffs, N.J.: Prentice-Hall.

Kennan, Kent. *Counterpoint*, 2nd ed. 1972. (ISBN 0-13-184291-9). Englewood Cliffs, N.J.: Prentice-Hall.

Mason, Neale B. *Essentials of Eighteenth-Century Counterpoint*. 1968. (ISBN 0-697-03605-7). Madison, Wis.: WCB Brown & Benchmark.

Merriman, Margarita. *A New Look at Sixteenth-Century Counterpoint*. 1982. (ISBN 0-8191-2392-7). Lanham, Md.: University Press of America.

Owen, Harold. *Modal and Tonal Counterpoint*. 1992. New York: Schirmer Books.

Parks, Richard S. *Eighteenth Century Counterpoint & Tonal Structure*. 2nd ed. 1984. (ISBN 0-13-246744-5). Englewood Cliffs, N.J.: Prentice-Hall.

Piston, Walter. *Counterpoint*. 1947. (ISBN 0-393-09728-5). New York: W.W. Norton.

Schenker, Heinrich. *Counterpoint, 2 Vols*. Rothgeb, John & Thym, Jurgen, trans. 1986. (ISBN 0-02-873220-0). New York: Schirmer Books.

Schönberg, Arnold. *Preliminary Exercises in Counterpoint*. Stein, Leonard, ed. 1982. (ISBN 0-571-09275-6). Winchester, Mass.: Faber & Faber.

Searle, Humphrey. *Twentieth-Century Counterpoint: A Guide for Students*. Reprint of 1954 ed. 1986. (ISBN 0-88355-763-0). Westport, Conn.: Hyperion Press.

Smith, Charlotte. *A Manual of Sixteen-Century Contrapuntal Style*. 1989. Newark, N.J.: University of Delaware Press.

Stewart, Robert. *An Introduction to Sixteenth Century Counterpoint and Palestrina's Musical Style*. 1994. New York: Ardsley House Publishers, Inc.

Westergaard, Peter. *Introduction to Tonal Theory*. 1976. (ISBN 0-393-09342-5). New York: W.W. Norton.

EAR TRAINING/SIGHTSINGING

Blombach, Ann K. *MacGAMUT, Intervals • Scales • Chords* 1988. Mountain View, Calif.: Mayfield.

Benward, Bruce & Kolosick, J. Timothy. *Ear Training: A Technique for Listening.* 4th Ed. 1990. Madison, Wis.: WCB Brown & Benchmark.

Carlsen, James C. *Melodic Perception: A Program for Self-Instruction.* 1965. (ISBN 0-07-009975-8). New York: McGraw-Hill Book Co.

Friedmann, Michael L. *Ear Training for Twentieth-Century Music.* 1990. New Haven: Yale University Press.

Gregory, David. *Melodic Dictator* (Macintosh program). 1988. Ann Arbor, Mich.: University of Michigan Center for Performing Arts and Technology.

Ghezzo, Marta A. *Solfege, Ear Training, Rhythm, Dictation & Music Theory: A Comprehensive Course.* 1980. (ISBN 0-8173-6403-X). University, Al.: University of Alabama Press.

Hindemith, Paul. *Elementary Training for Musicians.* 2nd Ed. 1949. New York: Associated Music Publishers.

Horacek, Leo & Lefkoff, Gerald. *Programmed Ear Training.* 4 Vols. 1970. (texts & tapes). San Diego, Calif.: Harcourt Brace Jovanovich.

Kelly, Robert. *Aural & Visual Recognition: A Musical Ear Training Series.* 1972. (ISBN 0-252-00073-0). Champaign, Ill.: University of Illinois Press.

Olson, Robert G. *Music Dictation: A Stereo Taped Series.* 1970. (ISBN 0-534-00671-X). Belmont, Calif.: Wadsworth.

Ottman, Robert W. *Music for Sightsinging.* 3rd Ed. 1986. (ISBN 0-13-607532-0). Engelwood Cliffs, N.J.: Prentice-Hall.

Trubitt, Allen R. & Hines, Robert S. *Ear Training & Sight-Singing: An Integrated Approach.* 1979. (ISBN 0-02-870810-5). New York: Schirmer Books.

Wittlich, Gary & Humphries, Lee. *Ear Training: An Approach Through Music Literature.* 1974. (ISBN 0-15-518707-4). (has records, tapes or cassettes). San Diego, Calif.: Harcourt Brace Jovanovich.

Listen 2.0 (Interactive Ear Training Software for the Apple Macintosh). 1989. Menlo Park, Calif.: Resonate.

FORM/ANALYSIS

Berry, Wallace. *Form in Music.* 2nd ed. 1986. (ISBN 0-13-329285-1). Englewood Cliffs, N.J.: Prentice-Hall.

Cook, Nicholas. *A Guide to Musical Analysis.* 1987. (ISBN 0-8076-1172-7). New York: George Braziller, Inc.

Cooper, Paul. *Perspectives in Music Theory: An Historical-Analytical Approach.* 1973. (ISBN 0-06-041368-9, HarpC). New York: Harper & Row.

Dunsby, Jonathan & Whittal, Arnold. *Musical Analysis.* 1987. (ISBN 0-300-03713-9). New Haven, Conn.: Yale University Press.

Epstein, David. *Beyond Orpheus: Studies in Musical Structure.* 1987. (ISBN 0-19-315150-2). Fairlawn, N.J.: Oxford University Press.

Forte, Allen & Gilbert, Steven E. *Introduction to Schenkerian Analysis: Form & Content in Tonal Music.* 1982. (ISBN 0-393-95192-8). New York: W.W. Norton.

Green, Douglas M. *Form in Tonal Music: An Introduction to Analysis.* 2nd ed. 1979. (ISBN 0-03-020286-8). New York: Holt, Rinehart & Winston.

Hutcheson, Jere T. *Musical Form & Analysis.* 2 Vols. 1972, 1977. (ISBN 0-8008-5454-3; 0-8008-5455-1). Boston: Taplinger.

Mason, Robert M. *Modern Methods of Music Analysis Using Computers.* 1985. (ISBN 0-9615669-0-6). Peterborough, N.H.: Schoolhouse Press.

Narmour, Eugene. *Beyond Schenkerism: The Need for Alternatives in Music Analysis.* 1980. (ISBN 0-226-56848-2, P893, Phoen). Chicago: University of Chicago Press.

Spencer, Peter & Temko, Peter M. *A Practical Approach to the Study of Form in Music.* 1988. (ISBN 0-13-689050-4). Englewood Cliffs, N.J.: Prentice-Hall.

Wade, Graham. *The Shape of Music: An Introduction to Musical Form.* 1982. (ISBN 0-8052-8110-X). New York: Schocken Books, Inc.

Walton, Charles W. *Basic Forms in Music.* 1974. (ISBN 0-88284-010-X). Sherman Oaks, Calif.: Alfred Publishing.

Warfield, Gerald. *Layer Analysis: A Primer of Elementary Tonal Structures.* 1978. (ISBN 0-582-28069-9). New York: Longman.

White, John D. *The Analysis of Music.* 2nd ed. 1984. (ISBN 0-8108-1701-2). Metuchen, N.J.: Scarecrow Press.

GENERAL

Barra, Donald. *The Dynamic Performance: A Performer's Guide to Musical Expression & Interpretation.* 1983. (ISBN 13-221556-X). Englewood Cliffs, N.J.: Prentice-Hall.

Baur, John. *Music Theory Through Literature.* 2 Vols. 1985. (ISBN 0-13-607821-4; 0-13-607847-8). Englewood Cliffs, N.J.: Prentice-Hall.

Beach, David. *Aspects of Schenkerian Theory.* 1983. (ISBN 0-300-02803-2). New Haven, Conn.: Yale University Press.

Cogan, Robert. *New Images of Musical Sound.* 1984. (ISBN 0-674-61585-9). Cambridge, Mass.: Harvard University Press.

Cogan, Robert & Escot, Pozzi. *Sonic Design: The Nature of Sound & Music.* 1976. Englewood Cliffs, N.J.: Prentice-Hall.

Fotine, Larry. *Contemporary Musician's Handbook & Dictionary.* 1984. (ISBN 0-933830-03-3). Sepulveda, Calif.: Poly Tone Press.

Halloran, Mark, Ed./comp. *The Musician's Business and Legal Guide.* 1991. Englewood Cliffs, N.J.: Prentice-Hall.

Harder, Paul O. *Bridge To Twentieth Century Music,* 1973. (ISBN 0-205-03639-2). Boston: Allyn and Bacon, Inc. (Rev. ed. now published privately by Tierra del Music, 1000 N. Denmark Dr., Muncie, IN 47304.)

Harder, Paul O. *Harmonic Materials in Tonal Music, Parts I & II,* 7th ed. 1994. (ISBN 0-205-15802-1 [v. 1]. — ISBN 0-205-15804-8 [v. 2]). Boston: Allyn and Bacon.

Helm, Eugene & Luper, Albert T. *Words & Music: Form & Procedure in Theses, Dissertations, Research Papers, Book Reports, Programs, & Theses in Composition.* 1971. (ISBN 0-913574-00-7). Valley Forge, Pa.: European American Music.

Hofstetter, Fred T. *Computer Literacy for Musicians.* 1988. Englewood Cliff, N.J.: Prentice-Hall.

Kostka, Steven. *Materials & Techniques of 20th Century Music.* 1990. Englewood Cliffs, N.J.: Prentice-Hall.

Marin, Deborah S. & Wittlich, Gary E. *Tonal Harmony for the Keyboard: With an Introduction to Improvisation.* 1989. New York: Schirmer Books.

Moore, F. Richard. *Elements of Computer Music.* 1990. Englewood Cliffs, N.J.: Prentice-Hall.

Pellman, Samuel. *An Introduction to the Creation of Electroacoustic Music.* 1994. (ISBN 0-534-21450-9). Belmont, Calif.: Wadsworth Publishing Co.

Rahn, Jay. *A Theory for All Music: Problems & Solutions in the Analysis of Non-Western Forms.* 1983. (ISBN 0-8020-5538-9). Toronto: University of Toronto Press.

Reti, Rudolph R. *The Thematic Process in Music.* Reprint of 1951 ed. 1978. (ISBN 0-8371-9875-5, RETH). Westport, Conn.: Greenwood Press, Inc.

———. *Tonality, Atonality, Pantonality: A Study of Some Trends in Twentieth-Century Music.* Reprint of 1958 ed. 1978. (ISBN 0-313-20478-0, RETO). Westport, Conn.: Greenwood Press, Inc.

Schafer, R. Murray. *The Thinking Ear.* 1986. (C86-093409-8). Arcana Ed., Indian River, Ontario, K0L 2B0, Canada.

Schwartz, Elliott & Godfrey, Daniel. *Music Since 1945.* 1993. (ISBN 0-02-873040-2). New York: Schirmer Books.

Simms, Bryan R. *Music of the 20th Century.* 1986. (ISBN 0-02-873020-8). New York: Schirmer Books.

Taylor, Clifford. *Musical Idea and the Design Aesthetic in Contemporary Music: A Text for Discerning Appraisal of Musical Thought in Western Culture.* 1990. Lewiston, N.Y.: Edwin Mellon Press.

Toch, Ernst. *The Shaping Forces in Music: An Inquiry into the Nature of Harmony, Melody, Counterpoint, Form.* 1977. (ISBN 0-486-23346-4). Mineola, N.Y.: Dover Publications.

MUSICAL ANTHOLOGIES

Benjamin, Thomas E. *Music for Analysis: Examples from the Common Practice Period & the Twentieth Century.* 2nd ed. 1984. (ISBN 0-395-34225-2). Boston: Houghton Mifflin.

Berry, Wallace & Chudacoff, Edward. *Eighteenth Century Imitative Counterpoint: Music for Analysis.* 1969. (ISBN 0-13-246843-3). Englewood Cliff, N.J.: Prentice-Hall.

Bockmon, Guy A. & Starr, William J. *Scored for Listening: A Guide to Music.* 2nd ed. 1972. (ISBN 0-15-579055-2, HC) records (ISBN 0-15-579056-0). San Diego, Calif.: Harcourt Brace Jovanovich.

Brandt, William; Corra, Arthur; Christ, William; DeLeone, Richard & Winold, Allen. *The Comprehensive Study of Music.* New York: Harper & Row.

Burkhart, Charles. *Anthology for Musical Analysis.* 5th ed. 1994. (ISBN 0-03-055318-0). Fort Worth, Texas: Harcourt Brace College Publishers.

De Lio, Thomas & Smith, Stuart Saunders. *Twentieth Century Music Scores.* 1989. Englewood Cliffs, N.J.: Prentice-Hall.

Hardy, Gordon & Fish, Arnold. *Music Literature: A Workbook for Analysis.* 2 Vols. 1966. (ISBN 0-06-042633-0, HarpC; 0-06-042634-9). New York: Harper & Row.

Kamien, Roger, ed. *The Norton Scores: An Anthology for Listening.* 2 Vols. 4th ed. 1984. (ISBN 0-393-95304-1; 0-393-95310-6). New York: W.W. Norton.

Melcher, Robert A.; Warch, Williard F. & Mast, Paul B. *Music for Study.* 3rd ed. 1988. Englewood Cliff, N.J.: Prentice-Hall.

Palisca, Claude V., ed. *Norton Anthology of Western Music.* 2 Vols. 2nd ed. 1988. (ISBN 0-393-95642-3; 0-393-95644-X). New York: W.W. Norton.

Ward-Steinman, David & Ward-Steinman, Susan L. *Comparative Anthology of Musical Forms,* 2 Vols. Reprint of 1976 ed. 1987. (ISBN 0-8191-5600-0). Lanham, Md: University Press of America.

Wennerstrom, Mary H. *Anthology of Musical Structure & Style.* 1983. (ISBN 0-13-038372-4). Englewood Cliff, N.J.: Prentice-Hall.

MUSICAL NOTATION

Harder, Paul O. *Music Manuscript Techniques, A Programmed Approach, 2 Parts.* 1984. (ISBN 0-

205-07992-X [pt. 1], 0-205-07993-8 [pt. 2]). Boston: Allyn and Bacon, Inc.

Read, Gardner. *Music Notation*. 1979. (ISBN 0-8008-5453-5). Boston: Taplinger.

Warfield, Gerald. *How To Write Music Manuscript in Pencil*. 1977. (ISBN 0-679-30332-4). New York: Longman.

MUSICAL NOTATION: COMPUTER MATERIALS

Deluxe Music Construction Set 2.5. (computer program for Macintosh), 1988. San Mateo, Calif.: Electronic Arts.

Encore 3.0. (computer program for Macintosh). 1993. Half Moon Bay, Calif.: Passport Designs.

Finale 3.0 and *Finale Allegro*. (computer programs for Macintosh and IBM). 1994. Eden Prairie, Minn.: Coda Music Software.

Freestyle (computer program for Macintosh).1994. Cambridge, Mass.: Mark of Unicorn, Inc.

Lime (computer program for Macintosh and IBM). 1993. Champaign, Ill.: Electronic Courseware Systems.

Metronome 3.2 & MetTimes 2.1 (music fonts to use directly in word processing for Macintosh and IBM). 1993. Thorofare, N.J.: DVM Publications, P. O. Box 399, Thorofare, N.J. 08086.

Music Printer (Apple IIe program) or *Music Printer Plus* (IBM program). 1987 & 1988. Bellevue, Wash.: Temporal Acuity Products, Inc.

Music Prose (computer program for Macintosh and IBM). 1992. Eden Prairie, Minn.: Coda Music Software.

Nightingale 1.x (computer program for Macintosh). 1993. Bellevue, Wash.: Temporal Acuity Products, Inc.

Notewriter. (computer program for Macintosh). 1993. Vancouver, B.C., Canada.: Keith Hamel, 449 East 37th Ave., Vancouver, B.C., Canada V5W 1E8.

Overture. (computer program for Macintosh). 1994. Palo Alto, Calif.: Opcode Systems Inc.

Personal Composer for Windows. 1994. Seattle, Wash.: Personal Composer, 3213 W. Wheeeler St., Suite 140, Seattle, WA 98199.

Professional Composer 2.3 and *Mosaic 1.4* (computer programs for Macintosh).1994. Cambridge, Mass.: Mark of Unicorn, Inc.

Score. (computer program for IBM). 1990. Half Moon Bay, Calif.: Passport Designs.

Songworks by ARS Nova.

ORCHESTRATION

Adler, Samuel. *The Study of Orchestration*. 2nd Ed. 1989. (ISBN 0-393-95807-8). New York: W.W. Norton.

Blatter, Alfred. *Instrumentation-Orchestration* 1980. (ISBN 0-582-28118-0). New York: Macmillan.

Burton, Steven D. *Orchestration*. 1982. (ISBN 0-13-639500-7). Englewood Cliff, N.J.: Prentice-Hall.

Kennan, Kent & Grantham, Donald. *The Technique of Orchestration*. 3rd ed. 1983. (ISBN 0-13-900308-8). Englewood Cliff, N.J.: Prentice-Hall.

Polansky, Larry. *New Instrumentation & Orchestration: An Outline for Study*. 1986. (ISBN 0-945996-01-2). Oakland, Calif.: Frog Peak Music.

Read, Gardner. *Style & Orchestration*. 1979. (ISBN 0-02-872110-1). New York: Schirmer Books.

Stiller, Andrew. *Handbook of Instrumentation*.1985. Berkeley, Calif.: University of California Press.

Note that there are many musical computer programs based on both Apple and IBM systems appearing all the time which may relate to one or more of the above bibliographical areas. Please check with an instructor or musical computer listings for what might be currently available.

Subject Index

About the Authors

Dr. Paul O. Harder (1923–1986) received a Master of Music degree in Music Theory from the Eastman School of Music, University of Rochester, where he performed as oboist with the Rochester Philharmonic Orchestra. Later he was a fellowship student at the University of Iowa, where he received his Ph.D. in Music Composition. He was also a student of composition with Mlle. Nadia Boulanger at the École des Beaux Arts de Fountainbleau, France, and studied at the Royal Academy of Music in Copenhagen, Denmark.

Dr. Harder held the post of Chairman of Music Theory at Michigan State University prior to his position as Assistant Vice President and Professor of Music at California State University, Stanislaus and Professor Emeritus at Michigan State University.

In addition to approximately fifty compositions for a variety of media including orchestra, band, chorus, and chamber groups, Dr. Harder was the author of *Harmonic Materials in Tonal Music,* Parts I and II, fifth edition; *Basic Materials in Music Theory,* sixth edition; *Music Manuscript Techniques,* Parts I and II; and *Bridge to 20th Century Music,* all published by Allyn and Bacon except *Bridge...,* which is now published privately by Tierra del Mar Music, 1000 N. Denmark Dr., Muncie, IN 47304–9302 (see *Bibliography*).

Dr. Greg A Steinke is Director of the School of Music and Professor of Music at Ball State University, Muncie, Indiana. Professor Steinke holds a Bachelor of Music degree from Oberlin Conservatory, a Master of Music degree from Michigan State University, a Master of Fine Arts degree from the University of Iowa, and a Doctor of Philosophy degree from Michigan State University.

Formerly, Dr. Steinke was Assistant Director of the School of Music at the University of Arizona, Chairman of the Music Department at San Diego State University, Director of the School of Music at the University of Idaho, Chairman of the Music Department at Linfield College, and a faculty member at The Evergreen State College, California State University, Northridge, and the University of Maryland.

Dr. Steinke is the author of numerous articles, has done the revisions to the Paul Harder *Harmonic Materials in Tonal Music* (sixth and seventh editions) and holds membership in a number of professional organizations. Currently, he is serving as the National Chairman of the Society of Composers, Inc. Professor Steinke is active as a composer of chamber and symphonic music with a number of published works; as a speaker on interdisciplinary arts; and as an oboe soloist specializing in contemporary music for oboe.

NOTES

NOTES

NOTES

NOTES

NOTES

NOTES

NOTES

NOTES